SHAKING
HANDS
with
HISTORY

ALSO BY JAMES E. ROGAN

"Dear President Truman"
(*American Heritage*, 1994; *Readers Digest*, 1995)

My Brush with History
(Contributor, 2001)

Rough Edges
My Unlikely Road from Welfare to Washington
(2004)

Catching Our Flag
Behind the Scenes of a Presidential Impeachment
(2011)

And *Then* I Met...
Stories of Growing Up, Meeting Famous People, and
Annoying the Hell Out of Them
(2014)

"On to Chicago"
Rediscovering Robert F. Kennedy and the Lost Campaign of 1968
(2018)

Shaking Hands with History:
My Encounters with the Famous, the Infamous, and the
Once-Famous but Now-Forgotten
(2020)

SHAKING HANDS *with* HISTORY

MY ENCOUNTERS WITH *the* FAMOUS,
the INFAMOUS, *and the* ONCE-FAMOUS
but NOW-FORGOTTEN

JAMES ROGAN

SHENANDOAH
PRESS

SHAKING HANDS WITH HISTORY

Copyright © 2020 by James Rogan

Library of Congress Control Number: 2020949989

Hardcover ISBN: 978-1-7346385-9-2
Paperback ISBN: 978-1-7351317-0-2
eBook ISBN: 978-1-7351317-3-3

Printed in the United States of America

For Ellie Grace and Ava

CONTENTS

AUTHOR'S NOTE

Imagine discovering the locked diaries of someone who recorded in them his unvarnished, candid stories of behind-the-scenes encounters with some of the most famous people of his generation: world leaders, explorers, iconic movie and sports stars, even two canonized saints. How badly would you want to locate that key? How hard would you look for it?

Your search is over.

Since the 2014 publication of my third book, *And Then I Met… Stories of Growing Up, Meeting Famous People, and Annoying the Hell Out of Them,* I intended to write this sequel, but my plan diverted when I began researching and writing a historical novel surrounding the 1968 presidential campaign and assassination of Senator Robert F. Kennedy. My fourth book, *On to Chicago: Rediscovering Robert F. Kennedy and the Lost Campaign of 1968* debuted on June 6, 2018, the fiftieth anniversary of RFK's death. When that project completed, I returned to this planned sequel.

Readers of my books know that I have always been a history buff. Growing up in downtown San Francisco, as a young boy I often cut school and took advantage of the many times notables rolled into town. I became adept at sneaking through police barricades, Secret Service checkpoints, and evading hotel security guards to meet the objects of my interest and get them to share memories of their careers. As a kid I met everyone—presidents, Hollywood royalty, sports greats, astronauts, and even the last surviving witness of "Custer's Last Stand." My camera and my notebook memorialized these events.

Four decades later, in *And Then I Met*, I opened those diaries and photo albums to share some of these early experiences with the greats, the near-greats, and the former greats now long-forgotten. I also included the recollections they shared with me of the famous whom they knew such as FDR, JFK, Laurel and Hardy, even Mussolini. Such a fun book!

And Then I Met ended with stories predating my own high-level foray into government. After winning elective office, and especially after entering Congress, the opportunities to meet historical figures and have meaningful discussions with them multiplied. Unlike my boyhood high jinx, these encounters were far different from what I experienced as a kid sneaking into places carrying a plastic Kodak Instamatic camera (complete with rotating flash cube) and an autograph album.

Shaking Hands with History is my first sequel to *And Then I Met*. Since I have more stories in my repertoire than I had room between the covers of this book, I'll save those for a future volume. (Spoiler alert: in the next installment, I'll tell you how I pranked Pope John Paul II—and how he got back at me!)

I hope you enjoy reading *Shaking Hands with History* as much as I enjoyed writing it for you.

—J.R.
Orange County, California,
November 26, 2020

1

"Godspeed, John Glenn"

—Scott Carpenter at NASA liftoff, February 20, 1962

Let your imagination take you back to the 1950s. You are a military pilot who flew combat missions during World War II and in Korea, and you live in an era when rocketry and missile technology remains primitive. A new government agency approaches you with a proposal:

They have designed a seven-foot-by-nine-foot metal container with only enough room inside for a man to squeeze into the coffin-tight compartment. They want to attach that capsule (with the man inside) atop a long-range missile designed for nuclear warheads, and then launch the missile into outer space. If the missile makes it that far, they hope to have the capsule break away, orbit the Earth repeatedly, reenter the atmosphere, and splash down into the ocean using pop-up parachutes. Of course, there are some problems. They have never sent a man into outer space, and they have no validated research available on how to do it and bring him back safely. Of their five previous missile tests, two of them failed on the launch pad and exploded into fireballs. Also, without any available medical testing, they worry that prolonged exposure to G-forces and zero gravity will crush his eyeballs or make them pop out of their sockets, as well as cause severe brain and skeletal damage. Mostly, they fret that the estimated 10,000-degree Fahrenheit reentry heat might vaporize both capsule and passenger. After explaining these multiple dangers, and in the interest of science and exploration, they ask you to climb into that glorified tin can atop the missile and let them light the fuse.

What kind of man would take such a catastrophe-beckoning gamble?

Meet John Glenn.

Born in 1921, as a Marine Corps pilot he flew fifty-nine combat missions during World War II, and ninety more in Korea. In 1959, NASA named him to its first group of astronauts, the *Mercury 7*. After two earlier launches completed successful suborbital flights, on February 20, 1962, he became the first American to orbit the Earth. His spaceship, *Friendship 7*, completed three revolutions in under five hours. Returning to a hero's welcome and tickertape parades, Ohio voters elected him to the U.S. Senate a dozen years later.

Project Mercury first day postal cover canceled from the NASA launch site at Cape Canaveral, Florida, on February 20, 1962, 3:30 p.m., the precise moment of Glenn's reentry into earth's atmosphere and fourteen minutes before his splashdown in the ocean. He signed this for me during our dinner over forty years later.

Glenn ranked as one of my earliest boyhood heroes. I wasn't yet five years old when he launched, but I still remember his death-defying, Buck Rogers-styled adventure. During his flight, I watched the live television coverage of his elderly mother waving at the sky as her son's capsule soared 162 miles above. When the TV newsman reported that in some cities people could view a glint from his spaceship as it passed, I begged my grandmother to bring me outside our San Francisco flat to see him sail across the heavens. As I stood on the sidewalk in front of 2718 Bryant Street holding Grandma's hand and staring upward, she never imagined that one day Little Jimmy would serve in Congress with the astronaut orbiting overhead.

• • •

When I made my first trip to Washington as a teen in 1975, rookie U.S. Senator John Glenn had arrived at the Capitol only eight months earlier. With no expectation of success, I wrote him and asked if I could drop by and meet him. To my delight, he said yes.

I arrived at his Senate office on a muggy afternoon and told his young and bubbly secretary that I was nervous about meeting her boss. "Relax," she said. "He's the nicest man in town. The word's already out among the staffers. They all want to work for him." After she led me into our meeting, I understood why.

He sat behind his desk reading a document when I entered. He looked up, removed his eyeglasses, and sprinted across the room to welcome me. Instead of having his aide rush me in and out for a perfunctory handshake and photo, he invited me to join him on the couch while he asked about my background and future ambitions (a paternal grin crossed his face when I told him I wanted to run for Congress someday).

After sharing with him my childhood recollections of his 1962 flight, he led me over to a table displaying a model of *Friendship 7*. "This is a 1/10 scale replica," he said, "which gives you an idea of how small the original was when it was flying over you and your grandmother."

"How did you ever fit inside?"

He laughed while pointing to his thinning hairline. "I don't know how I got in, but I think I lost a few hairs climbing out!" We walked over to the mantel over which hung an oil painting of *Friendship 7* orbiting Earth. Moving his finger over the painting, he traced the course of his three orbits while describing its various stages for me.

"Were you ever afraid?" I asked.

He shrugged. "I had so many procedures and tasks to accomplish before and after the launch that I really didn't have much time to think about that. The one time I grew concerned was near the end of the flight. Our ground station received an alert that the heat shield on my capsule had come loose. If it fell off, the ship would burn up during reentry. In the original flight plan, I was supposed to jettison the capsule's retro-pack before reentry, but once they got the warning signal, NASA engineers told me to leave it in place. They hoped that it might help secure the heat shield if it were loose. As it turned out, the ground signal was faulty. The heat shield remained secure. Still, it was quite a sight watching chunks of that retro-pack burn off and fly by my small window during reentry."

He signed a few autographs, we posed together for a photo, and I left awed at spending over twenty minutes alone with an icon. He couldn't have been more gracious to a young fan who wasn't even a constituent.

Over twenty years later, when I joined him in Congress, I looked forward to telling him so.

John Glenn and I posed for this photo in his Senate office in front of an oil painting depicting his 1962 *Friendship 7* capsule orbiting Earth. He used this painting to illustrate his flight description for me, September 10, 1975 (Author's collection)

• • •

In an unfortunate twist, Glenn's phenomenal 1962 success grounded him from all future Mercury, Gemini, and Apollo missions. President Kennedy and NASA officials secretly blocked him from future space flights, fearing that his accidental death would smother national enthusiasm for the program and risk its congressional funding. With no future opportunities available, he left NASA in 1964 for a career in business and politics, but his desire to return to space never waned.

In the mid-1990s, he began lobbying NASA to reverse its ancient blackballing of him. In time, the agency relented and announced that he would join the STS-95 crew aboard the Space Shuttle *Discovery* in October 1998, which was thirty-six years after his *Friendship 7* flight. At age 77, he would become the oldest person in space. Ironically, his advanced age tipped the scale in his favor because it gave NASA the chance to study the impact of space flight on the elderly.

Glenn's upcoming flight, scheduled during my first congressional term, made my encountering him around the Capitol difficult because he missed much of his final Senate year for NASA training. The chance came finally when an educational group invited me to a reception honoring him during one of his infrequent Washington visits. I stopped by his Senate office a few days before the event and left a copy of the old snapshot of us, along with a note explaining the circumstances of our 1975 meeting, my recent election, and my hope of seeing him at the reception in a few days.

At the celebration (held in the Dirksen Senate Office Building), well-wishers cheered and applauded his arrival. He made brief remarks after accepting an award, and then his staff tried to steer him toward the exit as a crowd surrounded him for autographs. "Last one, folks, sorry," an aide kept repeating with each one he signed, "but we have to go." Admirers ignored her efforts to extricate him.

To Jim Rogan —
— with best regards —
John Glenn

April 29, 1998: Twenty-three years after our first meeting, we took this updated photograph when I returned to Washington as a freshman congressman (Author's collection)

During this ongoing fanfest, a Senate staffer approached: "Excuse me, Congressman Rogan, but Senator Glenn hoped to see you. We're trying to move him out of here now. Do you have the time to meet with him?"

Do I have the time? Do winos have the DTs?

She brought me to an adjoining room where he joined us a few minutes later. "Jim, we meet again!" he called out. Pulling our old photo from his coat pocket, he held it alongside my face for a brief comparison before calling over a photographer: "I need an updated picture with the congressman," he said. "And quickly, before I get balder!"

He was as friendly as I remembered him from my youth. When I asked how, after almost four decades, he managed to land a shuttle crew slot, he told me, "A few years ago I began lobbying NASA Director Dan Goldin. He said he'd approve me if I could show a scientific basis justifying it, so I assembled my evidence. My studies showed that weightlessness has the same impact on the human body in space as the regular aging process has on Earth, including diminished balance, and muscle and bone mass loss. I argued to NASA that they could experiment on me to determine the impact of space flight on the elderly."

"It sounds as if you pitched yourself as a geriatric guinea pig."

"I wish I had thought of it that way," he chuckled, "because I might have talked Goldin into it sooner!" He said that although he looked forward to the adventure, he regretted that the intensive training required him to miss much of his final year in Washington.

In the event our paths did not cross again before his flight, I wished him luck and thanked him for taking the time to see me— now and in 1975.

"Welcome back to Washington, Jim," said the Democrat senator to the Republican freshman congressman. "I'm thrilled to see you again, even though you came here as a member of the wrong Party!"

• • •

I saw him around the Capitol occasionally before his flight. On October 29, 1998, STS-95 and its seven-person crew, including Payload Specialist 2 John Glenn, launched from the Kennedy Space Center. They returned safely from their nine-day mission; he retired from the Senate two months later and went home to Ohio to write his memoirs.

In November 1999, two weeks after its publication, my wife Christine, our seven-year-old twin daughters Dana and Claire, and I spent part of our Saturday shopping at the Pentagon City, Virginia, Price Club (now Costco). Clad in my typical weekend attire of faded jeans, sweatshirt, baseball cap, and day-old beard growth, I bore no resemblance to an incumbent congressman. As I pushed a cart down an aisle, John and his wife Annie approached from the opposite direction. He didn't recognize me as they walked by. I waited until he passed before calling to him, "Hey, mister, ain't you John Glenn? Can I have a free book? I'll trade it for a sandwich." He turned and studied my face momentarily before recognizing me.

"Well, Hobo Jim!" he replied, "I guess your voting record requires that you travel incognito." I introduced him to my family as my girls rode on the front of my cart. "You really have a basketful," he said as he patted their heads. "Are they for sale?"

"I don't know. I can't find their barcodes."

I congratulated him on the recent successes of both his shuttle flight and new book. He said the ongoing publication promotional tour was hectic but fun, and that he enjoyed meeting people at his signing events. Pointing to the opposite side of the warehouse where hundreds of people had lined up, he added, "That's why we're here today. I'm doing a book signing in the next few minutes." I hadn't known of his scheduled appearance, so our encounter proved coincidental.

"Wow, your turnout's impressive," I said. "If that line were any longer, we'd be at Disneyland in July waiting to ride the *Pirates of the Caribbean*." I told him that I had already bought copies of his book for my family and had planned to mail them for signatures when his travel schedule relaxed.

The store manager interrupted us. She welcomed the Glenns and said that they were ready to begin the event. "Don't mail them to me," he said as they left. "Call my office, and when I'm in D.C., bring the family for a visit and I'll sign them."

"That will be an honor for all of us."

Twenty minutes later, with our shopping completed, we headed for the checkout stand, which took us near the area where he signed books. I stood back and watched for a couple of minutes as he thanked each person individually, and then stood and posed for pictures with everyone who asked.

"Just like 1975," I said to myself.

He looked over as we walked away. He winked and blew a kiss to my girls. I removed my baseball cap and returned to him a military-precise acknowledgment.

"What are you doing, Daddy?" Claire asked.

"Honey, I'm saluting a hero."

• • •

Between Glenn's return to Ohio, my congressional and campaign obligations, and then my later domestic and international responsibilities while serving in the Bush Administration, it was a few years before our schedules meshed. The opportunity came because my Commerce Department duties included co-hosting the National Inventors Hall of Fame's annual induction ceremony at their Akron, Ohio museum (now located in Alexandria, Virginia). The 2003 ceremony inducted Maxime "Max" Faget, the engineer who designed Glenn's 1962 Mercury capsule, as well as the later Gemini and Apollo spacecrafts. At the same ceremony, we would honor John Glenn with a lifetime achievement award. For space exploration aficionados, this awards banquet promised a feast.

A month before the ceremony, Glenn came to Washington to address a small college seminar at the local offices of Ohio State University's John Glenn Institute for Public Service. He and I had arranged to meet before his seminar to go over the proposed Akron agenda, as well as for me to collect that book-signing raincheck. Along with my chief of staff Wayne Paugh and my twin daughters, we waited for him in the conference room where his seminar would take place later. A staffer directed students arriving early for the class to remain in an adjoining room until summoned.

During this lull, ten-year old Claire picked up a newspaper and read it silently. When another student entered the room for the lecture, the staffer directed her next door to wait with the others. At that very moment, an impolite sentence in the newspaper caught Claire's attention. Its rudeness shocked her, and she read it aloud, and loudly, to express her indignation at such printed language:

"Get the hell out of here RIGHT NOW!"

Everyone turned. Sensing that she stumbled into trouble, Claire pointed sheepishly to the newspaper. "Daddy," she said innocently, "*I* didn't say it! A man in the newspaper said it!" Everyone laughed except the flustered student who fled at Claire's apparent directive.

John and Annie Glenn arrived a few minutes later. "Hey, look, Annie!" he said while pointing to me, "There's my fellow member of the Congressional Has-Been Caucus!" I introduced

Dana and Claire Rogan, along with their Dad, join the Glenns in a "thumbs-up" (the *first* version of the pose), Washington, D.C., April 8, 2003 (Author's collection)

him to Wayne, and he hugged my daughters. "I remember you girls," he told them. "The last time I saw you both, you were riding on a shopping cart."

"Come on, girls," he called out while settling into a chair. "Let's get a family picture." They climbed into his lap as Annie and I flanked them. "Okay, let's give the photographer a thumbs-up," he directed, and everyone followed his instruction. The camera flashed, and then he suggested we take one more. Just before the shutter clicked, mischievous Claire dumped both thumbs downward (a prank I did not notice until the developed film came back from the processing lab).

After he and I went over the Akron agenda, he inscribed books for each of us. I also brought for autographs two original newspapers from his 1962 launch. "Oh, man," he exclaimed as he studied the front page and the artist's portrayal of him jammed inside the cramped capsule. "This brings back a lot of memories! They don't make 'em tight like that anymore, much to the modern astronauts' great pleasure."

With his class ready to begin, I told him with feigned sadness, "Sorry, John, but your seminar may be short one student. She got scared off before you arrived." When I told the story of Claire's newspaper recitation, he and Annie laughed. Giving Claire a "high-five" handclap, he asked, "Claire, may I borrow you for all my future meetings?"

• • •

A month later, Wayne and I flew to Akron for the black-tie dinner at the National Inventors Hall of Fame. We joined John and Annie at the two private VIP cocktail parties preceding the banquet. The first, an intimate gathering, was for the inductees and former NASA space shuttle astronauts Guion "Guy" Bluford and Kathryn Sullivan.

The Glenns asked about my daughters, and then he insisted that I tell the other astronauts about Claire's "Get the hell out of here" faux pas that scared away one of his students. "And she never did come back for my seminar!" he added.

I asked Annie about her memories of John's 1962 flight: "In those days," she said, "NASA officials wouldn't allow the astronauts' family members anywhere near the launch site. We were kept huddled some distance away from where John was preparing, and it added to the tension." When I asked how she coped with the pressure, she laughed and then looked at her husband. "During his flight, I did the physically impossible. I held my breath for almost five hours!"

I shared with Annie my boyhood memory of watching John's mother waving at the sky during his flight. Growing sentimental, he said, "When I went up in '62, both my Mom and Dad were still alive, so they got to see it." His eyes grew misty, and he paused for a moment before continuing. "I've always been glad that they lived to see the flight and all the accolades that came to their son. It meant *a lot* to them."

Changing the subject, he asked if I ever saw his *Friendship 7* Mercury space capsule at the Smithsonian Air and Space Museum. "My family and I are habitués there, so we've seen it many times," I replied.

"The next time you bring the girls to see it, check inside the capsule window and you'll see an interesting relic. Look for the small eye chart card on the control panel. NASA put it in there because they had no idea what would happen to the human eyeball in space at negative Gs and traveling at high speeds. They didn't know if I'd go blind or if my eyes would blow out of the sockets, so they rigged that small eye chart on the panel. Every fifteen minutes in space, I had to read the chart to the monitoring crew. They told me in advance that if I couldn't read the chart properly, I must abort the mission immediately."

He showed me the gold Mercury pin that he wore on his tuxedo jacket lapel. "NASA gave the original *Mercury Seven* astronauts a silver version of this pin when they selected us in 1959 for the space program. Once we flew, they gave us the gold version. They presented this to me after my 1962 flight. I've treasured it for a long, long time."

Soon we moved our intimate gathering to the general reception, where Glenn introduced me to Max Faget, the new Hall of Fame inductee, and told me, "Max designed my Mercury capsule." Slapping the short, elderly engineer on the back, he added, "We're old friends. I'm one of Max's satisfied customers!"

Glenn recalled the day during astronaut training when Max approached and said, "Hey, John, I think I figured out how to bring you back without you burning up in the atmosphere." He said that Max handed him a small honeycomb plug that he had invented and designed for insertion around the skin of the capsule to insulate it. "Max told me that the plug would only burn partially, but he warned me that if his calculations proved incorrect and it burned below where he thought it would go, then the capsule and I would be lost."

"That's true," Max told me. "And do you know what John replied? He said, 'Great! Put them on and send me up!'"

John reached into his coat pocket and produced one of Max's plugs encased in plastic. The marshmallow-shaped black plug's bottom resembled a used barbeque charcoal briquette because the 10,000-degree atmosphere had burned it white during the capsule's reentry. Showing the plug to Max, he told him, "When I got back [from the 1962 flight], NASA gave me this plug from *Friendship 7*. It's part of the heat shield you designed. I've kept it displayed on my desk since

With John Glenn and Max Faget at the National Inventors Hall of Fame, Akron, Ohio, May 3, 2003 (Author's collection)

that day." Turning to me, he added, "Those heat shield plugs Max designed burned down to the exact amount that he had estimated. If he had been off even slightly, I wouldn't be here today."

Max examined John's plug, handed it back, and smiled. "You know, John, I never told you this, but my calculations were off.

Actually, it burned farther than I had anticipated. Based on its actual burn rate and my original projections, you should have been turned into space dust forty years ago.

"Oh, well," Max added, "no harm, no foul."

Near the end of the reception, the Hall of Fame director welcomed everyone, and then he invited me to address the crowd. I stepped to the lectern and said that since I was speaking later at the award ceremonies, I would defer my remarks. However, I mentioned that I would be introducing Glenn later that evening, and that we had served in Congress together from different parties. Addressing him directly as he stood near the rear of the room, I added, "And John, if between now and my speech tonight you happen to reregister from Democrat to Republican, I can promise you a far more affectionate introduction!"

"Not a chance!" he shouted back amid laughter.

• • •

During the banquet, I sat between Glenn and Kathy Sullivan, who shared with me her experiences as an astronaut aboard three different space shuttle missions (STS-41-G, 1984; STS-31, 1990; STS-45, 1992). She said she spent almost three weeks in space and loved every minute. Her only regret was that NASA imposed severe restrictions on the personal items that astronauts may carry aboard their flights as souvenirs for friends and family. "There was a scandal years ago when some Apollo astronauts flew postal covers on their flight," she explained. "They returned to Earth and sold them for big money. It created a scandal, and because of it, NASA now limits what astronauts may carry to just a few medals and small flags. Back in John's day, things were different. When he returned in 1962, NASA gave him the control stick from his Mercury capsule as a souvenir. I wish I could have gotten a memento like that from the space shuttle!"

During this memorabilia discussion, Glenn talked with his wife

Annie, so he had not heard Kathy share with me the control stick information. I couldn't resist playing a joke, so I waited until he and I were speaking about something unrelated when I pretended to have my memory jogged: "Oh, John, I almost forgot. President Bush called me yesterday and said to tell you that NASA needs back the control stick from *Friendship 7*. They say you made off with it after splashdown, and now they want it back. Bush wants me to come to your house and pick it up. Shall I ride home with you tonight to get it?"

Here I am about to break the news to John Glenn that he needed to give back *Friendship 7's* control stick, National Inventors Hall of Fame, Akron, Ohio, May 3, 2003 (Author's collection)

John and Annie stared at me in silence for a moment, and then she replied, "But you can't! They *gave* that to John!"

"Well, I don't know about that," I deadpanned. "I only know President Bush wants it back."

Glenn's brow furrowed as he shook his head in dismay. "I— I just can't believe they'd do this," he protested. I couldn't hold back laughing, which gave away the joke. Everyone joined in, and a relieved Glenn added, "Whew! It's a good thing you were kidding, because I'd *never* give that back. It's been sitting on my shelf at home for forty years. I was going to tell you to call President Bush and tell him and NASA where to go!"

During dinner, he discussed with me the advances in aviation from the Wright Brothers to modern space flight. "When I flew aboard the shuttle in 1999," he said, "I carried a piece of the Wright Brothers' original plane with me." In a story that he repeated in his later speech, he described how the Wrights developed and refined their invention: "They had incredible problems on that first airplane. They didn't know how to control it laterally, meaning the side-by-side movement. They solved it by watching the birds to see how they did it. They figured out a way to imitate the birds by putting a yoke around the pilot's hips with a cable that went to the edge of the wing. When the pilot wanted lateral control, he slid his hips back and forth." He demonstrated the motion, shifting from right to left repeatedly in his chair.

"You make it look like they mastered lateral control and the *Samba* at the same time!"

"Pretty close. Their hip cable created the same motion for the trailing edge of the upper wing that the birds can do with their feathers. It's a good thing we improved on that invention, because I'd hate to fly a jet today with that same contraption!"

"That first Wright Brothers flight covered only one-half the length of the fuselage of a modern 747. That's how far we've come. It's hard to believe that the top speed on their first plane was only thirty-one miles an hour. A few years later the Army ordered a fleet of airplanes from the Wrights, and in their specs they contracted for delivery of planes that could fly *forty* miles an hour. In fact, the Army promised that if the Wrights delivered planes that could go forty-four miles an hour they'd pay them a big bonus. Just as amazing is that the Army specs for those first planes fit on *a single page*. One page—imagine such a thing today!"

He discussed the differences he experienced from flying aboard (as he called it) "the sardine can" Mercury capsule in 1962 and the much roomier shuttle almost four decades later: "The biggest differences were in communications and roominess. I could email my family and speak to them aboard the shuttle, which of course was impossible aboard Mercury. Also, on the shuttle, once in space we weren't strapped in, so we could move about in what was very much like a flying hotel. It had a bathroom, a gym, and sleeping quarters. All I had in the Mercury capsule was a strapped-in and cramped chair."

I recalled from our 1975 meeting the story he told me about the loose heat shield scare that occurred prior to *Friendship 7's* reentry. He downplayed the safety concerns from that flight. "Once Alan Shepard [the first American in space, whose brief suborbital flight preceded Glenn's orbital flight] went up and came back, we knew the capsule worked. As for the four-minute blackout in communications during my reentry, some have played that up as a nerve-wracking event to ground controllers, you know, 'Did he burn up during reentry?' It really wasn't that terrifying for the ground crew. They expected a communications blackout during reentry."

During that first flight, he said his primary concern wasn't safety, but instead whether he'd get off the launch pad. "We had many disappointing launch false starts," he said. "They suited me up six or seven different times for that flight. One day there was a problem with the weather. The next time there was a problem with the capsule. Then it would be the weather again, and then the capsule, and so on. NASA scheduled the launch *eleven* times. It had the buildup of a Hollywood movie premiere."

Throughout dinner, people interrupted our conversation to get his autograph, including a large group of children who lined up patiently at our table. He signed for everyone. During a break in these requests, I asked if, back in 1962, he had anticipated such enduring fame. He shook his head: "Not at all. I thought they might do some parades for a month or so, and then it would be over. The truth is I haven't had anonymity anywhere in the world for the last forty years. I never dreamed that a five-hour flight would bring such lasting recognition."

I took advantage of sitting with him during dinner to ask other questions, and later I recorded in my notes some historic tidbits that he shared:

"I greatly admired President Kennedy, but I was very disappointed in one thing he did to me. After my 1962 flight, I wanted to go back in space again. I petitioned repeatedly, but NASA stalled me year after year. I finally told them that if they weren't going to give me another mission, then I wasn't going to hang around. Eventually, I left NASA. It wasn't until years later, and long after Kennedy's death, that I learned that he had secretly ordered that NASA not allow me to fly again. Because my flight had attracted such fame and turned me into something of a hero, Kennedy feared that if I were killed on a later mission, it might end our future space program. I was deeply disappointed when I learned the truth."

As for JFK's brother, Senator Robert F. Kennedy, a longtime friend of Glenn's, he reminisced about campaigning for the martyred senator during his ill-fated presidential run in 1968. When I asked what RFK was like, he paused before answering: "Well, let's just say Bobby was a different kind of guy." His hesitating tone told me that there was more to the story than he wanted to share. "But I'll tell you this," he added. "Bobby was one of the few white men I knew who could go into an African-American church in Oakland and move the crowd to tears. I was with him and I saw it, and he did it during a time of great racial upheaval. I was also with him at the Ambassador Hotel in Los Angeles on the night that Sirhan Sirhan assassinated him. After the shooting, President Johnson sent a plane to Los Angeles for the Kennedy family's use. Bob died the next day. I was the one that the Kennedys asked to tell his children, one by one, that their father was dead. It was the worst day of my life."

When I asked if he ever met Charles Lindbergh, he shared this story: "I got to know him during World War II. Lindbergh had designed combat planes that developed the reputation of being dangerous, so he flew one himself out to the California air base where I was stationed. He allowed my fellow pilots and me to fly the plane ourselves, and he went up with us when we did to prove he had confidence in their safety. He even joined me later on a bombing mission overseas.

"Lindbergh was a recluse. I think that pattern developed after someone kidnapped and murdered his baby son. It grew worse over the years. He finally moved to Maui and lived like a hermit. When he died, his will instructed that he be buried in an unmarked grave."

"Speaking of aeronautical recluses," I asked, "do you stay in touch with Neil Armstrong?"

"Only occasionally. Neil is another one who doesn't like the limelight. He's always maintained a very low profile. I see him occasionally, but he pretty much keeps to himself."

When dinner service ended, a staffer escorted me backstage to begin the program. In anticipation of tonight's event, I had written to several former astronauts who were Glenn's contemporaries and invited them to send congratulatory letters for me to read at the ceremony. During the program, I shared some of these sentiments from his former NASA colleagues:[1]

> "Congratulations, John. Once again, you are receiving well-deserved recognition. I know that you and I both have mixed feelings about honors that we as astronauts receive, when so many others did the real inventing and hard work for Mercury, Gemini and Apollo, and other endeavors in our lives. You are, however, one of the best choices your hosts would have made to receive a lifetime achievement award on behalf of the 450,000 Americans who dedicated themselves to one of the most significant achievements in human history, the landing on and exploration of the Moon. Not only did they meet the original challenge delivered to our generation by President Kennedy, they made a major contribution to the end of the Cold War by convincing our adversaries that Americans can and will do whatever is necessary to preserve freedom. The ongoing demonstration of this same dedication in Afghanistan and Iraq underscores the remarkable

---

1   At the end of the evening, I offered the file folder of these original congratulatory letters to Glenn. He told me I could keep them. "You're the collector," he said, "and my scrapbooks are big enough. It's the sentiments that matter." The letters remain preserved in my historic memorabilia collection.

ingenuity, bravery, and compassion of another generation of young Americans in bringing freedom to others while protecting our own. With best personal regards, Jack Schmidt." [Apollo 17 astronaut and former U.S. Senator]

"Dear John: I'm so sorry that Marilyn and I will not be able to attend this evening. Congratulations on another special honor. I cannot think of another person more worthy to receive the lifetime achievement award in celebration of the centennial of flight. It is with respect and admiration that I add my congratulations to you on this very fitting honor, recognizing your contributions. Your brilliant career has expanded over fifty years, and to this day, you continue to give back to your country. Best wishes, Jim Lovell." [Apollo 13 astronaut]

"I am delighted to learn that the National Inventors Hall of Fame will be presenting a lifetime achievement award to John Glenn. He is certainly a worthy recipient, although he has been blessed with a very long life in which to achieve! John was an avid physical fitness fellow during the Mercury program and his colleagues claimed that he was the inventor of running. If true, this would be an excellent additional qualification while being presented at the National Inventors Hall of Fame. I'm disappointed that the scheduling gods have ruled against me joining you for this special occasion, but I trust it will be a memorable evening. I send my very best wishes for the success of the occasion. Sincerely, Neil Armstrong." [Apollo 11 astronaut and first man on the Moon]

In my introduction of Glenn, I spoke extemporaneously and from the heart about his profound contributions to science, exploration, and country. I no longer recall what I said, but I remember fondly that Wayne said later that Glenn told him as I wrapped up, "That's one of the best introductions anyone ever gave me. It was very kind of him, and very, very nice."

The audience stood and applauded as Glenn joined me on stage. I presented his award, and then resumed my seat at our table as he delivered his speech.

"'Lifetime Award' makes it sound like it's all over, but I ain't ready to quit yet!" he quipped. In prepared remarks, he paid tribute to tonight's Hall of Fame inductees, and then he discussed how innovation revolutionized flight almost overnight: "It's hard to believe that only twelve years separated that first Wright Brothers flight at Kitty Hawk from the aerial dogfights of the Red Baron, the *Lafayette Esquadrille*, and Captain Eddie Rickenbacker in World War I. In only sixty-six years we went from Kitty Hawk to the Moon—an amazingly rapid advance."

His words that night hit the mark: curiosity leads to invention and exploration, and that combination improves the quality of life for all of mankind. On that score alone, John Glenn made a vast contribution to both his and future generations.

• • •

As noted earlier, John Glenn missed much of his final Senate year. By then the bipartisan goodwill he had always enjoyed with his Republican colleagues had diminished, so perhaps it was just as well.

In 1997, the Senate authorized its Governmental Affairs Committee, under the chairmanship of Senator Fred Thompson (R-TN), to investigate foreign government money-laundering into Bill Clinton's 1996 reelection campaign. Thompson, who had served as Senator Howard Baker's chief counsel during the 1970s *Watergate* hearings, hoped to model his investigation on the same bipartisan template developed by Baker and the Democrat Chairman, Senator Sam Ervin. Thompson assumed that the ranking Democrat on his committee, his boyhood hero John Glenn, was the perfect counterpart to approach the inquiry with balance and judiciousness.

Thompson's fantasy collapsed minutes into the first session.

In a jaw-rattling blast, Glenn denounced the investigation and accused his Republican colleagues, and not Clinton, as the ones offering daily favors for special interest money. Glenn's atypical nastiness stunned Thompson. During the hearings, Glenn's continued assaults, coupled with his procedural foot-dragging, led to a *Wall Street Journal* rebuke. The paper accused him of turning the proceedings into "a partisan circus" and contributing "to a cover-up of [Clinton's] misdeeds[.]"[2]

Speculation over the cause behind Glenn's unexpected personality transformation pointed to White House pressure. Andrew Ferguson of *The Weekly Standard* was one of those who accused Clinton of holding hostage Glenn's desire to return to space in exchange for Glenn's help in torpedoing the Thompson hearings, branding it a "blatant political payoff."[3] Reporters and pundits weren't the only ones believing the extortion narrative.

Fred Thompson believed it, too.

During a private meeting with me in early 1998, Thompson told me that he was convinced Clinton blackmailed Glenn into adopting slash-and-burn tactics in exchange for approving Glenn's shuttle flight later that year. "That Clinton would play this card against a man of Glenn's stature makes me mad enough to cut off Clinton's balls," Thompson fumed through clenched teeth. He added, "These guys in the Clinton White House will do whatever it takes to win. When they can get a man like John Glenn to do what he did and behave as badly as he behaved during my hearings, you see just how dirty they can be."[4]

Other senators subscribed to the blackmail notion. "John Glenn

---

2   "Glenn's Reward," *The Wall Street Journal*, October 27, 1998, https://www.wsj.com/articles/SB909440576130281500 (accessed August 11, 2019).

3   Andrew Ferguson, "John Glenn," *The Weekly Standard*, July 6, 1997, https://www.washingtonexaminer.com/weekly-standard/john-glenn (accessed August 11, 2019).

4   See James Rogan, *Catching Our Flag*, 68-69.

used to be a hero," I heard a Republican senator grumble to a group of his GOP colleagues at the time of the hearings. I looked to see the others' reactions: each nodded in agreement.

• • •

Writing these personal reflections of John Glenn decades later, what do I make of this alleged Clinton arm-twisting and Glenn's possible submission to it?

It is true that during the hearings, Glenn's disruptive approach shattered Thompson's naïve hope of a bipartisan investigation. Such behavior from Glenn was, to say the least, uncharacteristic.

Further, the chronology shows that NASA, controlled by Clinton, withheld its announcement of Glenn's return to space until the press lost interest in the Thompson hearings and they sputtered into irrelevancy.

I know from my personal experience of battling and impeaching Clinton how dirty he and his team played. They would not have hesitated to throw sharp elbows into anyone, including a hero senator, if they

Presenting John Glenn his lifetime achievement award, National Inventors Hall of Fame, Akron, Ohio, May 3, 2003 (Author's collection)

needed something and if they had the leverage to compel submission. Given all this, do I believe that Clinton pressured John Glenn to turn the Thompson hearings into a sideshow, and that Glenn yielded to it?

Yes.

Can I prove it?

No.

If I *could* prove it, would it diminish my lifelong admiration and respect for John Glenn's seventy-five-year record of incalculable service to country?

Not one bit.

• • •

A year after the National Inventors Hall of Fame inducted Max Faget into its ranks, he died of bladder cancer at age 83 on October 9, 2004.

Fred Thompson retired from Congress in 2003. He returned to his earlier career of motion picture and television actor; he also hosted a talk radio show, wrote a syndicated column, and made an unsuccessful run for the 2008 Republican presidential nomination. He died of lymphoma at age 73 on November 1, 2015.

After leaving the Senate in 1999, John Glenn helped to educate future leaders through the John Glenn College for Public Service, as well as continuing his advocacy for America's space program. Awarded the Presidential Medal of Freedom in 2012, the last surviving member of the original *Mercury 7* astronauts died at age 95 on December 8, 2016 from complications following a stroke. When Marine Corps pallbearers laid him to rest at Arlington National Cemetery, a nation in mourning recalled Scott Carpenter's 1962 prayer as *Friendship 7* cleared the launch pad:

Godspeed, John Glenn.

2

The Champp

I was just a boy when he hit his athletic prime and I couldn't stand him. I thought him anti-American and a draft dodger, and I longed to see someone flatten him in the ring. At a time when most sports heroes were humble and unassuming, boxer Cassius Clay (who later changed his name to Muhammad Ali after converting to Islam) was a loudmouthed braggart. I disliked him so much that I felt guilty whenever I caught myself smiling at his outrageous and often hilarious antics and commentaries. In later years Ali supposedly credited his shtick to the advice given him at age 19 by "Gorgeous George" Wagner, whose boastful ways made him the highest-paid and most famous professional wrestler of the 1940s and 1950s: "A lot of people will pay to see someone shut your mouth, so keep bragging, keep sassing, and always be outrageous."

My favorite Ali rhyme came from the Vitalis hair tonic television commercial he made with his upcoming opponent, world heavy-weight boxing champion Joe Frazier. It aired during the final days before their title bout in March 1971, aptly called (then and now), "The Fight of the Century." The split screen image showed Frazier and Ali taunting each other during a telephone call. As Ali riffed about how he would demolish Frazier, the champion couldn't keep up with the challenger's fast-running mouth, so he called Ali "Clay" to get a rise out of him. (Since his conversion to Islam, Ali resented anybody calling him by what he termed a derogatory "slave name.")

"What'd you call me?" Ali barked into the telephone handset at Frazier, who then repeated the gibe. Ali then got in a final rhyme that I can still recite from memory almost five decades after hearing it only once: *Joe Frazier, I say this with no malice. When I get done with your head you gonna need some Vitalis!*

It took me a long time to change my mind about Muhammad Ali, but when I did, along with millions of others, it was a complete reversal. By the end of his career I respected his unmatched athletic prowess, I enjoyed without guilt his theatrical antics, and I admired his philanthropic heart. He proved himself the consummate showman and, unlike most celebrities du jour, Ali remained one of the world's most recognizable and beloved figures decades after his time in the limelight ended.

He was an American Original, and my encounters with him remain a fond memory.

• • •

A native of Louisville, Cassius Clay, Jr. first gained national recognition as a boxer at age eighteen when he won a gold medal at the 1960 Olympics. After he turned professional, few gave him a chance when he signed in 1964 to fight the reigning heavyweight champion, Sonny Liston. Clay entered the match as a seven-to-one underdog against the thuggish brawler Liston, who served a prison stretch for robberies before earning a parole and turning to boxing. Despite the pre-fight prediction in a poll of forty-three out of forty-six sportswriters that Liston would win by a knockout, Clay beat him.

"I am the greatest!" Clay proclaimed that night while mugging for the cameras, and the legend was off and running.

After joining the Nation of Islam two weeks after his Liston bout, Clay changed his name to Muhammad Ali. He joined the 1960s civil rights movement and he became a vocal opponent of the Vietnam War. When his draft number came up, he refused induction and told reporters, "I ain't got no quarrel with them Vietcong."[1] A judge sentenced him to five years in prison (the U.S. Supreme Court later overturned Ali's conviction in 1971).

Stripped of his title because of a felony conviction, no state would issue him a boxing license while he remained free pending appeal. Thus, Ali was banned from the ring for over three prime fighting years, from March 1967 until the New York commission reinstated his license in late 1970.

After returning to the ring and losing the "Fight of the Century" in a decision to Frazier, Ali went on to regain the championship twice: once from George Foreman in 1974, and again from Leon Spinks in 1978 (after losing it to Spinks earlier that year), making him the only boxer to win the world heavyweight championship three times. He retired from boxing at age 39 in 1981 with a career record of fifty-six wins, five losses, and thirty-seven knockouts. In later years, *Sports Illustrated* magazine named him the greatest athlete of the twentieth century, while *Ring* magazine and the *Associated Press* named him the greatest heavyweight boxer of all time.

A few years after retiring, Ali revealed that doctors had diagnosed him with Parkinson's disease, which they attributed to the years of severe head blows he suffered in the ring. For the next three decades, Ali traveled the world, made public appearances, and engaged in charity work as the illness took its continuing toll. Despite his increasing physical limitations, he enjoyed meeting and delighting his fans wherever he went.

• • •

After winning a seat in Congress in 1996, I developed an interest in Parkinson's research. Ali had sent me a letter on the subject, and this put me in touch with his camp. I became friends with Kim Vidt, who worked for Ali as his personal assistant and family

---

1   Bob Orkand, *The New York Times,* June 27, 2017 (accessed June 17, 2020).

spokeswoman. Later, after I helped her son obtain a congressional internship, she repaid the favor mightily.

In June 1997 Kim called and told me that Ali and his family planned to make a quiet visit to Washington for a couple of days to attend a friend's wedding and to take a private tour of the Holocaust Museum before returning home to Michigan. She invited my family and me to join the Ali family on the tour. Sadly, pressing congressional business that afternoon precluding my going, so she suggested we visit at his hotel.

Along with my legislative assistant Myron Jacobson (who doubled as office photographer), we arrived at the Hay-Adams hotel in the late morning. I followed Kim's directions and asked the desk clerk to ring the room reserved under her maiden name. The clerk found no such registration. "For whom are you looking?" he asked. When I told him, he rechecked the record. "Oh, look at this, the room is registered under Mr. Ali's own name. That's unusual. I'll ring him." After calling and confirming my invitation, the clerk directed us upstairs to room 218.

Jill, Ali's bubbly publicist, greeted us at the door. "Where are your wife and daughters?" she asked. When I explained that the girls had a school obligation that kept them from coming, she said, "I'm so sorry. Muhammad wanted to meet the twins."

She escorted us into the suite, where random activity buzzed among the small crowd of people. A young girl covered by a blanket slept on the couch in front of a television set airing a black-and-white episode of the early-1960s *Andy Griffin Show*. Two young teenagers ran in and out of an adjoining bedroom while Lonnie Ali, Muhammad's wife, introduced herself quickly and apologized for the need to round up her children.

Howard Bingham, Ali's longtime friend and his photographer since the 1960s, welcomed me. "Come on, I'll introduce you to the Champ. He's been waiting to meet you." I followed Howard from the foyer to the bright living room, where Ali sat motionless in a

Meeting the Champ, Washington, June 24, 1997 (Author's collection)

chair next to an unlit marble fireplace. He wore an untucked yellow
polo shirt with dark sunglasses dangling from his collar. His face
looked round and full; his head was bowed but his eyes were open.
His large hands and forearms lay motionless on the chair arm rests,
and he weighed almost fifty pounds over his prime boxing weight.
The only discernable muscular movement came from his eyes, which
tracked me as I approached.

"Hey, Champ," Howard said, "this is Congressman Jim Rogan.
He's a good friend who's helped us." Ali raised his head slowly but
otherwise showed no facial muscle movement except for in his eyes,
which looked soft and comforting. He then lifted one arm slowly and

took my hand. This minimal task took obvious concentrated effort.

Howard told me that the progressive disease affected Ali's ability to speak by limiting his mouth and jaw muscle movements. When he tried to speak to me, the sound that came from him was almost indecipherable beyond the last word, which sounded like "laser." Fortunately, Howard was more than his photographer. He also played the role of interpreter. Ali's face remained expressionless, but his eyes twinkled as Howard explained what he had just said: "The Champ says you look just like Joe Frazier!"

I smiled. "I hope you don't mean I look like him after you beat both of his eyes swollen shut during your *Thrilla' in Manila!* Well, at least you didn't look at my stomach and say I resembled George Foreman!" (Ali beat Foreman for the championship in 1974; in 1997, at age 48, Foreman came out of retirement and earned a surprisingly impressive win record despite his age, corpulent physique, and a notorious training diet of hamburgers and milkshakes.) Ali laughed and squeezed my hand when I referenced his two former opponents.

At Kim's earlier suggestion, I had brought a few boxing gloves to have Ali sign for my daughters and me, along with an oversized copy of Neil Leifler's iconic photograph of Ali standing over Sonny Liston sprawled on the canvas after Ali's first-round knockout in 1965. "Hey, Champ, Congressman Jim wants these signed for his family," Howard told him. Ali took the first glove and, with pen in hand, began inscribing it for my daughter Claire.

Once I saw how slow and laborious the task proved, I felt terrible for asking. I whispered to Howard and begged off on the autograph request, but he brushed off my concern: "This is what the Champ does all day," Howard replied. "Look around." Stacks of photographs, books, boxing gloves, posters, and other memorabilia lay strewn against Ali's chair and on the ground near his feet. "He's been sitting in this chair all morning signing autographs for strangers. When you leave, he'll continue sitting in this chair for hours, day and night, signing autographs for strangers. He signs hundreds of things every day. He does it because he knows it makes people very happy. In the Muslim faith, these are good works, and good works are what help you get into Heaven. He *wants* to do it for you and your girls. He's going to sign stuff anyway, and he'd prefer doing it for friends. Don't worry about how long it takes him as long as you don't mind that it takes him a while to do it."

I didn't mind.

Ali inscribed and signed each item at a painfully slow rate. Sometimes he made noises that sounded more like a snore or throat clearing than talking, but his staff and family all understood what he said. While he signed away, Jill told me that even with his physical limitations, he maintained an extensive travel and public appearance schedule. "He was home only ninety days last year," she said to my amazement. "The truth is that he loves the crowds and attention, and he especially loves to meet the children."

• • •

Despite his condition, Ali's sense of humor, along with his penchant for practical jokes and doing magic tricks for visitors had not diminished. "I've read about your famous levitation trick, Champ," I told him, "and someday I want you to teach it to me. I'd like to levitate a bunch of guys out of Washington." His face softened as he laughed, and then he strained against his chair armrests as if trying to stand. Unable to accomplish the task without assistance, Howard and I gripped him under each arm to lend an assist. It took great physical effort to hoist 255 pounds of dead weight out of that chair.

Once standing, Ali mumbled something to Howard, who then told me, "The Champ wants you to stand behind him and watch his heels. He's going to levitate himself!" Ali walked a few paces in front of me and then turned his back. "Watch his heels! Watch his heels!" Howard repeated. Ali slowly raised his arms out to his sides, pointed his index finger downward, and began making an "OOOOHHHHHH" sound as he circled his fingers slowly as if conjuring a magic spell. He rose slowly on the ball of one foot with near perfect equilibrium, and then raised the other foot a few inches off the floor. Then, with only the ball of one foot providing stability, he raised and lowered his height several times. Watching his heels from behind created the optical illusion of Ali hovering over the carpet. For a man without enough strength or muscle control to rise form his chair unassisted, he demonstrated remarkable balance once upright.

"You're floating, Champ!" I encouraged him.

He lowered himself to the ground, turned, and mumbled, "Good trick!" With a childlike look of satisfaction in his eyes, he trudged back to his chair and fell into it with a thud.

Not wanting to overstay my welcome, I signaled my readiness to leave several times. Jill and Howard appeared in no hurry for me to go. Although Ali was unable to engage in conversation, he listened intently while both Jill and Howard asked me about my family and my life in Congress.

Ali doing his levitation trick for my amusement (Author's collection)

Eventually, the time came for me to get back to Capitol Hill. I thanked Ali for our meeting and for the courageous symbol that he became for millions. He struggled to rise, so again Howard and I took him under each arm and heaved him upward to his feet. I said what I thought was my final goodbye, but as I did so, he bent forward slowly, turned his cheek toward me, moved it within two inches of my mouth, and studied me from the corners of his eyes.

I wasn't sure what he was doing or what he wanted. He kept staring at me and didn't move. I smiled. Ali remained frozen in that position saying nothing.

"You know, Champ," I said, "I have four-year-old twin daughters. When they put their cheek up next to me just like you're doing, it's because they want me to kiss them goodbye."

Ali remained silent and motionless, but he kept looking at me with impish eyes.

I continued: "If that's what you want, then I'll do it. Is that what you want me to do, Champ? I'm asking because there's no way I'm going to kiss the three-time world heavyweight boxing champion unless I'm sure that's what he wants me to do."

Maintaining his sideward gaze, Ali moved his cheek even closer, so I kissed him. He dropped his head slightly, chuckled, and then turned his other cheek toward me. After planting a second kiss on him, I turned my head sideways cheek-first and now stared at him through the corners of my eyes. His laughter grew louder as he leaned forward and gave my cheek a return peck.

"Now we're engaged!" he mumbled.

Ali took my right hand. I didn't know what he was doing as he slowly, oh, so slowly, started bending inward my index finger down to the second knuckle. Once done he repeated the process with my remaining fingers and thumb. When he positioned all of them inward, he cupped his huge hand around mine and squeezed it gently until my hand formed a fist. Then, moving just as slowly, he took my fist, brought it up to the tip of his nose, and mumbled something indecipherable to me.

Howard assisted: "The Champ says get your left up and protect yourself!" I made a fist with my left hand and raised it. Ali then closed his fists, raised both of his arms slightly, and then he motioned with his head for Myron to take the photograph. This fun shot, which Ali created to make it look like I had broken through the defenses of the greatest boxer in history, remains one of my most treasured memories captured on camera. With that, he reached out his arms and gave me a bear hug.

One of my favorite pictures—here I am "sparring" with the three-time heavyweight boxing champion of the world (Author's collection)

As I turned to leave, a room service steward arrived with a tray filled with cans of Coca-Cola and large bags of M&M's candy. Ali studied the contents of the tray, and then he looked at me and spoke the only word that I understood without Howard's intercession:

"Lunch!"

• • •

Kim Vidt and I remained in touch, and she surprised me occasionally with signed memorabilia from Ali. She also told me she would keep me posted if he returned to Washington so that my family could meet him.

That opportunity arose two years later when ESPN hosted "A Salute to Sports Greats" reception for members of Congress at the Capitol. Kim called to tell me that Ali would attend and that he wanted to meet my wife and daughters if they were in town. The answer, of course, was yes.

ESPN lobbyist (and coordinator for the reception) Brian Kelly told me he was glad my family was coming because there might not be another opportunity. "Ali's family told us this will probably be his last public appearance," he said sadly. "He just can't do it anymore. His Parkinson's has gotten really bad, and they want to preserve his dignity in public." He suggested that we come to Room HC-5 a few minutes before the 5 p.m. start time to beat the crowd.

• • •

As we arrived at the reception, I tried explaining the circumstances of Ali's physical condition in a way that seven-year-olds would understand. I told them not to expect him to do much talking or moving because his illness made it very hard for him to do so. Dana grew teary-eyed and told Claire how sad he must feel at being so sick. Claire took her sister's hand and said, "Come on, Dana, we'll cheer him up. He'll feel better then!" With that, they marched together into the reception alongside us.

Taking Brian's earlier advice, I was the first congressman to arrive. A group of ESPN, Disney Company, and other sponsors welcomed us. Brian gave me the head's up that Ali was present, but I didn't see him anywhere in the already crowded room. Brian introduced us to Carl Lewis, the world record-holding track and field star named by *Sports Illustrated* magazine as the "Olympian of the Century." During his competitive career (1979 to 1996), Lewis won nine Olympic gold medals, one silver medal, and ten world championship medals.

While chatting with Lewis, I noticed Dana nudging Claire and pointing to something. I looked where she pointed and saw Ali seated in a metal folding chair alone on the opposite side of the room. He fed himself grapes from a small plastic plate, raising each one to his mouth slowly.

"There's the Champ!" Dana whispered to Claire excitedly.

I knew what came next.

"Excuse me for a minute, Mr. Lewis," I said, "but I have to avoid a catastrophe." I was too late. Before I could stop them, both girls bolted across the room. I tried to catch them, but they navigated around sets of knees faster than I could get around whole bodies.

My concerns elevated as they drew closer to their target. If nobody else had approached Muhammad Ali in this crowded room, it must be for a reason. Maybe he was unable to greet people and we were the only ones who hadn't received the memo.

Too late.

Before I could catch them, the girls scrambled onto his lap. Claire stroked his cheek. "Oh, Champ," she said, "you're so sweet. I hope you feel better now." Meanwhile, Dana threw her arm

Olympian Carl Lewis with my family; the photographer took this picture seconds before Dana and Claire (depicted below) spotted the Champ, September 30, 1999 (Author's collection)

around his neck, told him that she loved him and hoped he felt better, and then she kissed him.

Ali's expressionless face lit up suddenly. His mouth turned upward into a smile, and his eyes filled with warmth. He wrapped his long arms around my girls as they told him they would pray for him.

"I love you, babies," he whispered through lips that barely moved. "I love you, babies."

Christine and I finally caught up and apologized for the destructive force of Hurricanes Dana and Claire, but he appeared delighted by their unrestrained affection. Photographers converging on the scene, and camera flashes now illuminated the corner of the room.

Dana, Claire, and a smiling Muhammad Ali: the photos speak for themselves.

Ali nodded for Chris and me to join them for a family picture. After we posed, I told the girls it was time to go. I didn't want them to monopolize the Champ's time. Dana and Claire hugged him goodbye. He smiled warmly as he leaned forward and kissed both of them. "Bye, my babies," he whispered. "I love you, babies."

In our family, the feeling was mutual.

The Champ gets a kiss from Dana....

...and a caress from her twin sister Claire (Author's collection)

• • •

In late May 2016, Muhammad Ali entered a Phoenix hospital for respiratory issues. He died there of septic shock at age 74 on June 3, 2016. In an obituary that ran the next day, Robert Lipsyte of the *New York Times* summarized the boxer's legacy: "Loved or hated, he remained for fifty years one of the most recognizable people on the planet." That was true. When I met Ali at his suite in the Hay Adams hotel, he had last won the boxing crown over twenty years earlier. Later that afternoon, when he stepped from his hotel to leave for his museum tour, the sight of him on a Washington street stopped traffic in all directions.

Howard Bingham, Ali's photographer, and biographer, died at age 77 on December 15, 2016.

3

The Car in the Motorcade

S-100-X is the most famous car in automotive history. You have seen it many times, you would recognize its photograph instantly, and yet its name conjures in you no recognition. Unlike Ford's *Mustang* or Chevrolet's *Corvette*, when this car rolled off the assembly line it was assigned no catchy name: just a number. It set no speed records. At over twenty feet long and almost four tons, it moved with the nimbleness of a World War I tank. In fact, it took its place in history while traveling at only 11.2 miles an hour. It isn't its speed or design drawing almost two million people annually to view it on display in a museum.

SS-100-X began as a 1961 Ford Lincoln Continental four-door convertible. After major modifications, it joined the White House fleet of automobiles. On November 22, 1963, it transported President and Mrs. John F. Kennedy and Texas Governor and Mrs. John Connally along a seven-mile procession through Dallas, Texas. At 12:30 p.m. that afternoon, it became a macabre relic of American history.

SS-100-X: it was the car in The Motorcade.

Many years later, I came to know several people who rode in that fateful procession.[1] The recollections they shared with me about their experiences that day follow.

---

1   When researching this chapter, I learned that two journalists I had met in previous years, Peter Lisagor of the *Chicago Daily News* and David Broder of the *Washington Post*, both had traveled in the Dallas motorcade press bus. I was unaware of this at the time, so I missed the opportunity of asking them about it.

• • •

DAVID F. POWERS

Born in 1912 in Boston to Irish immigrants, Powers worked in the publishing business and served in the Army during World War II before meeting fellow veteran John F. Kennedy in 1946. When the future president returned home from the war and ran for Con-

gress that year, Powers joined the campaign and remained with Kennedy all the way to the White House. His formal administration title was Special Assistant to the President, but their relationship ran much deeper. He was a member of the "Irish Mafia," a tight circle of longtime Kennedy confidants. The year after

With Dave Powers in his JFK Library office, July 16, 1993
(Author's collection)

the assassination, Powers became the first curator and director of the John F. Kennedy Presidential Library and Museum.

Powers and I had connected through a mutual friend. In 1993, when he learned of my forthcoming Boston visit, he invited me to the library to join him for coffee.

Within minutes of arriving at his office, we were fellow Irishmen sharing jokes and stories of family connections to the old country. He told me he knew some Rogans from Ireland. Their name originally was Regan, but an immigration official at Ellis Island transposed the "e" to an "o" when their ancestors arrived here. He asked if they were any relation. "Only if they're rich Irish," I replied.

He laughed. "I know what you mean. I was a poor working-class shanty Irishman who just happened to know the president of the United States."

Dave Powers and I hit it off at once.

Our connection cemented when I showed him my copy of his 1972 book *Johnny, We Hardly Knew Ye* that he had signed for me when I was a teenager. "And you've kept it all these years!" he exclaimed with appreciation.

"Since I hear that you're a political memorabilia collector," he said, "I put together a few things for you." He handed me a large envelope of various JFK photographs from the library, along with a vintage *Life* magazine from December 1963, which was the JFK memorial edition. "I had a few of these left over, and I thought you'd like to have it." We stood over his desk as he flipped through the magazine and commented wistfully over many of the highlights of Kennedy's life depicted in the photos.

He turned yet another page, and then his expression changed. Gone was the smile, and a pained look overcame him. I looked down at the page that altered his demeanor. It was a photo spread from the 8mm Zapruder film, which was the only motion picture footage taken of the assassination. He closed the magazine. "I wish that wasn't in there," he said in a whisper.

"Dave, you were there that day. Are you ever able to shake the memory of it?"

"Never. Here at the library reminders surround me every day of what might have been. It's unavoidable."

We sat on the couch and he told me about that trip to Dallas. Because Texas was a key state for JFK's anticipated 1964 reelection campaign, Kennedy chose to make a two-day trip there to shore up his support. He described their hectic schedule after leaving Washington on November 21 for San Antonio, Houston, and Fort Worth (where the official party spent the night).

"The next day, after a speech to the chamber of commerce, we flew from Fort Worth to Dallas and landed at Love Field. The crowds were huge and friendly, and the president and Jackie beamed when they came off the plane. After shaking hands with people along the fence, they climbed into the limousine with Governor and Mrs. Connally. I was in the Secret Service car right behind them as we started the procession through downtown Dallas to the Trade Mart, where the president had a speech scheduled for 12:30.

"Along the way I took home movies of the crowds and the motorcade, but I ran out of film as we got closer to downtown. There the crowds grew larger and larger, and they were more and more enthusiastic. The president and Jackie rode in the back seat of their car. He waved to the people on the right, and she waved to the crowd on the left. We planned it that way so that nobody on the sidewalks would feel ignored.

"We turned off Main Street. We made a couple of sharp turns and proceeded onto Elm Street, which put us almost at the end of the route. We were going slowly on the turns. I checked my watch and saw it was 12:30, which was the time we were due at the Trade Mart a few miles away. That was good, I thought. We weren't too late. We'd be there in a few minutes.

"Then I heard what I thought was a firecracker. I looked up and saw the president's body start moving slowly to the left. Another shot rang out, and Governor Connally disappeared from view. I saw a nearby overpass in front of us and I thought that maybe someone was shooting at us in an ambush. Then I heard a third shot and saw it blow off the back of the president's head. The impact of the bullet sounded like a melon thrown against a cement wall.

"The cars all accelerated quickly. Jackie climbed onto the back of the limousine, but a Secret Service agent jumped on the rear of the car and shoved her back inside. It probably saved her life.

"When we arrived at the hospital a few minutes later, I ran over to the president's car. Several of us picked him up and put him on a stretcher. I knew he was gone when I saw him."

Powers pushed aside the magazine. "Come on," he said, "let me show you some happier memories." He gave me a tour of the photographs from the Kennedy years adorning his walls, which included signed pictures and mementos from John, Robert, and Edward Kennedy. One photo depicted JFK and Powers in a motorcade through Ireland a few months before the assassination, inscribed, "Dave Powers goes home. Best wishes from his travelling companion, John Kennedy." Nearby was a framed document bearing a seal and ribbon. During the Kennedy years, JFK promoted fifty-mile hikes for physical fitness. After Kennedy pressured Powers into making one of those lengthy treks, the president presented him with this unique certificate congratulating him for hiking fifty miles—to and from Kennedy's refrigerator to steal the president's Heinekens.

"Here's something that you'll *really* appreciate," he said, and then he led me around his desk to a rocking chair. "This was the president's actual rocker that he used in the Oval Office. When we closed down the library exhibits for refurbishing some months ago, I told the archivist to store this here." During JFK's presidency, he used it to ease his chronic back pain, and he loved it so much that his staff brought it on Air Force One whenever he traveled. I had seen countless photographs of him relaxing in this very chair. I mentioned that I recalled watching the TV news the day after the assassination and saw a mover wheeling this

Dave Powers' snapshot of me giving JFK's Oval Office rocker a spin, July 16, 1993 (Author's collection)

rocker on a dolly out of the Oval Office. When that image came across the screen, my tough-as-nails longshoreman grandfather wept.

Dave nodded. "Give it a try," he told me as he motioned with his head toward the chair.

"Are you sure?"

"Go ahead. The president wouldn't mind if an Irish kid from San Francisco sat in it."

"What if he knew the Irish kid was a Republican?"

He laughed. "Well, that might be a problem, but we won't tell him. Go on, try it out." Dave picked up my camera and snapped a photograph of me sitting in JFK's chair.

"That's a very historic chair," he said with a grin, "and you're adding to its history. You just became the first Republican ever to sit in it—

"—And, trust me, you'll be the last!"

• • •

EVELYN LINCOLN

John F. Kennedy hired Evelyn Lincoln as his personal secretary during his final months as a member of the House of Representatives. She remained in that sensitive post when Kennedy moved on to both the U.S. Senate and the White House. Like Dave Powers, she flew to Texas with the president and rode in the motorcade.

I struck up an acquaintance with Mrs. Lincoln (as the president always called her) through the mail when I was a teenager and after she had retired. In later years, we became friends and spoke over the telephone often. She was quite pleased that the young boy who used to write to her about his interest in history and politics later served in public office.

Although we had maintained a friendship for many years, we met only once. Over dinner with my wife and me in 1991, she shared many behind the scenes stories of the Kennedys, Lyndon Johnson, Richard Nixon, and other leaders of that era. Ironically, our evening together coincided with the twenty-eighth anniversary of Kennedy's assassination.[2] As the wine poured, she offered increasingly unvarnished recollections—until it came to Dallas. When I tried drawing out those memories, she couldn't go beyond generalities. The grief proved too much. It wasn't until a couple of years later during a phone conversation that she offered these limited comments about that day.

"We left the White House by helicopter for Andrews Air Force Base on Thursday morning, the day before he died, and we flew aboard Air Force One to Texas. During the flight, the president sat in his private office talking to a number of Texas congressmen joining him for the trip. Later that night, he spoke at a testimonial dinner in Houston, and then we spent the night in Fort Worth.

"On Friday morning, before he left the hotel, I had the chance to introduce him to a few of my relatives who lived in the area. They were thrilled to shake his hand and meet him. He looked so handsome in his blue suit, and he charmed them.

"The president made a breakfast speech to the chamber of commerce, and then we headed to the airport. The flight to Dallas was short—only fifteen minutes. I remember taking some memos into his private cabin for him to sign. He looked distracted as he chatted with the congressmen seated with him. While he listened, he signed the memos and handed them back to me. They were the last things he ever signed.

"Air Force One landed at Love Field. It had been raining when we left Fort Worth, but now there was sunshine. I knew Kennedy would be pleased, because without the rain he could ride in the limo without the bubbletop on it. He always preferred to ride in an open car with no covering so that the crowds could get a better look at him. Afterward, the press reported that the bubbletop would have

---

2   The details of Mrs. Lincoln's recollections that she shared during our dinner are recounted in my book, *And Then I Met...*, 181-188.

saved him from gunfire, but that's not true. The bubbletop wasn't bulletproof. Its only purpose was to protect him from the elements.

"By the time I got off the plane, I saw that he and Jackie were shaking hands with people along the fence. She wore a pink suit and matching pillbox hat, and she held a bouquet of red roses in her arm.

"I was already in my assigned car when the president and Jackie climbed to their limousine. Governor and Mrs. Connally were with them. The motorcade left for the Trade Mart, where the president had a 12:30 speech.

With my wife Christine and Evelyn and Abe Lincoln, November 22, 1991 (Author's collection)

"As we drove through Dallas, I was amazed at the crowd size and the wonderful response we received. We had worried about hostile protests, but I saw none. Everybody was cheering, smiling, and waving. My last memory of Kennedy alive was seeing him in the back of the limousine with a beaming smile as he waved.

"I remember him waving."

That was it. She went no further. During our earlier dinner, she hit the same termination point in her recollection: "As his car pulled out of Love Field for the ride through downtown Dallas, I saw him sitting in the back seat. He was waving his hand." Then she stopped. "After all these years," she told me during dinner, "it's still too painful to discuss."

With that, and just as she had during our later telephone conversation about Dallas, Mrs. Lincoln changed the subject.

• • •

JACK VALENTI

Jack Valenti met John Kennedy only once. It occurred on the last night of the president's life.

Born in 1921, Valenti flew over fifty combat missions during World War II. After obtaining a Harvard MBA degree, he returned home to Houston and began a career as an advertising executive and political consultant. His friendship with Lyndon Johnson dated back to the future president's congressional years. In late 1963, when Kennedy decided to make a political trip to Texas, Johnson recruited Valenti to organize the multi-city tour. Valenti rode in the Dallas motorcade. Immediately following the assassination, he joined the new administration as Johnson's presidential assistant. He remained at the White House until 1966, when he left government to become the president of the Motion Picture Association of America (MPAA). Holding that position for the next thirty-eight years, he was the public face of, and chief advocate for, the Hollywood movie studios.

I knew Jack from my time in Washington. With much of the entertainment industry sited in my Los Angeles district, I allied frequently with the studios in the battle to protect American intellectual property (IP) from piracy. My membership on the House Judiciary Committee's IP subcommittee gave me a position of legislative leadership on this issue. Later, in my capacity as U.S. under secretary of Commerce for Intellectual Property, I became the Bush Administration's de facto IP czar. Because of these positions, I worked closely with Jack for years, and we developed a close friendship.

Our relationship transcended partisan politics. During my 2000 reelection campaign, President Clinton targeted me for defeat as payback for his impeachment. Thanks to Clinton's help, my Democrat opponent, Adam Schiff, had campaign contribution reports that looked like a Who's Who of Hollywood. After Jack's death, one of his MPAA lieutenants told me that she attended a meeting with Jack and the studio heads during that campaign. The leaders told Jack that Clinton was lobbying them hard to support Schiff financially, as were all of their A-list stars. Jack (a lifelong liberal Democrat and a close friend of Clinton) listened politely for a few minutes, and then he ended the discussion. "Gentlemen," he said, "Jim Rogan has been the best friend Hollywood has had in Washington when it comes to protecting our interests. As long as I am head of this association, we will support him, and I don't give a damn what Bill Clinton thinks about it." That was that. Although Schiff collected checks from people like Barbra Streisand and Steven Spielberg, my campaign deposited checks from Disney, Fox, Warner, Universal, and Paramount.

One day, while joining him for lunch at his Washington office, I brought along a copy of the famous photograph of Lyndon Johnson, flanked by his wife and a dazed Jacqueline Kennedy, taking the presidential oath aboard Air Force One shortly after the assassination. I asked Jack (who was depicted in the photo standing a few feet from Johnson) to autograph it for me. After he obliged the request, he told me about his experience that nightmarish day.

"About a month earlier, Vice President Johnson called me at my ad agency office in Houston and told me that President Kennedy had decided to make a multi-stop visit to Texas that November. Lyndon wanted me to organize it. He wasn't happy about the trip. He thought it was a bad time for Kennedy to come. Governor John Connally and Senator Ralph Yarborough, both Democrats, were having a terrible feud, and their bitterness was causing intraparty divisions. However, the president needed Texas to win the 1964 election, so he decided to visit.

"I put my business on hold and spent the next month working out the details of each stop. I coordinated everything with senior White House staff, the Secret Service, the Democratic National Committee, the state Party offices, and so forth. It was a monumental task, and I knew Lyndon would expect perfection when he brought the president to his home state. This *had* to be a success.

"On Thursday, November 21, the official party landed in Houston. JFK and Jackie came off the plane, and the crowds went wild. I focused on getting everyone into the motorcade and then to the hotel without any problems, so I didn't meet him when he arrived. A big problem developed before the motorcade departed. At the last second Yarborough refused to ride in the same car with Lyndon. I couldn't believe that asshole! I shoved him into a car with some Texas congressmen, and then I jumped into a White House staff car and we all took off for the hotel.

"The reception at the Rice Hotel went off perfectly. Lyndon told me that the president was pleased with it. So was Johnson, so much so that he told my wife, Mary Margaret, to go home and pack a bag for me. Johnson wanted me to travel with the official party to Dallas and Austin the next day.

"That same night, we all attended a testimonial dinner for Congressman Albert Thomas. While everyone was backstage, Johnson brought me over and introduced me to the president. We had never met. He thanked me for my work in organizing the trip, and he said that I did such a good job that he might steal me away so that I could organize his other trips. Then he introduced me to Jackie, who was dazzling. Like every other man in America, she enchanted me. The president thanked me again, and I went back to overseeing the program. How ironic it is that the only time I ever met John Kennedy was on the last night of his life.

"The next morning, we were in Fort Worth for a breakfast. When that finished, Kennedy, Johnson, Connally, and the other politicians went outside in the drizzle and spoke from a makeshift wooden platform to the few thousand people who had congregated outside. Then we drove to the airport for the flight to Dallas.

"At Love Field, another great crowd awaited. I did a final motorcade check, and then I jumped into a car with Kennedy's personal secretary, Evelyn Lincoln. We were about six cars behind the presidential limousine when we departed.[3]

"Along the way the crowds were boisterous and cheering. Everyone was smiling. I knew Lyndon would be very pleased with the turnout.

"Near the end of the route, we made a couple of quick turns into Dealey Plaza. Suddenly, the car in front of me accelerated quickly. Police started waving at the cars behind, people started running in the street, and I wondered what the hell was going on. My first reaction was that the cars in front took off speeding to the Trade Mart because we were running late for Kennedy's speech.

"At that time, I didn't know anything bad had happened. Our driver took us to the Trade Mart. When we arrived and the president's limo wasn't there, I thought they must be running late, or maybe they stopped for some reason. Then I heard a guard say the president and Governor Connally had been shot. I couldn't believe it. I grabbed a deputy sheriff and told him I had the president's personal secretary with me and that we needed to get to the hospital right away. He put us in his squad car, and we rushed off to Parkland Hospital.

---

3 According to a schematic chart of the motorcade, both Jack Valenti and Evelyn Lincoln rode in the White House Official Party bus, which was twenty cars behind SS-100-X during the procession through downtown Dallas. See Todd Wayne Vaughan, Presidential Motorcade Schematic Listing, November 22, 1963, Dallas, Texas, vers. 9.00 (1993), www.jfk.hood.edu/Collection/Weisberg%20Subject%20Index%20Files/.../Item%2015.pdf, 34 (accessed July 15, 2019).

"It was bedlam at the hospital. Cars parked all over, Secret Service and police swarming about, people rushing in and out. I dropped off Mrs. Lincoln with some Kennedy people. One of Johnson's aides came over and whispered to me that Kennedy was dead. He said the vice president wanted to see me *right now*.

"I was fighting back tears when I found Johnson in a small room in the hospital basement. People entered and started speaking to him. A Secret Service agent pulled me aside and said that Johnson wanted me to get out to Air Force One immediately. I didn't know why. I just did what he told me.

"An agent drove me back to Love Field and I boarded the jet. Everyone on board looked shell-shocked. They spoke to each other in whispers. Soon after, Johnson boarded the plane. He grabbed my arm and said, 'Jack, I need you on my staff. You need to come to Washington with me right now. Tell Mary Margaret to send your clothes. You can live with me until you and your family find a place back there.' That was that. My life and career as a Houston ad exec were over forever, although I didn't realize it at the time.

"Once on the plane, Johnson took charge immediately. He started making phone calls and meeting with people in the office. I couldn't believe how calm he looked after what had just happened.

"The White House and Secret Service pushed Johnson to leave Dallas for Washington immediately. He refused, and he ordered that the plane not depart without Kennedy's body and Jackie aboard.

"While we waited for Jackie and the late president, another debate erupted as to whether Johnson should take the oath now or back in Washington. He decided to do it before we left. He wanted the oath ceremony photographed, and he wanted that photo given to the press outlets immediately so that the world, and especially our enemies, would know that there was a continuity of leadership.

"A hearse pulled up on the tarmac with a coffin. They carried it up the stairs, loaded it in the back of the plane, and covered it with an American flag. Jackie remained in the back with the casket.

Johnson sent someone to ask if she felt up to coming forward and joining him as he took the oath. When she appeared, she looked like she was in a trance. Judge Sarah Hughes from Texas had joined us, and I had obtained the oath over the phone from the Department of Justice. With everyone now assembled, Judge Hughes asked Johnson to raise his hand. Just before she administered the oath, Congressman Thomas pulled me next to him to get a better view of history being made."

"And," he added ruefully, "because of Albert Thomas's thoughtfulness, I ended up in one of the most famous photographs ever taken."

• • •

JIM WRIGHT

To say that Jim Wright's Republican colleagues disliked him when he was the Speaker of the U.S. House of Representatives understates the point. The third-ranking House Republican at the time, Congressman (later Vice President) Dick Cheney, said of him, "He's a heavy-handed son-of-a-bitch, he doesn't know any other way of operating, and he will do anything he can to win at any price, including ignoring the rules, bending the rules, writing rules, denying the House the opportunity to work its will. It brings disrespect to the House itself. There's no sense of comity left."[4] Congressman (later Speaker) Newt Gingrich called Wright the most corrupt speaker of the twentieth century,[5] and he recruited seventy-seven other GOP colleagues to file formal ethics charges against him.

Despite this onslaught, there was a lone Republican con-

---

4   Adam Clymer, *The New York Times*, May 6, 2015, https://www.nytimes.com/2015/05/07/us/politics/jim-wright-house-speaker-who-resigned-amid-ethics-charges-dies-at-92.html (accessed July 14, 2019).

5   John M. Barry, *Politico*, May 7, 2015, https://www.politico.com/magazine/story/2015/05/the-house-of-jim-wright-117718_full.html (accessed July 14, 2019).

gressman who liked Jim Wright, albeit one who never had to endure service under his ham-handed leadership.

I liked him.

Born in 1922 in Texas, he flew as a bombardier during World War II. After the war, he returned home and held several local political offices until 1954, when he won the first of seventeen terms in Congress. Elected speaker in 1987, his ruthless approach in ramming through his legislative agenda angered Republicans (and many Democrats). After ethics charged piled up against him, which ranged from improperly profiting from book sale royalties to unlawful foreign policy interference, he resigned from Congress while maintaining his innocence. Upon leaving Washington, he returned home and taught college.

My youthful appreciation for coaxing historical recollections from noted leaders didn't end when I arrived in Congress. If anything, it metastasized because senior colleagues who had witnessed history from front row seats abounded. During legislative downtime, I looked for opportunities to ask them about their experiences. Occasionally, I wrote to retired members whom I wanted to meet and invited them to lunch when they came to town. Soon after I wrote to Jim Wright back in Texas, he called me and said that he planned to be in D.C. for the annual Former Members of Congress Association gathering. Each year, the Association holds a two-day reunion for former House and Senate members. The agenda always includes a morning business meeting held in the House chamber before the legislative session. We set that date on the calendar to meet.

Incumbent congressmen never attended these Association get-togethers in the chamber. With busy schedules, and with no political benefit derived from schmoozing has-beens, they had better things to do. Unlike my colleagues, I'd come, stand along the back rail of the chamber, and point out for our teenage House pages all the notables from the past whom I recognized: "See that man over there in the tan coat? He ran for president in 1972. I got his autograph when I was a kid. See that tall guy in the aisle of the second row? He was secretary of the Treasury. See the lady in the red dress? She was the Democrat vice presidential nominee in 1984—the first woman nominated by a major party." Later, I watched with satisfaction as the pages brought autograph books over to the people I had identified for them. These once prominent and now largely forgotten old-timers smiled as they signed for the pages, many of whom were born long after their public careers had ended.

At the Association's 1998 meeting in the House chamber, I pointed out an elderly man. "Do you see that fellow over there in the light blue sports coat? That's Jim Wright. He was Speaker of the House ten years ago."

Later, when I walked over and introduced myself, he greeted me warmly, and then he fished around in his wallet for a piece of paper bearing my name and telephone number written on it. "See? I was going to call you today," he said with a slight speech impediment, which he explained came from his recent cancer surgery on his tongue and jaw.

I invited him to lunch. "Absolutely!" he responded. "Why don't I come to your office and pick you up, or else I can come to your committee room and wait for you?"

"Sorry, sir, but it's not appropriate having a former Speaker of the House wandering the Capitol halls looking for a freshman, especially when the freshman is the beneficiary of the meeting. I'll come to you."

"All right let's meet for lunch in the private Speaker's Dining Room across from the Members' Dining Room. The nice thing about being a former speaker is that I am allowed to reserve it."

At noon, we had the dining room to ourselves. As a favor for one of the House archivists, I asked him to sign for her a photograph of his formal portrait hanging in the Capitol. He inscribed it, "To Barbara, who takes care of the old things in the Capitol—like me!"

Throughout lunch, he shared stories about his career in Congress and some of the historical figures with whom he worked. The most memorable part of our discussion came when he told me about November 22, 1963.

"I represented Fort Worth in Congress for thirty-four years, which was the city where President Kennedy started his last day. It was such a big deal to have the president of the United States in my district. He gave a speech there that morning and paid tribute to me. Then we drove over to the airport and boarded Air Force One for the flight to Dallas.

"Governor Connally and other Texas congressmen were on the plane with us. We sat talking with the president during the flight, and he was very interested in discussing the different political dynamics of Fort Worth and Dallas. We were still discussing it when the plane landed at Love Field. As we prepared to leave, he turned to me and said, 'Jim, we'll finish this discussion later this afternoon when we get back to the plane.'"

At this point in his story, Wright wiped away a tear. When he continued, he said softly, "We never finished that discussion."

I asked about the motorcade. He recalled, "It was a beautiful day. The crowds all along the way were very enthusiastic. I was in a car behind the president, maybe five cars back.[6]

"Near the end of the motorcade, as we got closer to the Trade Mart, I heard a loud pop. At first, I thought it was a firecracker. Then I heard a second pop, and I assumed it was a twenty-one-gun salute. 'This is a strange place to do that,' I thought. Then I heard a third pop, and that was odd because, if this were a twenty-one-gun salute, the shots were out of cadence. My heart sank when I looked out the window and saw horror on the faces of the people standing along the grassy knoll. I didn't know it at the time, but they had just seen the president's head explode.

---

6   The car in which Jim Wright rode in the Dallas motorcade was twelve cars behind SS-100-X. See Vaughan, *Presidential Schematic*, 21.

"I turned to see the president's car. It looked as if it had stopped in the middle of the street, and then it sped off as a Secret Service agent climbed onto the back of it. I saw another Secret Service agent violently push Lyndon down in his car.

"When we arrived at Parkland Hospital it was pandemonium. I saw the president carried out of his car." Wright paused briefly and gazed toward the carpeting on the floor. Composing himself, he continued: "I looked inside of his limousine. Blood, brain tissue, and chunks of his head covered the back seat. I knew he was dead.

"A few minutes later, I saw Lyndon at Parkland. He was stunned by what had happened, but he recovered quickly. He handled himself well that day under terrible circumstances.

Former House Speaker Jim Wright recalling for me his Dallas motorcade memories, The Capitol, May 13, 1998 (Author's collection)

"After the doctors pronounced the president dead, Lyndon wanted to get back to the plane immediately. He didn't know if there was a conspiracy to kill the whole government or not. We called Judge Sarah Hughes, who came to the plane to swear him in. I was in the plane with him when he took the oath of office."

I asked Wright how that day impacted him as he reflected on it thirty-five years later. He shook his head. "It was the saddest day of my entire career. It had started on such a high note. I was hosting the president of the United States in my hometown. My adrenaline was flowing, and I was on cloud nine. Then it all was destroyed. I've relived the day in my mind many, many times over the last thirty-five years.

"And, sadly, I will again, many, many more times."

• • •

DAN RATHER

I wanted to hear about history even when I was in the middle of making it.

In January 1999, a few hours after I delivered my opening statement in the Clinton impeachment trial before the United States Senate, I appeared on *Larry King Live*, a television interview show broadcast live to an international audience on the CNN network. When I arrived at their Washington studio, I learned that King had invited two additional interrogators for our interview: Dan Rather, then the longtime anchorman of the *CBS Evening News*, and fellow CBS newsman Bob Schieffer, the host of the long-running news show, *Face the Nation*.

A producer introduced me to both Schieffer and Rather in the greenroom before airtime. I told Rather I looked forward to his questions because I was a longtime fan. He thanked me, but his eyes showed scorn for what he undoubtedly thought was a cheap effort to ingratiate myself. Conservative Republicans had for years bashed Rather and other media liberals, so the last person from whom he expected a sincere compliment was a conservative congressman. Still, he looked surprised and mildly impressed when I told him, "When you were a young reporter, you were in Dealey Plaza on November 22, 1963. That must have been an incredible experience."

His countenance changed from disdain to quizzical. "How did you know that?" he asked.

"I heard your reporting from that day. Like I said, I've followed your career for decades." Since we had time before going on air, I asked him to tell me about Dallas.

"Kennedy was scheduled to make a five-city Texas trip," he told me. "CBS assigned me to head up their coverage of the visit. At the Dallas portion, I positioned myself at the very end of the motorcade. I stood just beyond the grassy knoll in Dealey Plaza on the opposite side of an underpass. The motorcade would come down Elm Street, drive under the pass, and then head out to the Trade Mart for his speech.

"At 12:30, the motorcade turned onto Elm and started its approach to where I waited. It only had about forty yards to go until its end. Because of my location, I never heard any shots. The first sign I had that something was wrong was when Kennedy's limousine sped past me without any other cars behind it. It raced by so quickly that I wasn't even sure it was his car.

"Suddenly, there was confusion all around. I knew something bad had happened, but I didn't know what. I rushed back to the local CBS affiliate. When I got there, reports had come over the wire services of shots fired at the motorcade. We still had no information about whether anyone was hit.

"I knew Dallas, and I assumed that if any trouble had developed, they would take anyone injured to Parkland Hospital. I called Parkland on a hunch, and I got in my call before everyone else jammed up the switchboard. My source there told me that Kennedy died. I called the New York television studio with the news, but they refused to announce it on the air until the White House confirmed it. CBS Radio didn't wait for confirmation. They went live with me

CBS NEWS
A Division of Columbia Broadcasting System, Inc.
524 West 57 Street
New York, New York 10019
(212) 765-4321

Dear Mr. Rogan: August 7, 1974

Thank you for your thoughtful letter of June 24, 1974. As
requested, I have enclosed a signed photo to be included in
your collection.

Again, thank you for writing and I hope you will continue
to watch CBS News.

Sincerely,

Dan Rather
White House Correspondent

Mr. James E. Rogan
2664 Mendocino Drive
Pinole, California 94564

Dan Rather's 1974 letter to me helped vindicate my credibility with him twenty-five years later (Author's collection)

saying that the president died. The official White House announcement didn't come until later.

"I went back to the scene and learned that a guy at a local clothing store might have taken a movie of the shooting. I tracked down the photographer, Abraham Zapruder. Once he developed the film, he let me watch it just one time. The graphic nature stunned me. It showed the president's head explode upon impact from the final shot. Later, I gave an on-air verbal account of what I saw on the film during a live CBS broadcast. I contacted Zapruder again and tried to buy the film for CBS, but *Life* magazine had beaten us to it."

With that, Larry King's producer interrupted the discussion and escorted us into the studio.

A few days later, I sent a note to Rather and thanked him for sharing his memories of Dallas. I also wrote that I suspected my comment about being an old fan was cause for understandable cynicism, so I hoped to restore my credibility with an attachment: I enclosed a copy of the letter he wrote to me in August 1974 (when I was a teen) in which he thanked me for writing and expressing appreciation for his work at CBS.

A couple of weeks later, a large box arrived. Inside were autographed copies of every book Rather had authored, with each bearing a gracious inscription. He enclosed a letter thanking me for sending that old letter, along with a suggestion that we get together for coffee.

Once again, my boyhood hobby of collecting political memorabilia paid off a dividend in later life.

• • •

JOHN B. CONNALLY

Of all the people in the Dallas motorcade, I once met the man with whom I wanted to talk the most about that day. Unfortunately, our encounter was not under circumstances that allowed me to ask former Texas Governor John Connally about his recollections of riding with Kennedy in SS-100-X.

Born in Texas in 1917, Connally served in the Navy during World War II. Later, he obtained a law degree and became an aide to his longtime friend, Lyndon Johnson, during LBJ's congressional years. At Johnson's urging, Kennedy named Connally as secretary of the Navy in 1961, a position he held until he resigned the following year to run for Texas governor. He went on to win three consecutive terms in the statehouse, and in this capacity, he welcomed the Kennedys to his home state in November 1963.

When the presidential motorcade departed Love Field for downtown Dallas, Connally sat in the jump seat of SS-100-X directly in front of Kennedy. According to the official Warren Commission report, the assassin's second shot passed through Kennedy's neck and throat, and then it struck Connally's back, exited his chest, blew through his wrist, and then lodged in his thigh. Although seriously wounded in the shooting, Connally survived.

President Nixon named Connally (still a Democrat at that time) as his secretary of the Treasury in 1971. Sixteen months later, he resigned to head "Democrats for Nixon" for the Republican president's 1972 reelection campaign.

Three weeks before Election Day 1972, Connally came to San Francisco as a Nixon campaign surrogate. Along with two school friends, I waited outside KGO at dawn for him to arrive. The sun was just rising when a black stretch limousine pulled to the curb. We were his only welcoming committee when he exited the car.

Connally had a commanding, dignified presence. He was tall, with wavy white hair and a deep baritone voice. That he survived one of the most infamous crimes in American history added to his mystique. While shaking hands with the same man I had seen depicted in countless photographs seated with Kennedy in that blue Lincoln, I felt both awed and awkward. I wanted to ask about his experience on that fateful day, but when my opportunity arose, I fumbled about for a way to approach the sensitive subject. If I ask him about Dallas, will it upset him? Will it cause some traumatic reaction? I lost my nerve.

Connally stood on the sidewalk and signed autographs for us, which created for me an unexpected distraction. As his hand moved across our souvenirs, I stared at his wrist looking for the scars from the bullet's entrance and exit wounds. I couldn't see them, so subconsciously I started leaning closer and closer. While I fixated on his wrist trying to spot his gunshot scars, I noticed that his hand had stopped moving suddenly. A deep voice asked, "Is something wrong, son?"

I snapped this photo of Governor John Connally moments before I decided to get a better look at his, uh, cufflinks. Outside KGO Studio, San Francisco, October 12, 1972 (Author's collection)

I snapped back to consciousness with a start. Without realizing it, I had positioned my face about three inches from his hand! Now embarrassed, I glanced upward and saw Connally looking at me quizzically.

"Son? Are you okay?"

"Oh, I'm sorry governor, I was—I was—I was admiring your cufflinks! And I'm farsighted. I just wanted to get a good look at them. Boy, they sure are beauties."

"My wife gave them to me. I'll tell her you like them." He posed for a group picture, and then he disappeared inside the studio.

Damn! John Connally stood with me on a deserted street, but I was a kid and I lost my nerve. I never asked my questions. That was too bad because the opportunity never returned.

Although John Connally and I didn't meet again, I still got to see in person the man in the jump seat, along with a very, very good look at a nice pair of cufflinks.

• • •

ONE LAST RECOLLECTION

A final memory comes from the man whose photograph taken that day made headlines around the world. Although his image is seared into every memory of November 22, 1963, you won't recognize his name, but you know Clint Hill. At the first sound of gunfire, he was the Secret Service agent who jumped onto the rear of SS-100-X, pushed Mrs. Kennedy back into the car, and threw himself over the First Couple as the limousine sped to the hospital.

Born in 1932, the college athlete became a Secret Service agent in 1957 after a stint in Army intelligence. He served on President Dwight D. Eisenhower's protective detail and then, after Kennedy's election, the Service assigned him to guard First Lady Jacqueline Kennedy. On November 22, 1963, as the motorcade neared the sniper's perch, he stood on the left running board of the Secret Service car trailing behind SS-100-X, which put him in direct line with Mrs. Kennedy's position in her car.

At the sound of the first shot, Hill jumped from the running board and sprinted to the presidential limousine. He put his foot on the rear bumper and grabbed the handrail to pull himself onto the car, but the limo driver accelerated rapidly. Hill almost fell off, but he managed to pull himself onto it in time to save Mrs. Kennedy, who had climbed onto the rear trunk to retrieve a section of her husband's skull. Hill shoved her back inside, and then he protected the Kennedys with his own body until they arrived at Parkland Hospital.

I never had the privilege of meeting Agent Hill, but we did correspond some years ago. After the fiftieth anniversary of Dallas, I wrote and asked him about that day. He responded with an amazing handwritten letter that described November 22, 1963 as a routine day for presidential travel. The crowds they encountered in Fort Worth, San Antonio, Houston, and Dallas remained large and enthusiastic.

As the motorcade turned into Dealey Plaza, he heard a gunshot and saw Kennedy react to it by grabbing his throat. Hill rushed toward the presidential limousine to protect the First Couple from additional fire. He added a final, brief sentence to this most painful recollection:

"I was too late."

• • •

The Dallas Citizens Council

The Dallas Assembly

The Science Research Center

request the pleasure of

the company of

at a luncheon in honor of

The President and Mrs. Kennedy

The Vice-President and Mrs. Johnson

The Governor and Mrs. Connally

Friday, the twenty-second of November

at twelve noon

The Trade Mart

Official invitation to the Trade Mart luncheon honoring President and Mrs. Kennedy, Vice President and Mrs. Johnson, and Governor and Mrs. John Connally, Dallas, November 22, 1963 (Author's collection)

After thirty years at the helm of the John F. Kennedy Presidential Library and Museum, Dave Powers retired in 1994. He died at age 85 of a heart attack on March 28, 1998.

Evelyn Lincoln, President Kennedy's personal secretary, died at age 85 of cancer on May 11, 1995.

Jack Valenti ran the MPAA for thirty-eight years until his retirement in 2004. He died at age 85 on April 26, 2007 of complications after suffering a stroke.

Richard Nixon hoped to make John Connally his new vice president after Spiro Agnew resigned in 1973, but the Democrat-controlled Congress signaled it would not confirm the man who abandoned their Party to align himself with Nixon. In 1980, Connally ran for president as a Republican, but he garnered only one delegate to the national nominating convention. He died at age 76 on June 15, 1993 of pulmonary fibrosis.

Following Dallas, Clint Hill continued in the presidential protective detail. He went on to guard Presidents Lyndon Johnson, Richard Nixon, and Gerald Ford. The Secret Service promoted him to the position of assistant director before he retired in 1975.

After Kennedy's assassination, the FBI moved SS-100-X to the White House garage, where agents photographed the interior and searched it for evidence. It was cleaned, painted, and overhauled, and then it returned to presidential service. During the next fifteen years, it transported Presidents Johnson, Nixon, Ford, and Carter before the government retired it from the fleet in 1977. The next year, it went on display at the Henry Ford Museum in Dearborn, Michigan, where it remains to this day as one of the venue's most popular attractions.

4

Feeling the Buzz

Although the historic footprints left in 1969 by the second man on the Moon are often overshadowed by those imprinted a few minutes earlier by the first, Apollo 11 astronaut Buzz Aldrin's story, standing alone, is breathtakingly admirable.

A West Point graduate and Air Force fighter pilot during the Korean War, Aldrin flew over sixty combat missions and shot down several enemy aircraft. In 1963, after earning a doctorate at MIT, NASA selected him for their third astronaut group. In 1966, along with future Apollo 13 commander James Lovell, he orbited Earth for four days aboard Gemini XII. During their mission, Aldrin performed two successful spacewalks, and he docked their capsule with another unmanned craft, which were technically difficult and physically dangerous maneuvers that required mastery before NASA attempted a manned lunar landing. When Apollo 11 lifted off for the Moon three years later, Aldrin and his crewmates, Neil Armstrong and Michael Collins, left Earth as pilots. They came back icons.

Today, the worldwide acclaim and glory surrounding their return is hard to comprehend for those not alive to witness it. Perhaps even harder to digest is how that fame slowly devastated Aldrin. Becoming one of the most famous men alive while still in his 30s, having accomplished all of his life's professional goals, and seeing no worthy challenges on the horizon, he spiraled into clinical depression. Between his partying, infidelities, and declining mental state, his marriage crumbled, and he wound up an alcoholic. He suffered a nervous breakdown and underwent psychiatric hospital-izations. Enduring lengthy rehab treatment programs, he regained control of his life and shared this controversial backstory in his 1973 book, *Return to Earth*. Its promotional tour brought Aldrin to San Francisco that same year, which gave me my first opportunity to meet him.

• • •

As a boy growing up in San Francisco in the 1960s and 1970s, I started my early morning weekdays tuning in to Jim Dunbar's live television show on KGO, the local ABC network affiliate. From 6:30 to 8:30 a.m., Dunbar did in-studio interviews with news-makers, and then he opened the telephone lines so his viewers could call in questions. Whenever Dunbar booked famous politicians for his show, I cut school with my junior high school classmates and fellow history junkies, Dan Swanson and Roger Mahan, for a predawn bus ride to downtown San Francisco. We hiked through the darkened and wino-infested streets to KGO, and then we waited outside to meet Dunbar's guests to collect autographs and take photographs when they arrived, and (if we could slow them down long enough) to ask questions about their careers. By 1973 Dan, Roger, and I had trekked to KGO a couple dozen times over the previous two years, so our trio had become familiar to the staff while we waited to meet their guest du jour.

One morning I heard Dunbar announce that Buzz Aldrin would appear on the show that day, so Dan and I rushed down to KGO. We arrived late; by then he had already entered the studio for his interview, so we stood on the sidewalk awaiting his departure.

"Who are you here to see today?" asked Sam the doorman as he came outside to chat with us. When I told him Buzz Aldrin, he shook his head and grimaced. "I thought you guys only came to meet politicians. Anyway, don't get your hopes up with Aldrin. I'm not sure what to make of that bird. He's here pushing his new book. It just came out. Have you heard about it?"

"No. Is it good?"

"It's better than good. It's down and dirty. It tells all about how he came back from the Moon and went bat-shit. *Seriously* cracked up—mental hospitals, drunk tanks, cheated on his wife, the whole nine yards."

That sounded terrible to a young teenager who grew up idolizing our astronauts. With trepidation I asked, "Is he okay now?"

"Who the hell knows? He wasn't very friendly when he came in this morning. All business, no small talk. I took him up the elevator and he didn't say a word. Maybe he's keeping his mouth shut because this book has gotten him in trouble."

"What kind of trouble?"

"*Big trouble*—with the other NASA astronauts."

"They're mad because he cracked up?"

"No, they don't give a damn about that. I hear he wrote in his book about how the astronauts all had these clean-cut, church-going public images, but they were a bunch of horn-dogs and hard-ass partiers behind the scenes, banging chicks, cheating on their wives, racing cars, boozing heavy. The NASA boys are really pissed at him."

"You said he has mental problems. Do you think he's okay now for us to approach him?"

"Take your chances. I don't think he's mental *now*. But who knows? If you ask for an autograph or you mention his personal life, he might go off. I can't tell you how he'll respond."

We were about to find out.

The elevator doors open inside the lobby and Aldrin appeared. Sam dashed for the front door and held it open, and the former Moon explorer stepped wordlessly onto Golden Gate Avenue.

Without Sam's cue, I might not have recognized Aldrin. I remembered him from his Apollo 11 flight three years earlier. Back then, he was clean shaven, and his hairline receded back to his ears, with only a small tuft in the front. Today he wore a full beard, and hair encircled his forehead.

"Dan," I whispered in confusion, "where did that hair come from?"

"I don't know. Maybe it grew on the Moon."

I tried not to stare at this apparent scalp contradiction as Dan and I walked up nervously and introduced ourselves. I asked Aldrin to autograph some Apollo 11 mission photographs that NASA had sent me. He took my pen and began signing.

Imagine being a young teenager standing on an empty street alongside a guy who had walked on the Moon recently, and back in a time when, only a few years earlier, such feats lived only in the fantasy of science fiction writers. I wanted desperately to ask about his Apollo 11 flight, but I didn't know how to approach it. By the time Aldrin emerged from the studio, Sam had me half-convinced that I was standing next to a ticking time bomb ready to explode if I spoke out of turn. Still, with this unique opportunity about to end, I decided to take a chance.

Wanting to begin with a compliment, I started to say, "So, your new book, I hear it's a great read. I'll buy it when I can save up enough money." That's what I *started* to say.

I never got beyond "So your, uh… So, your, uh… So, your, uh…."

Each time I started my intended sentence, my reeling thoughts stopped me. What if my question triggers terrible memories of his psycho past? What if he becomes enraged with me? What if I say the wrong thing and he comes unglued?"

"So, your, uh…."

Aldrin stopped signing and looked up at me.

"Huh?" he asked.

Panicked now, I shook my head from side to side. "Oh, oh, nothing. Thank you for the autographs. Bye."

"So, your, uh… So, your, uh…." Apollo 11 astronaut Buzz Aldrin signing autographs for me, KGO Studio, San Francisco, October 16, 1973 (Author's collection)

Aldrin handed back my pen and the photos. "Okay, boys, thanks for waiting for me." He stepped into his waiting car and drove away.

Meeting Aldrin outside KGO that morning, I feared (thanks to Sam) that the ex-astronaut was as crazy as an outhouse rat. Decades later, I still wince over my impressionable silliness. Nowadays, fading celebrities rush toward the klieg lights to bombard us with the most intimate, embarrassing, and tragic details of their red-carpet lives, and usually as a publicity tool to jimmy themselves back into public consciousness. That was not true half a century ago. There were no syndicated daytime talk show hosts boosting their ratings with the self-reported tragedies or scandals of the once famous. There were no fawning studio audiences applauding wildly over each tale of downward-spiraling wretchedness. No favorable publicity awaited those who shared their personal bouts of mental illness and alcoholism. There was only embarrassment, whispers, and isolation.

Buzz Aldrin didn't care. He had a story to tell and, long before society was primed for such revelations from our heroes, he proved himself a trailblazer, first in space, and then on Earth. Both journeys took profound courage.

I'm still not sure which one took more.

• • •

Fourteen years later, I crossed paths with Buzz Aldrin again, and my purpose was the same—to get a photograph signed, but it was not just any photo. In my collection I had a NASA color photograph of all three Apollo 11 astronauts. A decade earlier, I had mailed this special photograph to each of the astronauts. This was back in a bygone day when one could obtain those now-coveted genuine astronaut signatures for the price of a polite letter and a postage stamp. Neil Armstrong and Michael Collins had obliged my request and signed it; I sent it to Aldrin with a plea to complete the trilogy. He returned my picture unsigned and with a preprinted note reporting that he no longer signed autographs (doubtless a policy adopted after I handed him six pictures to sign at KGO in 1973).

After this rejection, the deficient picture hung on my wall for years. Whenever anyone looked at it, they always asked me the same question: "Where's Aldrin?" Tired of the repetitive failure reminder, I took it down and stored it in my closet. Having Armstrong's and Collins' signature without Aldrin's was like having soap without water. A racetrack gambler needs all three horses to win the trifecta; I needed Aldrin's signature to hit the Apollo trifecta. I still hoped to get it one day. I just didn't know when or how.

That opportunity arose in 1987 when I was a young deputy district attorney for Los Angeles County and in the middle of a felony jury trial at the Pasadena courthouse. During a morning recess, I plopped down in an empty jury room and thumbed through the morning newspaper. There I saw a small article announcing Buzz Aldrin as the noon speaker at that day's California Bicentennial Luncheon at the Los Angeles Biltmore Hotel.

"I gotta do this."

I asked the judge for an early lunch recess to handle a personal issue. The defense didn't object. My opponent had an errand to run as well. When the judge took the break, I rushed home, grabbed the large photograph from my closet, removed it from the frame, and then sped down the freeway to downtown LA. I double-parked my car outside the hotel, ran into the lobby, checked the event calendar, and then sprinted to the Biltmore Bowl, where the pre-lunch reception had begun. There stood Aldrin posing for a photograph with former ABC News anchorman Howard K. Smith, the moderator of the first Kennedy-Nixon debate in 1960. While they stood together, and with no time to lose, I made a beeline toward Aldrin. I had run so fast that I was now out of breath as I thrust the photograph at him. Between my gasping for air and talking so fast, I hoped that the confusing combination might distract him away from his "no autograph" policy. "Mr. Aldrin," I panted, "I'm sorry to interrupt, but I'm a DA in Los Angeles County in the middle of a trial and I need to get back to court...." I spoke so rapidly that all the words ran into one: *"ItwouldmeansomuchtomeandIhavespentyearstryingtocompletethepicturewithallthreeApolloastronautsonitthatIknowyouwon'tsaynosojustpleasesayyesandsignthedamnedthing...."*

My words struck with the rapidity of a tobacco auctioneer as I stuffed a pen into Aldrin's hand, crimped his fingers around it, and then I took his wrist and moved his hand (with the clenched pen) on top of the picture where I wanted him to sign. Aldrin stared at me with a mystified look as I kept jabbering in unending run-together sentences right up until he finished scrawling "Buzz Aldrin" on the photograph.

A wonderful inscribed memento from three American legends, the Apollo 11 crew, signed for me during my later Washington years (Author's collection)

Taking back the picture from him, I pumped his hand enthusiastically and added, *"OhthisissogreatthankssomuchthismeanstheworldtomeandI'llneverforgetitwellIhavetogetbacktocourtnowanywaythanksagain."* I turned and ran from the ballroom and through the lobby, jumped into my car just as a tow truck appeared on the scene, and raced back to Pasadena in time to resume the afternoon session.

When I first met Buzz Aldrin in 1973, I feared he might be crazy. When our paths crossed that day at the Biltmore, I'm sure he felt the same about me.

• • •

I didn't see Buzz Aldrin again until the second year of my freshman congressional term. On April 30, 1998, House Speaker Newt Gingrich invited me to join him at a press conference in the Capitol's Cannon House Office Building to promote his newly formed Congressional Drug Task Force.

At the appointed hour, I arrived at Room 345 and joined Gingrich and a dozen of our House colleagues. When the cameras rolled, Gingrich introduced Buzz Aldrin, an unexpected guest, who read his brief remarks from prepared notes. He and Gingrich then enter-

Buzz Aldrin addressing the Speaker's Congressional Drug Task Force; I'm at far right. Washington, D.C., April 30, 1998 (Author's collection)

tained a few questions before the speaker adjourned the meeting.

As the House members dispersed and headed back to their offices, I found myself exiting the room alongside Aldrin. I introduced myself, told him of my admiration, and then thanked him for the autographs he signed for me when I met him as a boy.

"Where was this?" he asked.

"San Francisco, 1973. You were on a promotional tour for your first book, *Return to Earth*."

Aldrin shrugged his shoulders. "I've done a lot of book tours since then." With that, and to my dismay, he turned and walked away from me abruptly.

"Nice to see you again, too," I muttered to myself.

On the Aldrin-Rogan Awkward Encounter Scale, the score now stood Aldrin 2, Rogan 1.

• • •

It wasn't until 1999 that I came to know Buzz Aldrin, and the circumstance was fortuitous.

In mid-summer, I boarded an American Airlines red-eye flight from Los Angeles to Washington-Dulles. I checked into the gate and handed the attendant my coach ticket. She looked around, made an entry on her computer, and then handed me a new first-class ticket. "I appreciated your courage in the Clinton impeachment," she said with a wink. (I had served as a House Manager—a prosecutor—in the impeachment trial of President Bill Clinton a few months earlier.) Just before takeoff, Aldrin boarded my flight and took his seat a few rows ahead of mine.

Once airborne, and after the pilot turned off the *fasten seat belt* sign, I considered approaching him and taking another whack at the conversational ball, but while I wasted time dwelling on whether I should try again, he turned off his seat light, reclined his chair, closed his eyes, and went to sleep.

The next morning, as the airplane began its descent, Aldrin was still snoozing. A flight attendant awakened him in preparation for landing. While he freshened up in the restroom, I wrote him a brief note, which was a simple message expressing admiration for his contribution to flight, and letting him know that the picture he autographed for me as a kid still hung on my office wall. When he returned, I handed the note to a flight attendant and asked her to deliver it and just say it came from another passenger. She walked over and handed Aldrin the note; he turned on his cabin light, read it, and then placed it in his briefcase.

After landing, the airline directed its passengers onto a tram for a short ride to the terminal. While disembarking the tram, Aldrin approached and thanked me for the note. As a fellow Republican, he told me that he had followed the Clinton impeachment trial closely and appreciated my work.

We walked together to the baggage claim area. He said that he came to Washington to meet with Lockheed representatives about the feasibility of a reusable rocket. "Dan Goldin [NASA director] doesn't like the idea since he didn't think of it first," he groused. I asked if he planned to participate in NASA's upcoming Apollo 11 anniversary celebration in two weeks. "Yeah, but that's two trips to D.C. from now," he said. I mentioned that Goldin had invited me to the ceremony and that perhaps I would see him there.

Aldrin thanked me for my strong support for the space program. I told him that Goldin kept promising to do anything to show his appreciation, but whenever I lobbied him to send me on a shuttle flight, he insisted that civilians remained grounded permanently following *Challenger's* disastrous explosion in 1986 that killed the entire crew, along with a civilian high school teacher.

"Oh, that's bullshit," he exclaimed, insisting that the way to rebuild public interest in the program was to send civilians into space. He proposed a national lottery system giving any able-bodied American the opportunity to fly.

He said that he had read about the Democrats targeting me for defeat because of my role as a Clinton impeachment prosecutor. I replied that I hoped to convince my constituents to appreciate that their congressman took an unpopular stand in defense of the rule of law. [Note to reader: at the next election, my ambitious persuasion attempt failed miserably.] "Here, take this," he said as he handed me his business card with the Apollo 11 mission emblem emblazoned on it. "Maybe during your campaign I could help you out. I could come and do an event for you."

"You have no idea how honored I would be to have you, especially considering I stood outside a TV studio on a cold morning in

1973 just to shake your hand and get your autograph."

"Where was that?"

Hmmm. The last time I answered this question at Gingrich's Capitol presser, Aldrin gave me the bum's rush. Oh, well, here we go again:

"San Francisco," I said. "*Return to Earth* had just been released. In fact, I had heard that the book created such controversy that I was afraid to ask you about it when we met."

This time he didn't turn and walk away. He grew pensive. "You know, I wrote that book to share a terrible chapter in my life. I'm afraid it gave people the wrong impression, though. I've been sober and in AA for over twenty years now. Oh, well...."

When the luggage carousel began turning, I knew our time grew short, so I squeezed in one mission question: "When you look back on Apollo 11 from a thirty year distance, are you amazed that what we now view as primitive technology brought you and the crew to the Moon and back safely?"

"You have no idea!" he said with a laugh while pointing to the computer bag at my feet. "Your laptop there has about 10,000 times more computing power than we had in all of NASA Mission Control. Nowadays, the gyroscope on the space shuttle is a microchip the size of my thumbnail. On Apollo 11, the gyroscope was a *gyroscope*, a real one, you know, the kind that actually spins like a top."

Our bags arrived. We shook hands; he said he would look for me at the upcoming anniversary celebration. He took his luggage and began walking away, and then he turned, grinned, and added a final observation: "You know, those Apollo-Saturn V rockets that took us to the Moon were nothing more than big tin cans with a fuse. We've come a long way since 1969!"

Indeed, we had. Come to think of it, given that my first attempt to engage Buzz Aldrin in conversation never got beyond, "So, your, uh... So, your, uh...," I felt that I had come a long way with him as well.

5

Gold Rush

These days, bipartisanship in Congress has become a rare commodity. However, one area where bitter political fighting turns harmonious is when Congress votes to award a distinguished person the Congressional Gold Medal. According to the House of Representatives' History, Art, and Archives office,

> Since the American Revolution, Congress has commissioned gold medals as its highest expression of national appreciation for distinguished achievements and contributions. Each medal honors a particular individual, institution, or event. Although the first recipients included citizens who participated in the American Revolution, the War of 1812 and the Mexican War, Congress broadened the scope of the medal to include actors, authors, entertainers, musicians, pioneers in aeronautics and space, explorers, lifesavers, notables in science and medicine, athletes, humanitarians, public servants, and foreign recipients.

During my four years in the House of Representatives (1997-2001), Congress awarded gold medals to such luminaries as Frank Sinatra, the *Little Rock Nine*, former Presidents Gerald Ford and Ronald Reagan, former First Ladies Betty Ford and Nancy Reagan, Rosa Parks, Theodore M. Hesburgh, John Cardinal O'Connor, cartoonist Charles M. Schulz, Pope John Paul II, and the Navajo

Code Talkers. The ceremonies attending these presentations were always a pleasant, albeit brief, respite from the unending partisan knife-fighting that is the hallmark of divided government. I attended several of these presentation events, and two of the more memorable ones were for Mother Teresa and Nelson Mandela.

• • •

On June 5, 1997, Members of Congress gathered in the Capitol rotunda for the gold medal presentation ceremony honoring Mother Teresa, who founded the Missionaries of Charity in 1950, and who had spent the last half century caring for the sick and dying of Calcutta. She and her ministry came to world attention in 1979 when she won the Nobel Peace Prize.

It was uncertain for the weeks leading up to the ceremony whether the eighty-six-year-old Roman Catholic nun would be able to attend due to a prolonged series of major health setbacks, including a heart attack, three angioplasty surgeries, and lung infections. Despite her frail health, she had declared her intent to visit the United States once more before she died, and when Congress invited her to accept the medal, she made the trip from India.

On the day of the ceremony, the rotunda area filled with over 600 people awaiting her arrival. Two large replicas of the presentation medal depicting Mother Teresa holding a child in her arms hung on both sides of the stage. The host dignitaries included Speaker Newt Gingrich, Senate Majority Leader Trent Lott, House Judiciary Committee Chairman Henry Hyde, and South Carolina Senator Strom Thurmond. When Thurmond arrived, the audience applauded spontaneously in recognition of him becoming recently, at age 94, the longest serving member of the United States Senate.

Applause and cheers filled the rotunda when Mother Teresa arrived, looking frail and in a wheelchair. She was dressed in her trademark blue and white head scarf and sari; a simple black sweater draped her shoulders. During the ovation, she looked down at her

Medal given to me by Mother Teresa, The Capitol, June 5, 1997
(Author's collection)

folded hands resting in her lap.

Although feeble, when introduced she lifted herself out of the wheelchair. In brief impromptu remarks, she thanked Jesus Christ for her ministry, and she asked for prayers repeatedly while reminding her audience that the more we are in love with the poor, the closer we come to the heart of Christ.

As she spoke, Congressman Dave Weldon (R-FL), seated next to me, said, "Look at this frail old woman who spent her life taking the near-dead off the Calcutta streets. Now Congress is giving her a gold medal to go with her Nobel Peace Prize. If that doesn't show the power of God's love and Christ's ability to magnify the most obscure mortal acts, nothing can."

At the ceremony's conclusion, an assistant wheeled Mother Teresa off stage. A few minutes later, as I made my way through a Capitol corridor, I encountered her party as an escort pushed her wheelchair down the hallway. I introduced myself to Mother Teresa, thanked her for her work, and congratulated her on the award. She took my hand and pressed into it a small aluminum prayer medal that nuns from her order had handed out earlier to attendees. She asked for prayers, and then she and her escorts disappeared down the corridor. I needed a magnifying glass to read the minute inscription on the medal: *Oh, Mary, conceived without sin, pray for us who have recourse to thee.*

A week later, one columnist speculated that Mother Teresa would likely sell her $30,000 gold medal and give the proceeds to charity, just as she had done with her Nobel prize.

I can't think of a better use for it.

• • •

Another memorable medal ceremony occurred a year later, on September 23, 1998, when Congress presented the award to South African President Nelson Mandela. A South African lawyer and communist, as a young man Mandela joined the anti-apartheid African National Congress (ANC). Initially the movement sought change through nonviolence, but later shifted tactics in their campaign to overthrow the white apartheid regime. Sentenced to life in prison in 1962 for treason, Mandela spent the next twenty-seven years incarcerated. Meanwhile, the movement to end apartheid increased due to international pressure. In 1990 South African President F. W. de Klerk ordered Mandela's release, and together the two men negotiated apartheid's end. For their efforts at reconciliation, both Mandela and de Klerk won the Nobel Peace Prize, and a year later South Africans elected Mandela president, making him their country's first black leader. Now, as he neared the end of his term, Congress voted him a gold medal to go with his Nobel award.

Seated near me for the medal event were 1996 Republican vice presidential nominee Jack Kemp and his wife Joanne; former presidential candidate Jesse Jackson and his son, Congressman Jesse Jackson Jr.; actor Danny Glover; U.S. Attorney General Janet Reno, and Senator Edward Kennedy (D-MA). Among those escorting Mandela to the podium were President Bill Clinton, House Speaker Newt Gingrich, House Minority Leader Richard Gephardt (D-MO), Senator Strom Thurmond (S-SC), and Senate Minority Leader Tom Daschle (D-SD). Now seventy-nine, slender, and wearing a

"Congressional Gold Medal Ceremony"

Honoring

President Nelson Mandela

The Capitol Rotunda

10:00 a.m.

September 23, 1998

My program from Nelson Mandela's gold medal ceremony, which he
later autographed for me (Author's collection)

hearing aide, Mandela stood erect as he smiled and raised a clenched
fist to acknowledge the ovation when he appeared.

The assembled dignitaries on stage read speeches praising Mandela. The most emotional came from Gingrich, speaking without
notes on Mandela's nearly three decades in prison. "Politics in a
free society is a very rough-and-tumble business," Gingrich said,

"involving at times great personal pain. But when you contemplate twenty-seven years in prison, when you imagine walking out of that isolation with your heart larger and not smaller, President Mandela, you gave everyone on the planet a personal witness to how valuable freedom must be." While speaking about Mandela's triumph of forgiveness and reconciliation, Gingrich's eyes welled with tears and his voice broke. Too choked up to continue, he turned from the microphone and resumed his seat.

Clinton praised Mandela and his lifetime of accomplishments: "Americans as one today, across all the lines that divide us, join in tribute to your struggle." At the end of his remarks, he handed Mandela the medal, who then held it aloft amid the cheers. Ninety-five-year-old Strom Thurmond came over and held Mandela's arm aloft, as though they were presidential and vice presidential running mates. The audience laughed and applauded; Congresswoman Juanita McDonald (D-CA), a member of the Congressional Black Caucus, leaned over and said to me, "Look at that—ole' Strom the segregationist with Mandela.

"Now there's a photo op if ever there was one!"

• • •

Three months after Congress presented her with the Congressional Gold medal, Mother Teresa died of heart failure at age 87 on September 5, 1997. In 2002, on the fifth anniversary of her death, Pope Francis canonized her.

Nelson Mandela served as president of South Africa from 1994 to 1999. He died of a respiratory infection at age 95 on December 5, 2013.

Jack Kemp, the 1996 Republican vice presidential nominee, died of cancer at age 73 on May 2, 2009.

When Strom Thurmond retired from the U.S. Senate on January 3, 2003, he became the only member of Congress in history to reach age 100 while still serving. He died in his sleep on June 26,

2003, just six months after he left Washington and returned home.

Congresswoman Juanita McDonald (D-CA) and I served together in both the California State Assembly and the U.S. House of Representatives. Despite our strong political differences, our close personal friendship continued until her death from cancer at age 68 on April 22, 2007.

6

"Say Hey!" (or, "Strike One")

Like most young boys during my childhood, I loved baseball. Growing up in San Francisco during the 1950s and 1960s, my sports hero was Willie Mays, the star hitter and outfielder for the San Francisco Giants. My grandfather first brought me to Candlestick Park in 1962 to see the Giants play their rival, the Los Angeles Dodgers. I ate hot dogs and candy, drank barrels of Coca-Cola, and marveled at the enthusiasm from the tens of thousands of fans whenever *The Say Hey Kid* came to bat.

Willie Mays. You had to be there to appreciate the phenomenon. He played in the major leagues for twenty-three years, and all but his last two seasons were with the Giants. Twice the National League's most valuable player, and twenty times named to baseball's All-Star team, he retired in 1973 behind only Babe Ruth in career home runs (660 to 714). Whether socking a home run or striking out swinging, I never knew so much excitement existed on earth until I saw him at the plate. He was, in the eyes of a five-year-old sitting on his grandfather's lap, beyond mortal. After my first trip to the ballpark, Willie Mays replaced cowboy star Roy Rogers at the top of my boyhood pantheon. I wore a *Willie Mays Fan Club* badge on my shirt, and I coaxed Grandpa to mount Willie's bobble head on our station wagon dashboard. When local TV stations aired a public service announcement of Willie warning kids not to play with blasting caps found on the street, I walked around my neighborhood looking for them. I didn't know what they were, but I wanted to find one—so as *not* to play with it, all because Willie said so.

The luster diminished somewhat when, as a kid, I attended a game in which Willie played. Attendance grew sparse near its end because the Giants trailed badly, so at the bottom of the ninth I snuck into an empty seat directly behind the home team's dugout. Willie came to bat with two outs, the crowd roared for him, but he hit an infield fly and made the final out. The Giants lost, but who cared? We all saw Willie play.

He left the batter's box and walked directly toward me. I reached across the top of the dugout. "Willie!" I called to him, "I'm a big fan! Can I shake your hand?" He scowled, grumbled something, and passed by me. My older cousin who brought me to the game saw my disappointment.

"Don't be sad," she consoled me. "Willie's just had a bad day. Everyone has bad days."

• • •

My chance to meet him came a few years later when he scheduled an early-morning live interview at a local TV station in a run-down section of San Francisco. The studio shared the block with an alley, a soup kitchen, and a flophouse for transients. The low-rent setting didn't deter me, especially if I could see him without thousands of other fans around.

Two hours before sunrise, my younger brother Pat and I took the bus downtown, and then we fended off drunks and perverts on our walk to the studio. After waiting there an hour, a pink Avanti sports car pulled up to the curb. The personalized license plate "BUCK 24" gave away the identity of the driver before we saw his face. Willie's team nickname was "Buck," and his Giants jersey bore number 24. He parked in front of the studio and exited his car.

There he was, only a few feet away from Pat and me on an otherwise empty street. What a thrill for two young fans! For a moment, we remained speechless, and then I blurted out, "Willie, you're our hero! We come to your games! Will you sign our baseballs?" I extended my ball and pen.

He stopped, glowered at me, and said nothing for what seemed forever. The silence broke only when he summoned a guttural sound from the depth of his esophagus. After bringing forth a mouthful of phlegm, he spewed it onto the sidewalk an inch or so from my foot. My eyes widened as I absorbed the scene and tried unlocking its meaning.

"Maybe this is some sort of baseball ritual," I thought. "Maybe the players greet each other this way." When I looked up, Willie still stared at me.

My mind kept racing: "Am I supposed to greet him the same way?" I wondered. "I guess he's waiting for me to do it back to him. Well, okay, here goes."

Just as I was about to launch a return salute, Willie snatched the ball from my hand, scrawled his signature across it, and then smeared the writing with the side of his hand as he tossed it in the air. The ball hit the street and rolled down Golden Gate Avenue.

As I chased after my smudged trophy, Pat asked if he'd sign his ball, too. Willie spun around and jabbed his index finger toward Pat.

"No!" he barked. "You kids got enough." With that, he turned and approached the studio entrance.

By now I had retrieved my ball and was approaching the scene when Pat called out, "Hey, Willie." He looked back to hear Pat finish his thought:

"Screw you!"

Pat turned and ran down Golden Gate Avenue toward Hyde Street and the bus station. His older brother, clutching a smeared baseball, was right behind.

• • •

Many years later, when I was just out of law school, I attended a sports collectable show in Los Angeles. The schedule featured

Willie Mays signing autographs for what was then a top-dollar fee at such gatherings: $6 each. Since he was so unpleasant when Pat and I asked him for a free autograph long ago, maybe, I thought, he might be more chipper if people paid him for it. I decided to test my theory. Besides, six bucks was a small price to pay to replace the smeared and scuffed baseball in my collection.

Here I am paying Willie Mays to sign my baseball. He looks unhappy that someone snapped a picture of us. Perhaps that wasn't included in the six-dollar fee. Los Angeles, November 3, 1985 (Author's collection)

Dealers and cases of baseball memorabilia for sale crowded the hotel ballroom. Willie, now retired from the game for over a decade, signed at a corner table. The people in his long line carried baseballs, bats, cards, photographs, jerseys, gloves, and so forth. After fans paid their money and handed him their item, he signed without looking up or acknowledging any expressions of admiration or gratitude. Once the money hit the cash box, he wrote his name, handed back the autograph, and then he called out, "*Next.*"

A dad approached him with his young kid in tow. "Hey, Willie, will you make out the ball for my son Johnny?"

"No inscriptions. *Next.*"

From another fan: "I've followed you since you played for New York. It's such an honor to meet you."

"*Next.*"

This went on for the hour that I waited. The script never changed: "*Hey, Willie, you're my hero....*"

"*Next.*"

When my turn came, I paid my fee, handed over my ball, he signed it, I said thanks, and then I stepped away without waiting for him to tell me to keep moving.

• • •

Thirty years after Pat and I encountered Willie Mays on Golden Gate Avenue, my brother worked as the operations manager at PacBell Park (now Oracle Park, which is the home stadium for the San Francisco Giants). When I visited him one afternoon in his ground-floor office, I was surprised to see Willie Mays signed memorabilia decorating his walls. Pat told me that Willie, now old, stooped, and moving slowly, still attended most home games. He'd often stop by Pat's office to shoot the breeze and have a beer with my brother before the opening pitch. They became friends.

"In fact," Pat added, "he was here yesterday. I told him that my brother was coming to town for a visit, so he signed this for you." Pat handed over a baseball, un-smudged and un-scuffed, inscribed to me.

"Do I leave the six bucks with you?" I asked.

"No charge. He did it as a favor. Besides, he raids my refrigerator before the games, so we're even."

"Did you ever mention how rude he was when we met him as kids, or that he once spewed his phlegm at my shoe?"

Pat shrugged. "No, I never bothered telling him—

"—Why tell him what he already knows?"

7

Happy Anniversary (or, "Strike Two")

On April 8, 1974, 53,775 people attending the Fulton County Stadium's baseball game watched the Atlanta Braves' left fielder, Hank Aaron, take his stance at home plate in the fourth inning. Al Cowling of the Los Angeles Dodgers threw his first pitch, Aaron swung, and the ball sailed over the outfield wall. With that, he broke a presumptively unassailable Major League record—Babe Ruth's 714 career home runs—which put him atop the totem pole of baseball's immortals.

Twenty-five years after that feat, the U.S. House of Representatives honored Aaron with H. Res. 279, which commemorated his smashing Ruth's record. I was in the House chamber when the resolution's sponsor, to my surprise, pointed to the visitor's gallery and asked everyone to welcome Aaron, who sat with his family. As he stood and waved, and as cheers rolled through the room, Ken Calvert (R-CA) pulled me aside and invited me to a private reception he was co-hosting for Aaron later that afternoon in the Capitol's Room S–111.

To this longtime Aaron fan, that sounded great. I had met him once before at a baseball card show almost a decade after he retired from the game. Our encounter was momentary but pleasant.

With *Hammering Hank*, Los Angeles, July 22, 1984. Eight years after retiring, he still had Popeye forearms (Author's collection)

• • •

After stopping by a sporting goods store to buy two baseballs (to ask him to sign for my daughters), I arrived at S-111 a few minutes after the 5 p.m. start time. Upon entry, the scene appeared awkward. Less than a dozen people, all my House colleagues, were in the room. So was Aaron, who stood alone in the far corner and away from all of them. Hmmm.

Calvert broke the ice and approached the legend first. He congratulated him on the anniversary, told him that he helped get the congressional resolution passed, and then he held out his copy of H. Res. 279 and asked Aaron to sign it.

"They didn't tell me I would have to do that here," Aaron replied curtly.

"I'm sorry, do what?" Calvert asked.

"They didn't tell me I would have to sign things if I came to this reception."

Calvert looked nonplussed. "Well, uh, I sure don't want to

inconvenience you," he pleaded, "but like I said, we worked hard getting this resolution through. We had to collect hundreds of signatures to bring it to a vote. I just wanted you to sign it as a keepsake to frame in my office."

"I really shouldn't have to do this."

Flummoxed by the unexpected pushback, Calvert apologized. "Mr. Aaron, I've been a fan of yours my whole life. Congress just passed a resolution honoring you. There aren't a lot of people in this room, let alone people asking you for autographs. But if you don't want to, that's fine. I'm sorry for asking."

Sighing in resignation, Aaron took the resolution from Calvert and scrawled his signature on it. "Okay," Aaron said as he handed it back. "Here you go, but I really shouldn't have to do this."

I had already joined the small line to meet Aaron that had formed behind Calvert, so I witnessed this uncomfortable exchange while holding two baseballs for an autograph! I wasn't a cosponsor of the resolution, I didn't lift a finger to get it passed, I didn't organize the reception. Hell, I didn't even know it was Aaron's anniversary. Once I saw Calvert's predicament, I tried hiding the balls in my pocket, but they wouldn't fit. Desperate to conceal them from Aaron, I shoved them down the back of my pants.

Congressman Jay Dickey (R-AR) was the next victim to approach Aaron. With a House photographer standing nearby, Dickey asked if he could have his picture taken with the honoree. Aaron rolled his eyes and snapped sarcastically, "*Oh sure.*" The photographer took the shot and Dickey moved away quickly.

"I might as well take pictures with each of you right now," Aaron announced to the rest of us, "so we can get this over with quickly."

Guess who was next in line.

I approached Aaron slowly while hoping to keep my elephantine-sized ass cheeks from dislodging and rolling down my trouser legs. I introduced myself and the photographer snapped our picture. I was mid-sentence offering congratulations on his milestone when he turned away and struck up a conversation with someone standing nearby. I walked away, fished out the baseballs from my britches, and tossed them into a nearby wastebasket.

"Great reception, Ken," I said as I walked over to the buffet table where Calvert and Dickey sulked.

Had this photograph with Hank Aaron captured us below the beltline, you'd see my bum sticking out an extra half foot. The smiles belied the uncomfortable situation. October 19, 1999 (Author's collection)

"Did you guys hear the way he talked to me when I asked for a picture?" Dickey asked. "I was so embarrassed. I wonder what that was supposed to mean?"

Placing my hand on Dickey's shoulder, I told him, "Jay, it means *I'm in the Baseball Hall of Fame, and the rest of you can go to Hell.*"

"That's not what it means," Calvert said. "It means, '*I'm Hank Aaron, and you're all assholes.*'"

Happy anniversary, Hank.

• • •

What to make of my encounters with baseball greats Hank Aaron and Willie Mays? I suspect that decades-long worldwide fame takes its toll, especially when an unending parade of well-meaning fans fill those years with nonstop impositions. At some point even the most fan-friendly celebrities must come to begrudge these intrusions. Although my experiences with Aaron and Mays were less than ideal, I'd bet that countless other fans could testify to their acts of kindness, generosity, and patience when they met them. I choose to believe that I experienced the exception with both of them instead of the rule. As my cousin told me at Candlestick Park on that long-ago afternoon, everyone is entitled to a bad day.

Play ball!

8

The First Men (Part One)

On Sunday, July 20, 1969, I was eleven years old and staying with my great-aunt, Della Glover, in her 700-square foot apartment in Daly City, California. Sitting at her small laminate kitchen table and chain-smoking Bel-Air cigarettes, my spinster aunt spent all morning remonstrating with me to back away from her 23-inch black and white Magnavox television set. "Jimmy, I can't see through you," she repeated with increasing frustration. "You're not a window." After retreating to the sofa, I'd inch my way slowly back toward the screen to get a closer look at its wavy images. Before cable television, TV viewing quality depended on the strength of an analog signal picked up by a "rabbit ears" antenna sitting atop the set, so the reception in Aunt Della's apartment complex was always marginal.

From the moment Apollo 11 launched from Cape Kennedy four days earlier, Aunt Della and I, along with a billion viewers worldwide, remained mesmerized by the coverage of astronauts Neil Armstrong, Buzz Aldrin, and Michael Collins hurtling toward the Moon. Unlike today, when astronauts blast off and return from space in virtual anonymity and with public indifference, our 1960s astronauts dominated the headlines. Their flights preempted scheduled television programming, and their splashdowns garnered celebrations, ticker-tape parades, and international fame. But this mission, Apollo 11, topped them all. For the first time in mankind's history, astronauts sought to leave a human footprint on another celestial body. It took millions of years to progress from the caveman's wheel to Henry Ford's assembly line. Advancement, yes, but humans remained chained to the earth. Then, in the span of less than one lifetime, men went from a twelve-second soar above a Kitty Hawk sand dune to exploring space. For Aunt Della and her generation, born before the Wright Brothers cracked the code for controlled powered flight, living to see mankind end the Moon's nearly 5 billion years of isolation (in Neil Armstrong's words) was a staggering notion.

And so, in the minutes leading up to 1:17 p.m. on that Sunday afternoon, the world joined me in inching closer to the television screen.

We watched the coverage on Channel 5, San Francisco's local CBS affiliate, because Aunt Della liked anchorman Walter Cronkite, whom Dr. Gallup's poll proclaimed America's most trusted man. On that momentous day, Cronkite shared the anchor desk with Walter Schirra, one of the original seven Mercury astronauts and the commander of the 1968 Apollo 7 flight.

Hearts raced as the epic moment drew near. The astronauts hovered just above the lunar surface when a serious problem developed. In this final landing phase, Armstrong looked out the window and saw that the onboard computer system was guiding their lunar module (LM) to set down in a deep crater filled with automobile-sized boulders. He overrode the computer, took the controls, and steered the LM manually away from the preordained touchdown spot while burning through his rapidly dwindling fuel supply. With Aldrin acting as navigator, Armstrong kept searching for a safe landing site even after NASA's Mission Control radioed a warning that they had only fifty seconds of fuel left. Both astronauts knew that if they depleted their rationed descent tanks, they would not have enough remaining fuel to lift off from the Moon and dock with the command module (piloted by Collins) sixty miles overhead. As the critical seconds ticked away, Aldrin called out the changing altitude and speed coordinates while keeping one hand poised anxiously over the capsule's "abort" button.

With a chilling sixteen seconds of fuel remaining, Armstrong found his spot. It is no exaggeration to say that mankind held its collective breath in those final moments until Armstrong's voice crackled over the television:

"Houston, Tranquility Base here. The Eagle has landed."

The force of the cheers rumbling throughout Aunt Della's apartment building rattled her windows, while a CBS camera caught Schirra wiping a tear from his eye. "We're home," he said quietly. Cronkite, an experienced and rugged reporter who parachuted with the invading force into Normandy during World War II's D-Day invasion, and who covered every major news story since, was left uncharacteristically speechless. When he recovered, the newscaster could only come up with, "Man on the Moon! Whew! Boy, oh boy!" while shaking his head in disbelief.

Later that evening Armstrong opened the LM's hatch, climbed down the ladder, and then entered the pantheon of exploration heroes. After planting his boot into the lunar soil, he spoke the memorable words, "That's one small step for man, one giant leap for mankind."

If ever someone deserved the world's admiration, it was Neil Armstrong. He was Columbus and Marco Polo and Lindbergh all rolled into one and then some. I remained in awe of him from that day, and to the extent that a sixth grader can have a "bucket list," shaking his hand was at the top of mine. From the day I sat in front of Aunt Della's television until thirty years later when I sat in Congress, that goal never changed, and it remained just as elusive.

• • •

Neil Armstrong retired from NASA in 1971, returned home to Ohio, taught aerospace engineering at the University of Cincinnati, but otherwise became something of a recluse. Three decades after Apollo 11, the *Washington Post* called him, "The world's most private famous person." Unlike many other astronauts who spent the decades after their missions commercializing their fame by giving paid speeches, writing books, and selling their autographs for exorbitant prices, Armstrong eschewed the limelight. His interviews and public appearances were rare, and he seemed painfully uncomfortable as the center of attention. One of his colleagues at the University of Cincinnati recalled the time Armstrong joined fellow faculty members for lunch at the nearby Skyline Chili Parlor. Someone in the restaurant recognized him and asked for an autograph. He was very polite, but after accommodating the request he excused himself from the table. When he didn't return, his colleague went looking for him. They found that he had left the restaurant to wait in the car while everyone else finished their lunch.

My desire to meet Armstrong appeared to be a bigger hurdle than landing the LM in a crater full of Chevy-sized boulders.

• • •

Early in my congressional career, and after I was instrumental in helping to save funding for the International Space Station, NASA director Dan Goldin visited my office to thank me. "Let me know if I can *ever* do *anything* for you," he said. "Would you like astronauts to visit your district? Would you like us to consider you for a private citizen slot on a space shuttle flight? That's a very unlikely thing, by the way, but we have let a couple of members of Congress go up previously. I'm here to find out what can we do for you. Just name it."

"I don't need any big-ticket items like those," I told the director. "I just want one thing. I want to shake hands with Neil Armstrong."

Goldin's face froze. "Anything but that," he gasped. "If you want to meet any other astronaut, it's a done deal. Ask me anything but that. We never get Neil for anything. He doesn't come to the reunions or other NASA events. He avoids the limelight. He's basically a hermit." Goldin then rubbed his chin thoughtfully before asking, "Are you sure you wouldn't like to go up on the space shuttle?"

• • •

A year later, I received a telephone call from a NASA congressional liaison officer: "Congressman Rogan, Director Goldin asked me to tell you that the Apollo 12 astronauts will be near your district this weekend. Since he knows of your interest in the Apollo program, he wanted you to know they will attend an autograph show in Southern California. They'd like to meet you to say thanks for your great help to NASA if you have time in your schedule to drop by and see them."

The Apollo 12 astronauts, Charles "Pete" Conrad, Richard Gordon, and Alan Bean made man's second Moon landing four months after Apollo 11, with Conrad and Bean becoming the third and fourth men to walk upon the lunar surface. Conrad, an experienced astronaut, had flown into space twice previously, on the Gemini V (1965) and Gemini XI (1966) missions; later he made his fourth and final spaceflight as commander of Skylab 2 (1973). Bean later flew aboard Skylab 3 (1973). Gordon, who remained in orbit piloting the Apollo 12 command module while his crewmates explored the Moon's surface, had flown with Conrad previously aboard Gemini XI.

It wasn't Neil Armstrong, but it would do for now.

• • •

My June 27, 1999 meeting with the Apollo 12 crew, ostensibly for them to thank me, wasn't exactly as advertised.

I cleared my late afternoon schedule that day and drove to North Hollywood to meet the three astronauts at the Beverly Garland Hotel. Upon entering the hotel's theater, I saw them seated at a long table and talking among themselves. They all dressed casually, with Conrad in an open-neck shirt and sweater, Gordon in a short-sleeved shirt, and Bean in a button-down shirt and sport jacket. All three had aged and put on weight, but I still recognized them as the space jockeys of my boyhood.

It was late, the theater was nearly empty, and the autograph show was wrapping up. No line of fans waited to meet the astronauts when I approached the table and introduced myself to Conrad. He shook hands with me and said, "It's nice to meet you. Would you like a photo?" while pointing to a stack of vintage Apollo 12 crew pictures before him.

"Sure, that would be great."

"Would you like us to sign it for you?"

"Absolutely. Thank you."

Conrad penned his name on the photograph, and then slid it over to crewmates Gordon and Bean, who did the same. Bean handed it back to me. "That will be $65," he told me.

"I beg your pardon?"

"It's $65. Five dollars for the photo, and $20 per signature." At first, I thought he was ribbing me, so I looked at Conrad and Gordon, both of whom sat expressionless.

"Thanks for saving the space station," I grumbled to myself as I reached into my wallet hoping I had enough cash to pay for it. I peeled out three twentys and a five and put the money on the table. Each astronaut took a twenty and stuck it in his pants pocket, and the fiver went into a cash box.

With the mercenary aspect of our meeting out of the way, I began what I thought was the "They'd like to thank you" segment of the encounter. I said I was honored to meet them and that I was pleased to support the space program in Congress. "That's great," Conrad said, and then he and the other two astronauts turned away from me and started discussing where they should grab dinner that night. I picked up my $65 photograph and walked away. Nobody at the table noticed my exit.

My $65 thank you gift: photograph signed for me by the Apollo 12 crew: Charles Conrad, Richard Gordon, and Alan Bean, Beverly Garland Hotel, June 27, 1999 (Author's collection)

A few days later, and after I had returned to Washington, my colleague Dana Rohrabacher (R-CA) asked how my meeting went with his longtime friend (and constituent) Pete Conrad. "Divine," I told Dana. "I drove down from an event in Malibu to North Hollywood in heavy L.A. traffic, and all for the pleasure of having him and his buddies clip me for sixty-five bucks before they gave me the bum's rush." I reported my experience to Dana, who seemed perplexed.

"There must be some confusion here," he said. "Let me look into it."

Later that week Conrad called me and apologized, telling me that the crew had spent long hours that day sitting at the table signing autographs. They were ready to wrap up their appearance when I showed up and introduced myself. He said he recognized me from somewhere but didn't make the connection, and he really hadn't heard my name when I introduced myself. He and the others assumed I was a last-minute guy in line who came to buy a signed photograph. "Let's get together in the next few weeks when you get back to California, congressman, and I'll make it up to you, and I'll also refund your money." I told him to keep the money. After all, I got a signed photo for it, but I looked forward to meeting him under less materialistic circumstances.

Our future meeting was not to be. A few days after he called me, on July 8, 1999, Conrad mounted his motorcycle and departed his Southern California home for the long drive up the coast to Monterey. When he reached Ojai, he lost control and crashed; he died from his injuries a few hours later.

• • •

On behalf of Conrad's family, NASA's congressional liaison officer invited me to his funeral service at Arlington National Cemetery on July 19, which fell the day before another NASA event to which I had been invited previously—the thirtieth anniversary celebration of Apollo 11's Moon landing. The officer said that Conrad's family held off scheduling the funeral an extra week so that his former astronaut colleagues who planned to come to Washington for the anniversary commemoration could attend. He also told me that, as usual, Neil Armstrong had not planned to participate in the reunion (despite press reports that he might come). However, because the ceremony now overlapped with Conrad's funeral that he did plan to attend, NASA officials persuaded the reluctant Armstrong to remain in town an extra day for the reunion. There was, he added, no guarantee of my meeting Armstrong there.

"Maybe not," I thought, but at least I had a chance to see him in person, albeit under unhappy circumstances.

. . .

The Conrad family scheduled the late astronaut's service for 11 a.m. on July 19 at Fort Myer Chapel on the Arlington cemetery grounds. I arrived at 10:15 a.m. and found a seat in the middle of the sanctuary. The chapel soon filled with the aged, balding, white-haired icons of my youth. Apollo 11 astronauts Buzz Aldrin and Michael Collins entered together, along with Conrad's Apollo 12 crewmembers Richard Gordon and Alan Bean. All four sat in a pew to my left. John Glenn arrived—the first American to orbit the Earth (1962), later a U.S. Senator, and, in 1998, the oldest human to travel to space (at age 77 he flew aboard the Space Shuttle *Discovery*). Glenn embraced and greeted other aging veterans of the Mercury, Gemini, and Apollo missions before taking a seat. Other astronauts that I recognized were Scott Carpenter (Mercury II); Walter Schirra (Mercury VIII, 1962; Gemini VI, 1965; Apollo 7, 1968); Eugene Cernan (Gemini IX, 1966; Apollo 10, 1969; and Apollo 17, 1972); Thomas Stafford (Gemini VI, 1967; Gemini IX, 1966; Apollo 10, 1969; and Apollo-Soyuz, 1975); James McDivitt (Gemini IV, 1965; Apollo 9, 1969); James Lovell (Gemini VII, 1965; Gemini XII, 1966; Apollo 8, 1968; Apollo 13, 1970); Thomas Mattingly (Apollo 16, 1972; STS-4, 1982; STS 51-C, 1985); Frank Borman (Gemini VII, 1965; Apollo 8, 1968); Rusty Schweickart (Apollo 9, 1969); and Joseph Kerwin (Skylab 2, 1973). It was impressive to see so much of America's space history assembled in one place, but my eyes kept sweeping the room looking for The One who was not there. I had a sinking feeling that Armstrong had succumbed to his crowd aversion and doomed my hope of seeing him.

Dan Goldin and Dana Rohrabacher entered the chapel together through the door to my left just as the service began. After they settled into their pew, I glanced back to that doorway and saw a nondescript lone man standing there: eyeglasses, silver-haired, portly, plain blue suit. His appearance suggested retired accountant, not daredevil explorer. I looked around to see if anyone else took note of him. They didn't, I did.

But then, I'd know Neil Armstrong anywhere.

He proved himself a loner even in the chapel. When Michael Collins spotted him in the doorway, he nudged Buzz Aldrin. The two former crewmates motioned for him to join them. He smiled and nodded to them, and then he sat in a pew two rows *behind* them even though there was plenty of room alongside Collins and Aldrin. Collins waited a few minutes, and then he turned and again beckoned to Armstrong, who relented and joined them in their pew.

I didn't know what to make of this bizarre kabuki dance, but it didn't matter. There sat the Apollo 11 crew twenty feet away. The boyish astronauts depicted in their famous crew photo from 1969 were now gray and old. Aldrin sported wavy white locks. Collins, now bald, was rail-thin and wore two hearing aids.

The service began with a Navy honor guard wheeling Conrad's flag-draped casket to the front of the chapel. Both Goldin and Rohrabacher spoke, and then Armstrong paid tribute to his late comrade. Unlike the previous speakers, he used no notes and his remarks were brief, recalling that he and Conrad had been partners on three early Gemini missions "with him as my backup and me as his backup." Then, abruptly, he returned to his seat. I was unsure if he had ended his remarks from emotion overcoming him or because he had nothing else to add.

Alan Bean, Conrad's crewmate aboard Apollo 12, shared the last time he saw Conrad three weeks earlier when they spent a weekend together in Los Angeles (coincidentally, it was when I met them at the Beverly Garland Hotel). He said that after Conrad's death he traveled to California to inspect the site of the fatal motorcycle crash, and then his voice broke and he was unable to complete the

Charles "Pete" Conrad, Jr.
1930 – 1999

An Original

Memorial Service
Fort Myer Memorial Chapel
July 19, 1999 – 11:00 am

Order of Service
 Musical Prelude
 Call to Service
  Chaplain Frank Johnson, CDR USN
 Special Remarks
  NASA Administrator Daniel Golden
  Representative Dana Rohrabacher
  Mr. Neil Armstrong
  Captain Alan Bean USN (RET)
  Captain Richard Gordon USN (RET)
  Captain James Lovell USN (RET)
  Mr. James Rathmann
  Mr. Stockton Rush
 "Amazing Grace"
  Mr. Willie Nelson
 Recessional
 Internment – Arlington National Cemetery
  Graveside Service
  Memorial Fly Over

A reception for family and friends will be held at Fort Myer,
Spates Hall, immediately following the ceremony.

In Loving Memory
July 19, 1999

Program from the Fort Myer Memorial Service for Astronaut Charles "Pete" Conrad, July 19, 1999,
with my handwritten notes taken during the service (Author's collection)

story. After composing himself he choked out, "He was the best man I ever knew. I loved him."

Richard Gordon, the third Apollo 12 astronaut, spoke next, saying, "Many of you came today to bury a friend or relative. I came to bury a brother." He said that when Conrad was selected for NASA and he had been passed over, Conrad sent him a photo of himself inscribed, "To Dick, until we serve again."

"Now, there is a new picture," Gordon concluded. "It is inscribed, 'To Pete, until we serve again.'"

James Lovell, the commander of the ill-fated Apollo 13 mission, delivered a polished eulogy, and he drew big laughs with his recollection of the Gemini flight he piloted during his wife's pregnancy. After strapping into his space capsule, he opened the flight plan and found a *Life* magazine cover featuring a newborn baby. Someone had taken a pen and labeled the picture, "Baby Lovell." Taped over the baby's face was a cutout picture of Conrad's face with his wide, gap-toothed grin. Conrad had written on the photo, "Lovell, you've been away too long!"

Following additional attributes, country music legend Willie Nelson sang, "Amazing Grace" a cappella. Long braided pigtails bordered Nelson's deeply lined (haggard, really) face. Dressed in black clothes, he looked the part of a rebellious old hippie that had been his mien for decades. As he sang his head jerked from side to side, but his vocal delivery was flawless and moving.

When the service ended, the honor guard wheeled Conrad's casket outside as mourners lined up behind it for the walk to the gravesite. I exited the chapel directly behind John Glenn and the three Apollo 11 astronauts; walking alongside me were astronauts Frank Borman and Joseph Kerwin. As the honor guard placed the casket on a horse-drawn caisson, our transition from the air-conditioned chapel to the oppressively hot and humid outdoor air felt brutal. The slow march to the burial site commenced.

I walked alongside Dana Rohrabacher who, like me, felt awed

by seeing Armstrong in person. We both expressed mutual disbelief that the ordinary-looking man a few steps in front of us was the Columbus of our time. If one expects sophisticated congressmen, when meeting famous people, to portray celebrity indifference, Armstrong shattered that veneer for both of us.

I worried about the scores of aged guests trudging along as we walked the long trek to the gravesite under a broiling sun. Gratefully, everyone withstood the heat and made it to Conrad's final resting place without incident, but by the time we got there my shirt was soaked. I had perspired through my suit jacket and necktie knot.

Burial ceremony for Astronaut Charles "Pete" Conrad, Arlington National Cemetery, July 19, 1999 (Author's collection)

Conrad's family sat in folding chairs positioned next to the casket while the rest of us stood quietly during the final prayers. The honor guard fired a volley, jets appeared overhead in a memorial flyover, and then a guard folded the casket flag and presented it to the family.

During the closing ritual Buzz Aldrin stood next to me, with Michael Collins directly behind. They chatted during the service, and I overheard comments like, "There's Rusty [Schweickart]. I haven't seen him in years," and "Did you see Borman? He looks pretty good." Aldrin interrupted my eavesdropping when he turned and recognized me. He grasped my hand and then introduced me to his wife Lois: "This is Jim Rogan, the congressman I was telling you about last week," he told her. Mrs. Aldrin bemoaned to me the lack of appreciation she felt America showed for Apollo 11, especially when compared to the level of appreciation the Europeans held for the mission. "Why isn't July 20th a national holiday?" she asked. "It marks one of America's greatest triumphs."

When the graveside service concluded, we walked back toward the chapel, where a group of young onlookers approached Armstrong, who greeted each with a smile and handshake. Despite his reputation as a reclusive figure, he was very friendly to everyone, although he declined politely an autograph request. "I'm sorry," he said, "but I stopped signing in 1994. I just don't do that anymore."

• • •

By now, I had spent almost two hours in the company of Neil Armstrong, but we had not met. I didn't want to intrude on his privacy at a friend's funeral, but with the service now over I expected him, at any moment, to make a quick getaway. If, after a thirty-year wait, I missed what might be my only chance to meet him, my regret would be profound and lifelong.

Just as I feared, while I contemplated my intrusion, he pivoted suddenly and walked toward a nearby waiting car. "No way," I muttered to myself. I hated to do it, but his abrupt exit with no handshake was a nonstarter. I bit the bullet.

"Excuse me, Mr. Armstrong. My name is Jim Rogan. It's such a great honor to...."

"*Oh, of course! Congressman Rogan!*" he replied.

Cliché notwithstanding, my jaw dropped.

Aunt Della would have liked this photo: here I am with Neil and Carol Armstrong, Arlington National Cemetery, July 19, 1999 (Author's collection)

Because of my work on President Clinton's impeachment, there existed a brief window in my life where I experienced a high level of public recognition. During that period, strangers often recognized me at times, but it caught me flat-footed when Neil Armstrong proved to be one of them. I never dreamed *he* would know *me*. Holy cow.

Armstrong introduced me to his wife, Carol, and then, *bingo!* I shook the hand of the first man on the Moon.

Somewhere, Aunt Della smiled.

• • •

After our brief exchange of pleasantries, the Armstrongs departed in their car. Everyone had been out in swamp-like weather for so long that nobody wanted to linger outdoors. I turned to go when John Glenn, with whom I served in the 105th Congress during his final two years in the Senate, came over to say hello. A cemetery official handed us cold bottles of water. "Just in time," Glenn said as he mopped his brow. While sipping water he told me he missed Capitol Hill since retiring from the Senate earlier that year. "Things are sure quiet for me these days," he lamented. While we spoke the same group of young onlookers who had approached Armstrong encircled Glenn and asked for autographs. While he obliged, I patted him on the back and told him I would see him inside.

John Glenn and I appreciated those cold water bottles. Arlington National Cemetery, July 19, 1999 (Author's collection)

• • •

The Conrad family hosted a reception for invited guests at nearby Spates Hall, located a few hundred feet from the chapel. All three of the Apollo 11 crewmembers attended: Armstrong and Collins stood alone outside the men's room in quiet, private conversation, while Aldrin and his wife moved through the buffet line.

It was there that I met Collins. "Congressman Rogan, I know you by reputation quite well," he said as we shook hands, leaving me

Meeting Apollo 11 command module astronaut Michael Collins, Arlington National Cemetery, July 19, 1999 (Author's collection)

again flattered. I told him I could prove I was a longtime admirer: on my first trip to Washington as a teenager in 1975, I wandered back and forth throughout the public floors of the Smithsonian's Air and Space Museum. "I knew you were the museum director at the time," I explained, "so I was hoping to get a glimpse of you in person!"

Collins laughed. "You should have just knocked on my office door! That was a long time ago. Now I spend most of my time down in Florida where I live."

As the reception wound down, it was time for me to return to the Capitol. I was leaving when Aldrin grabbed my elbow. "See you at the breakfast tomorrow morning?" he asked. I told him that I wouldn't miss that event for anything: tomorrow's "breakfast" was a private NASA reception at the Air and Space Museum commemorating the thirtieth anniversary of the day Apollo 11 landed on the Moon. Originally, only crewmembers Aldrin and Collins planned to attend. Now, with Armstrong in town for the funeral and staying overnight, all three Apollo 11 members would reunite on the historic anniversary. And, thanks to NASA's congressional liaison office, I had one of the hottest breakfast tickets in town.

For a space and history buff, it promised to be the photo op of a lifetime.

9

The First Men (Part Two)

The day after astronaut Pete Conrad's funeral, July 20, 1999, NASA hosted an invitation-only reception and ceremony at the Smithsonian's National Air and Space Museum to commemorate the thirtieth anniversary of the day Apollo 11 landed the first men on the Moon. Of all the official events I ever attended, this was a highlight.

I arrived at the Smithsonian at 7:30 a.m. and was escorted to a rear corner of the ground floor, where guests congregated for a continental breakfast. Security guards watched over the nearby area reserved for the later ceremony. A makeshift platform rested alongside the original Apollo 11 space capsule (on permanent museum display). Three empty chairs and a lectern awaited on the stage. John Glenn and Buzz Aldrin stood near the capsule conducting television interviews. Aldrin finished and joined the other guests for breakfast, while Glenn remained behind speaking to reporters.

(From left) Astronauts John Glenn and Buzz Aldrin giving television interviews on the thirtieth anniversary of the Apollo 11 Moon landing, July 20, 1999 (Photograph by the author)

After Neil Armstrong arrived, he saw me and walked over with an outstretched hand. When he again greeted me by name, I told him that I remained nonplussed that my boyhood hero knew me. Then, to sweeten my memory of the occasion, John Glenn joined us. While we talked about that July day three decades earlier, I stepped away to take a photograph of the first American to orbit the Earth alongside the first man on the Moon. As I lined up the two astronauts in my viewfinder, a NASA photographer tapped my shoulder, saying, "Excuse me, congressman, may I get a picture of you with Mr. Armstrong and Mr. Glenn?"

"Are you kidding?" I thought, and then put aside my camera quickly to accept the invitation. I posed alongside Armstrong and Glenn while thinking about how much I would treasure the photograph of this monumental life moment. Then, just as the photographer raised his camera and focused his lens, Senator Byron Dorgan (D-ND), Congresswoman Connie Morella (R-MD), and Con-

The original photo-bombed image (from left): Senator Byron Dorgan, Neil Armstrong, Congresswoman Connie Morella, John Glenn, Congressman Dana Rohrabacher, and yours truly, July 20, 1999 (NASA photograph)

gressman Dana Rohra-
bacher (R-CA) rushed
over and jumped into the
picture. "Thanks," the
photographer said after
he clicked the shot, and
then everyone dispersed.

I can't blame anyone
for wanting to be in the
shot with Armstrong
and Glenn on this his-
toric date, but over the
ensuing decades, my
teeth clenched whenever
I recalled how those three
interlopers hijacked my
once-in-a-lifetime photo.
While writing this book
I complained about it to
my friend and colleague,
Judge Jeffrey Ferguson.
Jeff, a digital *sensei* on
the computer, said he
could right the wrong.

Ahh...much better! *This* is the one hanging on my office wall today. Look closely and you will see that Fergie transplanted my left arm onto John Glenn's shoulder. This extra touch earned him a couple of beers.

He scanned the photograph, made some artistic adjustments, and poof! The interlopers disappeared. Yes, I know, historian purists are aghast that Jeff digitally evaporated three photo-bombers from my coveted picture.

The historian purists can go to hell.

Stewards arrived and rang small bells, signaling for guests to leave the breakfast area and take their seats for the ceremony, which was scheduled to begin at 9 a.m. We moved to the folding chairs facing the Apollo 11 space capsule. An usher seated Carol Armstrong and Lois Aldrin, the wives of the first two men on the Moon, directly in front of me, with John Glenn alongside me. Senator Ted Stevens (R-AL), sitting nearby, took a phone call, and then came over and said to me that some important issue broke and that the GOP leadership wanted all members back at the Capitol. "Would you like a ride back?" he asked me.

"Ted, I wouldn't go back right now if the British were burning the city again."

At 9:10 a.m. the three Apollo 11 astronauts took their seats on the stage next to their spaceship amid cheers and applause. A NASA spokesman apologized for the delay, saying, "We're waiting for Vice President Al Gore to arrive. The vice president is presenting medals to the astronauts, so we can't begin until he gets here."

(From left) Apollo 11 astronauts Michael Collins, Neil Armstrong, and Buzz Aldrin seated alongside their space capsule on the thirtieth anniversary of their Moon landing, July 20, 1999 (Photograph by the author)

Carol Armstrong turned to me and whispered, "I guess we're on *Gore Time.*"

Referencing Gore's anticipated presidential campaign in 2000,

I whispered back, "Not for long, I hope."

Once Gore's motorcade arrived, NASA Director Dan Goldin introduced the vice president. Gore stepped from behind the backdrop curtain, greeted the trio on the stage, and then began his remarks by acknowledging Glenn in the audience, along with Apollo 15 astronaut Al Worden. Gore read a lengthy tribute to the crew, and then he shared his memory of attending their July 1969 launch with his father, then-U.S. Senator Albert Gore, Sr.

Gore presented the three with NASA's Langley Medal, established in 1908 to honor those who have advanced aviation. Previous recipients of the solid gold award have included Orville and Wilbur Wright, Charles Lindbergh, astronaut Alan Shephard (the first American in space), and rocketry pioneer Wernher von Braun.

Armstrong stepped to the lectern and read from a prepared text. He thanked the Smithsonian on behalf of his crew, and then shared a brief history of the relationship between Langley and the Wright Brothers in the early days of flight. When he finished, the three astronauts stood together and displayed their medals for the photographers.

Once I learned that Armstrong planned to remain in town, I called in that chit I held for saving the space station. NASA Director Dan Goldin set up a private meeting for my family and me with the Apollo 11 crew at NASA headquarters later that afternoon. Since I had run out of film (a constant danger in the pre-digital camera days), and thinking I should get back to investigate Senator Stevens' apparent political emergency, I slipped out during Gore's concluding remarks and returned to the Capitol.

• • •

Two disappointments occurred prior to my family's afternoon NASA appointment with the Apollo 11 crew. First, my wife Christine called late that morning and told me our twin girls could not attend. Both had developed ear infections, so she was taking them

Obverse and reverse of the bronze version of the medallions that Neil Armstrong gave me on July 20, 1999. These were made of metal from the Saturn V tower that launched the Apollo missions to the Moon. (Author's collection)

to see the doctor. Second, a family emergency necessitated Collins' return to Florida, so he would not join his two colleagues for a discussion about their mission before an assemblage of NASA engineers. Only Armstrong and Aldrin would attend.

When I arrived at NASA, an aide escorted me into a conference room, where I found Armstrong and Aldrin awaiting the start of their program. Both welcomed me, and then Armstrong asked, "Where's the family?" I told him the reason for their absence. "I'll bet that thirty years from now they still won't forgive me for letting an ear infection keep them from this meeting," I said.

"Or they won't forgive their ears," chuckled Carol Armstrong, who had just entered the room.

"I'm really sorry," Armstrong said. "I was hoping to see the girls." Then he reached into his coat pocket and produced a fistful of bronze and aluminum tokens. "Here," he told me. "Give them these with my best and tell them how sorry I was to miss them." NASA had minted the silver dollar-sized tokens to commemorate the thirtieth anniversary of Apollo 11's flight. Each was made from metal taken from the

Saturn V launchpad used to blast the Apollo spacecrafts to the Moon. What a treasure getting these from him, and on this special day.

Armstrong, Aldrin, and I chatted while they awaited the start of the program. I asked Neil if he was still teaching college in Ohio. No, he told me, he gave it up some years earlier. He said he kept active these days serving on a variety of corporate boards as well as working on his Lebanon, Ohio farm. He pulled out his bulging brown wallet and fished through it until he found and gave to me one of his business cards.

I brought with me a treasure that NASA officials gave me five years earlier during my service in the California legislature. I showed Neil and Buzz the large certificate that NASA printed in 1994 to commemorate Apollo 11's twenty-fifth anniversary; attached to it was a cloth flag flown aboard the Space Shuttle Columbia on that earlier anniversary. Neil and Buzz agreed to sign it for me, which I considered a coup given Armstrong's "no autographs" policy. When I said that I hesitated to ask him to sign since I knew about his rule, he smiled. "I make an exception for friends," he said, and then he penned a bold, black signature onto the certificate. While signing he paused briefly after each pen stroke as if determining whether his umbrella-shaped autograph looked satisfactory. Then, to memorialize that day's historical significance, he wrote "7/20/1999" under his name, and then drew a small squiggle under the date as a final flourish. Buzz took the pen and also signed and dated it.

Buzz suggested that he, Neil, and I take a group photograph next to the flag in the corner of the room. As I stood between the first and second man on the Moon, I thought about how I had watched their Moon landing, thirty years earlier to the hour, in Aunt Della's apartment. (I also looked around to make sure that Byron Dorgan, Connie Morella, and Dana Rohrabacher didn't jump into the frame and ruin this photograph!)

A NASA employee entered and said it was time for the two astronauts to begin their program. Neil invited me to join them, but once

Presented to

JAMES ROGAN

This Apollo 11 25th anniversary flag was flown aboard the Orbiter "Columbia" STS-65, July 8–23, 1994 in commemoration of America's first Lunar Landing Mission.

Daniel S. Goldin, Administrator
National Aeronautics and Space Administration

Apollo 11 twenty-fifth anniversary flag and certificate, NASA headquarters, Washington, D.C., July 20, 1999 (Author's collection)

again, congressional business intruded on my fervent desire. Buzz mentioned to Neil that I was in for a tough reelection race in 2000 because of my leadership role in the Clinton impeachment, which proved very unpopular in my Democrat-dominated Los Angeles-based congressional district. "Yes, I know," Neil replied. "I've been reading about it. The Democrats are coming after you because of

Here's one photo that Jeff Ferguson didn't need to fix digitally! With Buzz Aldrin and Neil Armstrong, Washington, July 20, 1999 (Author's collection)

it. Hang in there." He nodded in a friendly and reassuring manner.

I thanked them again for all they had done to advance space exploration, and for giving me the memory of a lifetime. "There's more to come," Buzz said as the aide escorted them through the door to their presentation. "I'll see you back in L.A."

• • •

I didn't know it at the time, but Buzz was right. There was more to come. Over the coming years, I developed a friendship with Neil Armstrong and other astronauts, all of which would have been unimaginable to me as a boy. I will share more of these stories and recollections down the road. For now, we leave the realm of space and return to Earth.

• • •

Neil Armstrong died at age 82 on August 25, 2012 of complications following heart surgery.

Mercury astronaut Scott Carpenter died at age 88 on October 10, 2013 of complications following a stroke.

Mercury, Gemini, and Apollo astronaut Walter Schirra died at age 84 on May 3, 2007 of a heart attack.

Gemini and Apollo astronaut Eugene Cernan died at age 82 on January 16, 2017.

One week before Election Day 2008, a jury convicted Senator Ted Stevens (R-AK), a forty-year Senate veteran, on federal corruption charges. He went on to lose his reelection that year by a narrow margin, but his conviction was thrown out the following year based on newly discovered prosecutorial misconduct. The news broke too late to save his Senate seat. He died in a plane crash on August 9, 2010 at age 86.

10

Keeping a Promise

In the 1990s, I attended a banquet at the historic Roosevelt Hotel in downtown Hollywood, where my seatmate was Anita Page, one of MGM's great silent movie stars of the 1920s and early 1930s. Someone at our table mentioned that the ballroom in which we dined was the location for the first Academy Awards ceremony in 1929. Anita looked around the room, confirmed the trivia, and told us that she not only had attended that night, but she had a starring role in a picture nominated that year. She shared her memories of the event, and of how the stars laughingly accused the hotel chef of serving canned peas as part of the main course. She added her assurance that those attending that first Academy Awards banquet never dreamed that the annual event would "grow into a big deal."

By the 1990s, almost seventy years after that first gathering, the Oscars remained an international big deal, and especially to my wife Christine. Like millions of others, she grew up watching the annual televised production from the red-carpet arrivals to the concluding credits. During our courtship she once remarked wistfully that it was her dream to attend it just once, and then dance the night away at the afterparty Governors Ball. With the youthful bravado of an ardent suitor, I promised that one day I'd take her to both. The promise was an unlikely one coming from a junior-grade deputy county prosecutor with no connections to the entertainment industry, but a decade later I made good on it.

Each year the Democrat and Republican leaders of the California legislature are allotted two VIP tickets to the Academy Awards. In 1995, when I served as a member of the State Assembly, I persuaded GOP Minority Leader Jim Brulte to give me his tickets. Actually, I didn't persuade Jim. I begged him. He had a reputation for refusing any invitation that required him to wear a tuxedo. Since the Oscars are strictly black-tie, his orphan tickets cried out for a loving home. I hounded my besieged leader until, weary of listening to my unending pleas, he surrendered them.

When I announced the news to Christine with great fanfare, I assumed that this coup would allow me to press the marital cruise control button and ride the gratitude highway indefinitely. She showed surprise and appreciation, but not to a level that matched my expectation. Still, she hit the department stores for countless try-ons before settling on a Jessica McClintock gown of billowing gold lamé with a jewel-buttoned halter bodice and worn with black four-inch Stuart Weitzman stilettos. [Author's note: when Christine read the draft of this chapter, she crossed out my description of her Oscars-night wardrobe and added the one that you just read. In my version, I wrote that she wore a pretty gold dress and black shoes, and that she carried a purse so small that I had to carry her lipstick in my pocket.]

She refused to model her gown for me until shortly before we left for the event. When I saw her in it, I thought she looked stunning, but she moved stiffly. Something wasn't working. "Why are you walking so funny?" I asked.

"I have to move carefully," she replied, "or things might fall off when we get there." A few more saunters in front of the mirror brought a frown. "I don't need all this," she muttered, and with that she peeled off a pair of fake eyelashes and ten fake fingernails, and then she reached inside her dress and removed two medium-sized gel inserts. Tossing this collection of enhancements onto the kitchen table, she said, "That's much better. Besides, you'll see enough fake stuff tonight." After a few curative minutes before the bathroom mirror, we were on our way.

For those who have never attended an Academy Awards ceremony, its glamorous underpinnings go far beyond the attendees' wardrobe or glitzy arrival. Per the directions attached to our tickets, Christine and I arrived at a designated hotel in downtown Los Angeles for a private reception, where we joined fellow invitees for sumptuous (and complimentary) hor

Christine wearing her Oscar-night dress (just after leaving half of her "ensemble" on the kitchen table), March 27, 1995 (Author's collection)

d'oeuvres and champagne. At the appointed time, our personal chauffeur arrived and escorted us to our assigned black stretch limousine (the limo and driver also came with the tickets) for the ride to the Shrine Auditorium. I didn't know until I showed up for the reception that everyone attending the Oscars *must* arrive by limousine. That explains why, if you watched the ceremony on television that evening, you didn't see the Rogans toddle down the red carpet after exiting my 1971 Chevy Impala.

Our chauffer joined a procession of other limousines arriving at the Shrine shortly after 5 p.m. Giant gold-painted Oscar statues lined the entrance. Searchlight beams spun and danced overhead. Screaming fans in nearby bleachers cheered, took pictures, and clamored for autographs from everyone stepping from a limo and onto the red carpet, including us, which confirmed my suspicion that they do that automatically for whoever arrives; they sort out their photos and autographs of the famous from the nobodies later.

It took over ten minutes to walk the short distance from curbside to auditorium through the gauntlet of fans, television and still cameras, reporters, movie stars, and guests. The pace of entry slowed significantly because everyone walking the red carpet appeared to be in no hurry to reach the entrance (and thereby fall out of camera range). We didn't mind the slow pace because it gave us a chance to absorb the frenetic scene of too many movie stars occupying too little space.

The whole limo-and-red-carpet experience was, for a couple of non-celebrities, very Walter Mitty-ish. It proved so much fun that once we reached the auditorium, Christine suggested that we circle back to the curb and "arrive" again. After I vetoed that idea, and not wanting to surrender the moment too quickly, when we reached the end of the carpet Christine turned, faced the crowd, smiled broadly, blew a kiss, and called out, "Thank you—I love you all!" Another cheer erupted from the bleachers as she turned, smiled at me, and then entered the auditorium.

An usher escorted us to our reserved seats. Legendary movie actor Gregory Peck, looking frail and moving slowly, followed behind us down the aisle and took his seat near the stage. Movie and television stars were everywhere we looked. Even the snack bar line was unlike the ones I patronized at my local theater. At the Shrine, I waited to buy Milk Duds while chatting with two other chocoholics in line with me on a similar mission: four-time Oscar nominee Annette Bening, and Susan Sarandon (who took home the Best Actress award the following year).

The show began at 6:00 with a rambling speech by Academy president Arthur Hiller before comedian David Letterman took over as master of ceremonies. Although Letterman later received mixed reviews as host, I thought he did a great job. Some of his quips during the show included:

- [Referring to the nominated film, *Eat, Drink, Man, Woman*] "That's how Arnold Schwarzenegger asked his wife Maria Shriver out on their first date!"

- [While dragging a carpet onto the stage for a scene] "I suspect I'm not the only guy here tonight carrying his rug."

- After winner Roger Avery ended his acceptance speech with the crass comment that he now had to "go and take a pee," Letterman returned to the lectern and deadpanned, "I've had to take a pee since 6:15 and you don't hear me whining about it."

Another hit was Letterman's "Hints That a Film Would Not Win an Oscar," which included:

- It still has the time code from the camcorder on it.

- Any combination of the words "Police" and "Academy" in the title.

- Four words: *Dom DeLuise is Gandhi.*

The Oscar presenters during the three-and-a-half hour show comprised a "Who's Who" of 1990s Hollywood elite, including Tim Allen, Jamie Lee Curtis, Robert De Niro, Matt Dillon, Sally Field, Mel Gibson, Hugh Grant, Tom Hanks, Anthony Hopkins, Tommy Lee Jones, Paul Newman (who forgot to read the names of the nominees before presenting the Oscar), Jack Nicholson, Al Pacino, Gregory Peck, Keanu Reeves, Susan Sarandon, Steven Seagal, Steven Spielberg, Sylvester Stallone, Sharon Stone, John Travolta, Denzel Washington, Sigourney Weaver, and Oprah Winfrey. The show featured performances by entertainers such as Elton John, who played the piano and sang "Can You Feel the Love Tonight," his Oscar-nominated song from Disney's *The Lion King.* Arnold Schwarzenegger presented the Irving Thalberg Memorial Award to Clint Eastwood, who joked that Schwarzenegger (later California governor) was his illegitimate son.

Comedian Steve Martin got the loudest laugh of the night when he described how much the movies meant to him. He recalled fondly sitting in the back of one darkened theater with his sixteen-year old girlfriend as he tried to get to first base with her. "I even remember the name of the movie," Martin deadpanned. "It was called *The Lion King!*"

The excitement heightened with the announcement of the major awards: Best Supporting Actress Dianne Wiest gave the longest speech, while Best Supporting Actor Martin Landau rambled so much during his acceptance that the director cued the orchestra and cut to a commercial in mid-sentence. Jessica Lange took home the Best Actress award, and Tom Hanks won Best Actor for the second consecutive year (the first actor to do so since Spencer Tracy in 1938). After presenting the final Oscars for Best Director to Robert Zemeckis and Best Picture to *Forest Gump,* the ceremony concluded.

Aside from my limousine protocol ignorance, I also didn't know until now that attending the Oscars was easy when compared to scoring an invitation to the far more exclusive Governors Ball. Once the awards ceremony ended, an army of security guards deployed and steered Oscar attendees into one of two lines: the privileged line leading to the ball or the non-privileged line leading to the street. They kept busy chasing would-be crashers out of the ball line (I heard more than one rejected couple arguing with a guard by declaiming authoritatively, "Do you happen to know who *I* am?").

Since we clutched the coveted passes, we were waved into Valhalla, which in this case was a massive tent where an orchestra played, award winners posed with their trophies for photographers, and chef Wolfgang Puck served hors d'oeuvres to the guests inching toward their assigned tables. The dinner presentation was elegant—no canned peas on the menu that night—but I might have preferred otherwise. Since I am a picky eater with no appreciation for any food more continental than pizzas or hot dogs, I found little on the plates of fancy food that appealed to me beyond the solid chocolate Oscar statuettes served during dessert.

Surprisingly, for a woman who longed to attend the Academy Awards all her life, Christine showed little interest in remaining to savor the drinking, dancing, hobnobbing, and celebrity gawking. As soon as dinner and coffee ended, I suggested that we join the movie stars and assorted beautiful people on the dance floor. She had a different idea.

"I'm ready to call it a night," she said with a yawn. I looked at my watch. It was barely 10:30. When I expressed surprise at her premature ending to a lifelong fantasy, she shrugged. "When I told you that I dreamed of dancing the night away at the Academy Awards, I wasn't the mother of two-year old twins who will need me at 4 a.m. Let's go."

While waiting outside in the limo line for the ride back to our hotel, we stood alongside stars also awaiting their ride to an early exit. Pointing out that our line now included movie stars like John Travolta, Clint Eastwood, Holly Hunter, and Jeremy Irons, I told Christine with smug satisfaction, "Well, someone sure came through for you Big Time. You were promised the Academy Awards and the Governors Ball, and you got the Academy Awards and the Governors Ball."

She disabused me quickly of my expectation of coasting for decades on Oscar laurels score. "Honey," she replied, "it was a wonderful evening and I'll always be grateful for it. So, when you get to work tomorrow—

"—Be sure to thank Jim Brulte for me."

• • •

Actor Gregory Peck died of pneumonia at age 87 on June 12, 2003.

Actor Paul Newman died of cancer at age 83 on September 26, 2008.

Actor Martin Landau died of heart disease at age 89 on July 17, 2017.

Director Arthur Hiller died of natural causes at age 92 on August 17, 2016.

11

Animation Legends

While I attended UCLA Law School, the nearby Sherman Oaks Galleria (a local shopping mall) announced plans to host a Saturday animation art display and sale. This sounded interesting, and since it took very little to coax me away from law library drudgery, I abandoned my studies for a quick visit to the galleria.

Until computers overtook the industry, the traditional form of animating a cartoon involved artists drawing by hand each individual frame on a clear plastic sheet, a "cel", and then inking in the colors (also by hand) before photographing it. It could take twenty-five or more individual cels just to make up one second of film. For example, to create the first full-length animation movie, Disney's *Snow White* (1937), the studio employed over 750 artists who hand-drew and inked over 250,000 different cels for the eighty-three-minute film.

Now coveted by serious collectors and investors, back in the late 1970s most viewed animation cels more as curiosities than as art. That became apparent at the Sherman Oaks sale I attended, where thousands of original sketches, storyboards, and painted cels from countless movies and television cartoon programs were available for purchase. The character subjects ranged from the universally identifiable to the hopelessly obscure.

Flipping through one stack, I found an original hand-painted animation cel of Fred Flintstone and Barney Rubble used in the production of the classic early 1960s cartoon series *The Flintstones*. I bought it for $10 (about what I cleared in tips after working an all-night bartending shift at Filthy McNasty's in Hollywood).

I looked through another stack when a lanky older man with thin white hair wandered over and asked if I had found anything I liked. I showed him the Fred and Barney cel I had just purchased. "Hang on to that," he advised after admiring it. "Someday it might be worth something." As we chatted, he opened a case, pulled out and set up a collapsible artist's easel, and placed a large tablet on it. When I asked what he planned to do with it, he replied, "I'm an animator myself, although I've long since retired. They asked me to come to the show today and draw." When I asked what type of cartoons he drew, he began sketching several poses of the instantly recognizable features of Betty Boop.

"My name's Grim Natwick," he said. "I created this girl over fifty years ago. Ever hear of her?" When I said I was a fan of Betty's, he smiled. "I'm surprised that someone your age knows her. She was very big in the 1930s, but not so much now." As he completed the sketch, a small crowd formed. He put the final touches on her and then invited questions from the expanding crowd.

I wanted to ask if I might have the Betty sketch he churned out, but with his growing audience, I feared my request might touch off an avalanche of similar ones. I let the opportunity pass (an oversight I still regret forty years later, especially after I saw him crumple it up and throw it in the trash can when he left).

After Natwick finished his sketch-and-talk to appreciative applause, a nattily dressed elderly man used a portable public address system to invite everyone to gather at the nearby stage where he waited. When a small group of shoppers assembled, he encouraged all the children to sit in front to meet his special friend. He reached into a battered valise and pulled out a vintage ventriloquist-style Donald Duck doll dressed in his familiar sailor suit. "My name is

Clarence Nash," the man announced. "I've been the voice of Donald Duck in the Walt Disney cartoons for the last fifty years. Now, I'd like you to meet my special friend." Nash plopped the doll on his knee, and to everyone's delight, he began a conversation with his companion. His first few words in the familiar quacking voice evoked laughter and applause.

After "interviewing" Donald, he put away the doll. "I have some pictures of Donald that I will be happy to autograph for anyone who wants one," he said. "No charge!" A line formed at the stage quickly. He greeted each fan in Donald's voice, and he inscribed every picture individually. He proved as likeable and adorable as the famous duck into which he breathed both life and character for five decades.

• • •

In 1984, my future wife Christine went shopping at her local Glendale drug store. As she exited, a dapper old gentleman standing near the door bowed to her while tipping his tweed hat. "Good morning to a beautiful lady," he said in a Donald Duck voice.

Impressed at his talent, she told him, "Oh, how charming! Hey, you do that very well! I'm impressed." The man bowed politely, replaced his hat on his head, and then he went on his way.

The next night she tuned in to the annual Academy Awards ceremony and watched in disbelief as Clarence Nash, the man who greeted her the day before, appeared onstage with host Johnny Carson during an Oscar tribute to his half century of voicing the beloved character.

• • •

A few years later, I mailed my Flintstones cel to Hanna-Barbera Studios in Hollywood with a request that their creators, Bill Hanna and Joseph Barbera, sign it for me. After a lengthy wait, Hanna's secretary called me and said that both her boss and Mr. Barbera had autographed it. The delay, she said apologetically, was because she wanted to find an old background print used during the original show's production to match with my cel. After locating one in the archives, she matted my Fred and Barney cel atop it, and then she secured the autographs. "I hope you don't mind the delay," she said apologetically, "but it took a long time to find a production background."

I didn't mind.

My autographed original *Flintstones* cel, complete with production background, thanks to Mr. Hanna's secretary (Reprinted with permission, Warner Bros. Clip and Still Licensing; Author's collection)

In 1989, Christine and I celebrated our first wedding anniversary in San Francisco. While waiting for an available table at a Powell Street restaurant, something caught my attention at the chic art gallery next door. The gallery had a Fred and Barney original production cel signed by Hanna and Barbera displayed prominently in the entrance bearing a price tag of $1,500 (back then!).

Grim Natwick's advice to hang on to my $10 investment proved sound.

• • •

By the mid-1930s, as Walt Disney led the world in animation feature films, he dubbed his core group of studio animators as the "Nine Old Men," even though most of them were still in their twenties. Over the next half-century, these artists churned out some of the studio's best-loved classics.

The last two surviving members of this elite group, Frank Thomas and Ollie Johnston, were lifelong friends and colleagues. Both met while art students at Stanford University, where they worked together at the college newspaper. Both joined Disney studios only months apart: Frank in 1934 and Ollie in 1935. Over the next forty-five years, their combined contributions included immortal films such as *Snow White, Peter Pan, Cinderella, The Jungle Book, Alice in Wonderland, Mary Poppins,* and many others. They both retired in 1978; they co-authored four books, they were the subjects of documentary films, and they lived as next-door neighbors in a Los Angeles suburb for some sixty years.

By the time I entered the state legislature, both Frank and Ollie (as everyone called them) were long retired. When I learned that they were my constituents, I had the State Assembly prepare ornate resolutions to honor them for their lifetime achievements in art and entertainment. In appreciation for these legislative recognitions, they sketched and signed prints from of their best-known films for my family.

Once again, I obtained a wonderful memento of two animation legends only because I was in the right place at the right time.

• • •

Although I never met Hank Ketcham, the artist who created and drew *Dennis the Menace* for many decades, he drew this sketch for me when I was a young municipal court judge in Glendale, California. I include it here as an honorable mention only because I still appreciate his kindness:

Original sketch of *Dennis the Menace* done for me by creator Hank Ketcham (1920-2001) (*Dennis the Menace* cartoon syndicated by North America Syndicate; reproduced with permission)

• • •

Besides Betty Boop, during his lengthy career spanning from the 1920s to the 1950s, Grim Natwick also animated such iconic cartoon characters as Snow White, Popeye the Sailor, Mickey Mouse, and Felix the Cat. He died at age 100 on October 7, 1990.

Clarence Nash, the voice of Donald Duck for half a century, died of leukemia at age 80 on February 20, 1985.

William Hanna died of throat cancer at age 90 on March 22, 2001. His partner, Joseph Barbera, died of natural causes at age 95 on December 18, 2006.

Hank Ketcham retired from drawing Dennis the Menace in 1994 and turned the daily chore over to his former assistants. He died of prostate cancer at age 81 on June 1, 2001.

Frank Thomas died of natural causes at age 92 on September 8, 2004.

Ollie Johnston, the last surviving member of Disney's "Nine Old Men," died of natural causes at age 95 on April 14, 2008.

12

The Saturday Night Massacre

WATERGATE.

Writing this nearly half a century since that term first exploded across the headlines, I am mindful that this word, so ubiquitous throughout my life that it required no explanation, becomes increasingly hazy to readers born decades (or generations) after it collapsed Richard Nixon's presidency in 1974. Although its labyrinthine details are beyond the scope of this book, my experiences meeting key players from America's greatest political scandal are within its wheelhouse.[1] This chapter covers the four people involved in the drama's major turning point: Watergate's *Saturday Night Massacre*.

• • •

On June 17, 1972, police nabbed five men planting surveillance equipment in the Democratic National Committee located in the Watergate Office Building. In the months following, evidence connected the burglars to senior administration officials, which led to investigations by the FBI, both houses of Congress, and the press over possible White House involvement in either the original burglary or a later attempted cover-up.

---

1   I have excluded my stories of meeting both President Nixon and Vice President Spiro Agnew, whose separate scandal during Watergate led to his own resignation in 1973. I detailed my encounters with both in my book, *And Then I Met....* (2014).

In 1973, as the scandal percolated, President Nixon nominated Secretary of Defense Elliot Richardson as his new attorney general. After serving in the Army during World War II and participating in the Normandy invasion, Richardson finished Harvard Law School, became U.S. Attorney for Massachusetts under President Eisenhower, and then served as his state's lieutenant governor and attorney general. Nixon's election in 1968 brought Richardson to Washington, and he became one of only two men in U.S. history to serve in a president's cabinet as the head of four different departments.[2]

At his confirmation hearing, Richardson promised the Democrat-controlled Senate that he would appoint a special prosecutor to investigate possible Watergate crimes. He kept the promise on his first day at the Justice Department by appointing Democrat Archibald Cox, his former Harvard law professor. Cox, a campaign aide and speechwriter for John F. Kennedy, served in JFK's administration as solicitor general alongside Attorney General Robert F. Kennedy. With such deep ties to the Kennedys, Nixon harbored a well-deserved paranoia over the appointment and motives of the special prosecutor and his large staff of lawyers, virtually all of whom were liberal Democrat combatants.[3]

The scandal's levee began failing when former White House Counsel John Dean, whom Nixon had fired, told investigators that he helped coordinate the scandal's cover-up with Nixon and other high-ranking officials. Nixon denied any wrongdoing. Later, when Deputy Assistant to the President Alexander Butterfield revealed

---

2   Secretary of Health, Education and Welfare (1970-1973); secretary of Defense (1973); U.S. Attorney General (1973); and secretary of Commerce (1976-1977).

3   Attorney General Richardson chose Cox, "a known adversary to Nixon for the position of special prosecutor... [Richardson] poorly manag[ed] Cox while he staffed a special prosecution team made up almost entirely of liberal Democrats[.]" Robert H. Bork, *Saving Justice: Watergate, the Saturday Night Massacre, and Other Adventures of a Solicitor General* (New York: Encounter Books, 2013), 70.

that Nixon recorded all Oval Office conversations, Cox subpoenaed many of the tapes, including those from meetings that might corroborate Dean's claim of presidential culpability.

At first, Nixon and Cox negotiated over the tapes, but when those talks failed, Cox pushed forward with the subpoenas. Claiming executive privilege, Nixon refused to surrender the tapes. On October 20, 1973, after Cox held a nationally televised press conference and defied openly Nixon's order to withdraw the subpoenas, Nixon instructed Attorney General Richardson to fire him. When Richardson refused and resigned, his deputy attorney general, William Ruckelshaus, received the same order. When he also refused, Nixon fired him. The command next fell upon the third in line at the Justice Department, Solicitor General Robert Bork, who complied. The media quickly dubbed the resignation and firings as the *Saturday Night Massacre.* Its aftermath created a White House public relations nightmare while simultaneously driving the impeachment compass needle due north.

Richardson, Cox, Ruckelshaus, Bork. In 1973, every American with a pulse recognized those names and counted them as heroes or villains (depending on one's politics). I met them all, and each shared with me their versions of what happened on that fateful weekend night.

• • •

After Elliot Richardson resigned as attorney general in October 1973, the press and anti-Nixon forces (yes, I know—a redundancy) hailed him as a principled and fearless defender of the law. His public stock rose swiftly, and soon his name registered prominently in the 1976 presidential polls. If such adulation ignited Richardson's ambitions, he doused that fire by accepting President Ford's appointment as U.S. ambassador to the United Kingdom. This diplomatic plum removed him from the domestic scene and sent him overseas. By failing to exploit his newfound national popularity back home, he faded from public consciousness. He waited ten years to run for office again—an unsuccessful Senate race in 1984. By then, he was remembered, if at all, as a relic of a scandal people wanted to forget. Marjorie Williams later wrote, "The man who had once been thought a presidential contender, who had been lionized for standing up to Richard Nixon, would spend [his remaining years] more or less on the sidelines . . . in law firms."[4]

When I was in high school, I met Richardson at the apex of his political popularity. On January 15, 1974, less than three months after he resigned, the San Francisco Harvard Club honored him with a dinner. Along with my classmates Dan Swanson and Roger Mahan, I skipped school that day and took the bus into the city hoping to meet him and get his insights on politics. As usual, we had no ticket (or money to buy one), it was a sold-out event, security was tight, and a battalion of reporters encamped throughout the St. Francis Hotel trying to interview him.

The media interest in Richardson, already high, jumped off the charts hours before his San Francisco appearance. During the ongoing legal battle for Nixon's tapes, the White House had revealed previously the existence of an unexplained eighteen-and-a-half-minute gap in a recorded conversation between Nixon and his chief of staff three days after the burglary. Allegations flew that Nixon erased the tape intentionally to destroy evidence. Nixon claimed the erasure was accidental, and his secretary, Rose Mary Woods, posed for an infamous photograph showing how, through strained physical contortions, she might have erased it unintentionally. John Sirica, the judge overseeing the Watergate trials, ordered a panel of experts to review the tape. A few hours before Richardson's speech, the panel reported their conclusion of an intentional erasure. All hell broke loose in Congress and the media. By late afternoon, it seemed as if every reporter in America had crammed into the hotel

---

4   *The Washington Post*, July 29, 1990.

wanting to interview Richardson about the bombshell revelation. By the time we arrived, it was almost impossible to move about the lobby, and any chance to meet him privately appeared slim.

While looking for a way to sneak into the ballroom to hear his speech, I struck up a conversation with a busboy who mentioned offhandedly that he had delivered food to Richardson's party in rooms 935 and 936. That information came in handy later.

Meanwhile, patience paid off. The dinner and preliminary program ran too long. It was well after 9:00 p.m. when the emcee began Richardson's introduction. The late hour forced the print reporters to leave early to file their stories before deadline. As the grumbling correspondents filed out, we filed in and conscripted three empty seats at the press table in the back of the room.

Richardson began his talk by acknowledging the rampant speculation about a possible presidential candidacy in 1976, and then he teased the audience with what appeared to be a major announcement. "I am here among friends to declare that I will not remain politically inactive," he intoned. "Since there has been great pressure on me to seek this office, therefore, I am announcing tonight that I *will* be a candidate—

"—for overseer of Harvard University!" The initial gasp after his dramatic pause turned to laughter, but I felt disappointed over him cheating us out of a possible historic moment.

Despite a long, dull, uninspiring speech, well-wishers cheered and surrounded him afterward. Since the crowd proved too thick to meet him, and remembering what the busboy told me earlier, we took the elevator to the ninth floor and waited upstairs for our chance to meet him.

It was after 11:00 p.m. when Richardson and his companions emerged from an elevator. I turned on my tape recorder, introduced myself, and asked for an interview. He suggested that we attend his morning press conference instead, and then he asked how long we had waited. When he learned we had been at the hotel since early afternoon, he told his companions to order him a Michelob and wait for him in their rooms while he talked to us.

I didn't think that the requested Michelob would be his first brewski of the evening. During the interview, I smelled alcohol on his breath and he weaved slightly, but he was a good sport and answered our questions. I still have the audio tape preserved in a box in my garage:

ROGAN: Due to today's tape revelations, would you say now that President Nixon's credibility has been shattered to a point where he cannot repair it?

RICHARDSON: I don't feel able to make a forecast of it at this point. I haven't really assimilated the situation well enough. The matter, of course, is in the hands of the District Court of the District of Columbia under Judge Sirica, and I think we all ought to withhold judgment until we've all had a little more time to assimilate the situation.

ROGAN: Would you say now the actual chances for an impeachment resolution in the House are better than they were twenty-four hours ago?

RICHARDSON: Yes, I would, based on what I understand the situation to be. Certainly, the situation has not improved from the president's point of view, and there is another piece added to the accumulation of things that have been eroding confidence in his credibility and his administration.

ROGAN: Do you think that President Nixon will serve out the remaining three years of his term?

RICHARDSON: I have no good way of forecasting this. I think, and I have thought, that chances are somewhat better than even that he would, but again I really haven't factored into the odds that I would try to estimate just what the impact of this new finding is.

ROGAN: Several senators and others in government have said, in the words of one senator, to "Impeach him or get off his back."[5] Do you think that an impeachment resolution would be in order?

RICHARDSON: I think that the attitude to "impeach him or get off his back" has been a premature response to a situation in which the American public has not had all the facts, and neither has the Congress. And so, it has been my view all along that the investigative process should continue, that the president should cooperate with it, that he should make available whatever tapes and documents are relevant to these inquiries. And only after all this has been done, and after it's possible to sift the evidence and to develop a coherent picture of what happened out of it, should we draw conclusions about the president's own involvement or responsibility. These things remain to be done. And I personally believe that any judgment about what ought to happen procedurally by way of impeachment proceedings or under the direction of the District Court ought still to await the completion of that process.

ROGAN: Besides your "campaign" for Harvard Overseer, there has been a lot of talk over the past few weeks that you might be a candidate for president and that a strong draft movement might be developing. How would you respond to a draft?

---

5   "May I now pass on to this Congress advice which I received recently from a fellow Vermonter—Either impeach him or get off his back." Senator George Aiken (R-VT), November 7, 1973.

RICHARDSON: Well, of course, if a draft really developed, I would have to pay attention to it. I haven't seen this as a likely prospect. You asked me if I had any thoughts about the possibility of a candidacy besides overseer of Harvard. And the only answer is, yes, I've had thoughts, but the thoughts have certainly not amounted to plans. I'm not doing anything about it. I plan to spend the next year trying to distill out of my government experience what I think are some significant views and hopefully to find a way of expressing them that will be communicable and persuasive....

Former Attorney General Elliot Richardson submitting to my late-night interview, (Roger Mahan in background), San Francisco, January 15, 1974 (Author's collection)

ROGAN: Thank you very much, Mr. Richardson. Nice to meet you.

RICHARDSON: It was nice to meet you. You're bound to go far.

• • •

Fast-forward over two decades later. Along with fellow members of California's state legislative delegation, I attended a VIP breakfast in San Francisco held in honor of the U.N.'s fiftieth anniversary. As we mingled, I spied an elderly man standing near the buffet table in the corner of the room. Even when I pointed him out to one of my colleagues, his name failed to register with her. "Who's Elliot Richardson?" she asked.

Oh, Lord.

The former attorney general who once stood in the middle of Watergate's Ground Zero now stood among dignitaries unaccompanied and anonymous. I walked over and introduced myself, and then I recounted the circumstances of waylaying him in 1974 for an interview. "Oh, my gosh!" he exclaimed with a laugh, and then he expressed great pleasure to learn I had pursued a career in both the law and politics. "I like to think the time I spent with young people in those days encouraged them to follow a life of public service," he said. When he heard that I held elective office as a Republican, the center-left Richardson complained about his Party's conservative wing and their pursuit of "phony current political remedies" such as the "so-called war on drugs" and "three strikes" career criminal statutes. "We need politicians who stop giving easy answers like these," he grumbled. "We need leaders who will stand up and finally say, 'I'm gonna level with you, and now respect me for my candor in return.'" Then he stopped, reflected for a moment on his sermon, and shrugged. "Of course," he added with a grin, "if I were still in politics and running for office today, I doubt that I would want to be the one who tests this theory."

Richardson had aged, but from across the room he looked healthy. That impression faded when we spoke. His voice trembled and his words slurred. His nametag bore his signature written in a trembling hand when compared to the firm autograph he signed for me years earlier. Unlike our long-ago encounter, these were not objective signs of mild-to-moderate alcohol consumption. This was a man in declining health.

Grace Napolitano, my Democratic colleague, had wandered over a few minutes earlier and listened as Richardson bashed conservative Republicans and their anti-crime nostrums. When attendants rang the bells signaling it was time to take our seats in the auditorium, we shook hands and I thanked him again for his kindness long ago.

As I escorted Grace inside the theater, she told me that he seemed like a very reasonable Republican. "What do you think about him?" she asked.

"Gracie, I think he's a very nice man, and I think I'm very glad he never became president."

•••

Archibald Cox stood alongside Elliot Richardson in the 1974 liberal pantheon. After his firing, and with the Nixon impeachment coals burning white-hot, Cox's public reputation soared. When he came to San Francisco for a speech in June 1974, the Nixon presidency, already on life support, had seven weeks remaining.

Once again, my school chums Dan, Roger, and I wanted to meet him and seek his advice on entering the law and politics, but we knew that his appearance would generate an even greater press mania than that which surrounded Richardson's earlier visit, because by now the Watergate scandal was reaching critical mass. We might never have met Richardson but for the pure luck of a busboy casually telling me his room number. I didn't want to rely on chance a second time, so I tried a more direct approach. Before we left for the event, I called the hotel.

"Hello, St. Francis Hotel. How may I help you?" inquired the friendly operator.

[Clearing my throat] "Hello. This is Professor [mumbling an indecipherable name] from Harvard. I need to speak with Archie, oh, I'm sorry, Professor Cox. He's staying at your hotel."

"Who?"

"Professor Cox. Archibald Cox. Please ring his room, young lady, and hurry. I have a flight to catch."

"One moment, please." After brief silence, a telephone rang.

The ruse worked.

I was surprised that the switchboard didn't screen calls to his room more carefully, especially with every reporter in town trying to snag time with him. I covered the mouthpiece when the phone picked up on the third ring. "They just answered!" I whispered excitedly.

"Hello," came the clipped New England voice on the other end. "Archibald Cox speaking."

The unexpected startled me. "Oh, shit," I muttered. I had expected to pitch the understudy, not the lead. Sudden panic evaporated my memory retrieval cells, and I forgot what I had planned to say.

"Hello, who's calling, please?"

When nothing came out of my mouth, I hung up.

"What was that all about?" Roger asked. I told him.

"You hung up? You had him on the phone, and you hung up? That was stupid!"

As they say in court, so stipulated.

Defaulting to our original plan of attempting trespass into the event, we took the bus downtown and arrived at the hotel later that afternoon. As expected, national and local reporters swarmed the lobby trying to maneuver an interview.

Still smarting over my cowardly hang-up, and with my resolve now steeled, I picked up the lobby house phone and asked the operator to put me through to Cox's room. Again, she complied without any screening. This time the phone kept ringing without a pick-up. Five rings. Six rings. Seven rings, ten rings and no response. I planned to hold the line open until someone answered or until the call disconnected. Then, a click and a greeting by the same voice that had panicked me earlier. This time I didn't flinch. I introduced myself to Cox, apologized for disturbing him, and told him that we were three students in the lobby hoping to interview him. He thanked me for calling, and then explained politely that he now declined all interview requests. "If I didn't have this policy," he said, "I would be talking to reporters all day long."

Oh, well, I tried.

Hiding my disappointment, I said I understood and thanked him for taking my call. Before saying goodbye, I mentioned that we hoped to wangle our way in to see his speech and get his autograph later.

"Oh, you want an autograph. That's different. Why don't you come to my room? I'll be happy to sign for you. I'm in 933. Give me about thirty minutes and then come up."

Once again, brashness paid off.

We waited as requested before taking the elevator to the ninth floor. Coincidentally, it was the same hotel location where we had bushwhacked Richardson for an interview earlier that year. In fact, Cox occupied the suite next door to the one used by his former boss.

We knocked on 933 and Cox greeted us at the door. He invited us to join him in the living room so he could comply with our requests. I handed him a card bearing Richardson's autograph. "Oh, you already got Elliot on this," he commented as he signed it. Dan mentioned that Richardson had been here earlier in the year, and that he had announced in his speech that he planned to run for Harvard Overseer in 1976.

"Well," Cox chuckled, "I think Elliot is running for something a little higher than that in 1976."

While he signed, I asked about the Saturday Night Massacre and if he had advance warning that Richardson would refuse any presidential order to fire him. "Yes, I knew ahead of time that Elliot would refuse," he replied. "In fact, I knew that he planned to let Nixon fire him when he refused. He and I had discussed the scenario in advance."

"So, you weren't shocked by it."

"No, not by the firing. What shocked me was the degree of public outcry over it. I never expected that."

146

To quell the firestorm fueled by Cox's firing, Nixon approved the appointment of another Democrat, Leon Jaworski, as the new special prosecutor. Once selected, Jaworski resumed the subpoena battle with Nixon over the White House tapes. Dan asked Cox's opinion of the man who succeeded him. He praised Jaworski for doing a fine job and added that he wouldn't have handled Watergate matters any differently had he retained the job. "Leon is a very courageous man," he said, and then he shared a story about dealing with Jaworski in 1962. At the time, Cox was solicitor general and Jaworski was a partner in a Texas-based law firm. He recalled that during the height of the civil rights marches, a young black student named James Meredith tried to enroll in the whites-only University of Mississippi—*Ole Miss*. Riots broke out, and eventually federal marshals intervened to protect Meredith. "The governor of Mississippi, Ross Barnett, pretended to work with us at the Department of Justice to avoid a clash, but he did more to exclude Meredith from Ole Miss than he did to help him enter. President Kennedy asked Jaworski to go to Mississippi and bring legal action against the governor to force him to enroll Meredith."

"Why did President Kennedy send a private lawyer rather than a Justice Department lawyer?"

"The Southern states had great apprehensions about 'damned Yankee' lawyers from Washington coming down there and interfering. Jaworski was a Texan. And, by the way, before Jaworski agreed to the assignment, he raised

Here I am "interviewing" the man who refused interviews, former Watergate Special Prosecutor Archibald Cox, San Francisco, June 17, 1974 (Author's collection)

the issue with his law partners, all of whom voted against it. They feared losing their southern clients. Jaworski went anyway." He added that Jaworski later prosecuted successfully the contempt charges leveled against Barnett when he defied a federal court order to integrate the campus. The courts fined Barnett and sentenced him to jail. "Barnett never went to jail or paid the fine, but, eventually, Meredith won admission to the college."

After sharing these and other vignettes, he added, "Those were matters I dealt with way back then. These days I no longer have to worry about such things, especially Watergate. My only task now is to grade exams in my Harvard law classes." When Dan and I shared that we wanted to attend law school one day, he extolled the virtues of a legal education and urged us to pursue it, especially if we wanted to enter politics. "Become a lawyer first," he advised. "That way, should a political race prove unsuccessful, having knowledge of the law and being part of the legal profession will give you something else to do. I know from experience. When I finished law school, I ran for local office in my small Boston suburb. I lost, but that experience led to several appointed positions in government, which included the Kennedy Administration in 1961."

During our twenty-minute talk, Cox remained relaxed and showed no inclination to hurry us along. He continued chatting and answering questions until Roger reminded him that he needed to get downstairs for his event. He looked at his watch, apologized for keeping us so long (!), and then he escorted us to the door. "Boys," he added, "it was very nice to meet you, and I'm sorry that I couldn't give you an interview." Dan, Roger, and I looked at each other and laughed.

"I'm no expert," I said, "but I think that was an interview."

His face grew solemn. "Whatever you do," he said, "*please* don't tell any of the reporters downstairs."

Back in the lobby, we passed the gaggle of frustrated newshounds still coveting an exclusive with America's most famous lawyer. We kept our mouths shut.

Later that evening, we snuck into the ballroom in time to catch the end of Cox's speech. After he finished, a woman seated at his table approached and asked if we were the ones who visited his room earlier. She said he talked about us during dinner and expressed pleasure at meeting boys so interested in government and law, and then she revealed why it took him so long to answer my telephone call. "He told us that the phone kept ringing because he was in the shower, and he had to come out of the bathroom soaking wet and with a towel wrapped around him to take your call!"

Later, when the crowd of well-wishers thinned, I went over and apologized to Cox for the shower interruption. "Oh, she shouldn't have told you that," he said. "Besides, getting out of the shower is never a problem—

"—when the cause is worthwhile."

• • •

Many years later, Cox and I reconnected after I became a lawyer. He followed my career as a gang murder prosecutor in the Los Angeles County District Attorney's Office with interest, and it pleased him to know that his "other boys" went on to careers in law and government. Dan became a partner in a prestigious law firm, and Roger worked on Capitol Hill as a senior congressional committee staffer.

In 1993, when I was the presiding judge of our municipal court, I attended a national judicial conference at Harvard in the midst of Boston's worst heat wave in a century. Two decades after I pulled him out of the shower to get his autograph, and with Cox still teaching law school there, we made dinner plans for when I visited Cambridge.

When I reached town a couple of weeks later, he called my hotel and apologized for not being able to keep our date that evening. The heat was taking a toll on his wife, he said, and she wanted to get away to the Maine coast for a respite. Since they were leaving that afternoon, he asked if we might visit at his office before they departed. I skipped my morning seminar and walked over to the Harvard campus.

By the end of the four-block walk, my clothes stuck to my body from the awful heat and humidity. Entering Langdell Hall offered no relief. The building's air conditioning system had broken down. I found Cox's office on the third floor with some difficulty, because

Reunited twenty years later, Harvard Law School, July 14, 1993
(Author's collection)

tall stacks of library books obscured his door almost completely.

When I entered, Cox rose from behind his desk and strode across the room to welcome me. With no ceiling fan and all of his office windows closed, the lack of ventilation felt suffocating, but it did not appear to wilt the erect, lanky professor. He was coatless, yet otherwise dressed in a yellow bow tie and a crisp dress shirt. "Well, Judge, you haven't changed much from that fresh-scrubbed kid who visited my hotel room!" he said. I returned the compliment with sincerity. Although grayer, he had changed little in the ensuing decades.

After we reminisced about our long-ago visit, he retrieved from his desk a Los Angeles newspaper article praising my work as presiding judge for refunding to the taxpayers almost $700,000 in unspent revenues from our $4 million budget. "I keep tabs on you," he said. "These things never happen in Massachusetts. Here the politicians, not the judges, run the court budgets."

Cox walked down the hallway and asked a secretary to take an updated picture of us. We posed in front of his desk, and when I commented on its antique appearance, he pointed to an old wooden frame hanging on the wall. It displayed two faded photographs, each of a distinguished man seated at a desk. "The top photograph is of my grandfather in his law office," he said. "The bottom one is my father in his law office many years later." Pointing with pride to his Langdell Hall desk, he told me it was the same one depicted in both photographs. I asked why he didn't have a pic-

Archibald Cox behind Grandpa's family desk, July 14, 1993 (Photograph by the author)

ture of himself seated at the heirloom included in the montage. He said that he never got around to taking one.

"Well, I brought a camera, so let's correct the deficiency." He posed behind the desk and I took the photo for his family posterity.

"This is so great," he said with thanks. "I have a daughter who is a Colorado attorney. One day I hope that she will use this desk in her own law office." Then he shook his head, adding, "I don't know if she will. She has this New England streak of independence. I'm afraid she gets it from me."

I didn't want to hold up his Maine vacation plans. Besides, with sweat now pouring down my neck and back, I couldn't take much more of his office sauna. The visit was wonderful, but I was ready to go. I thanked him for letting me drop by, and I promised to welcome him to a more hospitable climate when he visited me on the west coast. "When I come to see you in Southern California, round up my other two boys," he said. "We'll have a reunion."

"That'll be fine, but to make it authentic, you'll have to come out of the shower soaking wet and wearing a towel when I call."

• • •

Although we remained in touch, I never saw Archibald Cox again. Still, I took great pleasure when the legal icon who encouraged me as a boy to study law endorsed my 1994 judicial retention election.

And, he told me, so did he.

• • •

Like Richardson and Cox, William Ruckelshaus enjoyed a distinguished career. The former Indiana prosecutor and state legislator earned a Justice Department appointment when Nixon won the presidency. Next, the president tapped him as the first head of the newly created Environmental Protection Agency. Following J. Edgar Hoover's death in 1972, Nixon again reached out and appointed him acting FBI director, and then later named him deputy attorney general, making him the number-two man at the Justice Department. It was from this position that he collided with his political benefactor over Cox's firing.

I met Ruckelshaus a couple of times when I was a kid. The first was only six days after the Saturday Night Massacre, on October 26, 1973. The local San Francisco ABC television network affiliate, KGO, scheduled an early-morning live in-studio interview with the newly fired deputy attorney general. Coincidentally, also scheduled for the same program (but in a different segment) was Earl Butz, the current U.S. secretary of Agriculture.

My school friends and I took the bus into town hoping to meet Ruckelshaus at KGO. Whenever we met dignitaries, we always asked for an autograph for two reasons: we collected them, and it made them stop long enough to answer our questions. That plan didn't work with Ruckelshaus. We were a block away and heading toward KGO when we saw Ruckelshaus arrive in a taxicab at 7:00 a.m. He carried his two suitcases inside the building and was behind locked doors by the time we reached the studio.

While we waited for him to leave, dozens of reporters arrived and congregated outside. Technicians set up TV cameras on tripods. I assumed they came to interview Ruckelshaus, which would make getting any time with him very difficult. To my surprise, they converged on Secretary Butz when he arrived. I hadn't heard that the morning news revealed an investigation now underway against Butz for allegedly interfering with a federal probe of high-level GOP donors. The reporters swarmed Butz and shouted questions. He denied wrongdoing as his staff pushed him through the crowd and into the studio. An aide appeared outside later and announced that Butz would hold a formal press conference at the nearby Cow Palace in an hour to answer the allegation. The reporters rushed off in a pack for that event.

And so, less than a week after the Saturday Night Massacre press uproar, the only people waiting around for Ruckelshaus were three young political nerds. The press had moved on to their next scandal.

Our wait proved in vain. When Ruckelshaus exited, he headed directly for a waiting taxicab. When we asked for an autograph, he declined politely and explained that he was running late to catch an airplane flight. He tossed his suitcases in the trunk, jumped into the cab, and it sped away.

Eight months later, Ruckelshaus returned to San Francisco to appear once again at KGO. Just as before, we were in sight of the location in time to see him leap from a taxi with his luggage and bolt inside. Again, we missed meeting him on his way into the studio, so we waited outside. An hour later, a cab with no passenger pulled to the curb. Out rushed Ruckelshaus with his suitcases, and he made a beeline for the back seat. This time I stepped between him and the cab and asked him to sign a card autographed for me previously by Richardson and Cox. He scrawled his name on it as he apologized for not having time to stop and talk to us.

"That's okay," I said. "Thank you for the autograph. I hope you get to the airport in time to catch your plane."

"How did you know I was late for my flight?"

"I have psychic powers."

• • •

Twenty-five years later, when I served in Congress, the Republican leadership asked its House and Senate members to attend a gala GOP fundraiser in Washington. I had decided to skip it initially, but I changed my mind when I saw that the guests assigned to my table included Ruckelshaus, who was now chairman of a waste industry corporation.

This time he wasn't going to escape from me in a taxicab.

We ended up seated together at the dinner, and I shared with him my youthful efforts to get his autograph and talk about Watergate. He laughed when I produced an old photograph of us from 1974, and he joked that the slick black hair and long sideburns he wore in those days had given way to thinning gray hair. From that moment, he treated our evening as a reunion of old friends, and it proved delightful.

Before the program commenced, I asked about the Saturday Night Massacre. He described Richardson's and his efforts to work out a compromise between Nixon, the Department of Justice, and Special Prosecutor Archibald Cox over the White House tapes. "That all fell apart when Cox went on TV and held a live press conference stating he would keep pushing for the tapes in court. When he did that, he was in open defiance of the president's order. Any chance for a compromise ended at that moment." He and Richardson stood together watching Cox's press conference on TV, and they both knew instantly that Nixon would demand they fire Cox for insubordination. When I asked how an "independent" prosecutor could be "insubordinate," he replied, "Well, law professors still debate the point today. In fact, [then-Solicitor General] Robert Bork argued that because Richardson appointed Cox and had the authority to fire him, and because Nixon appointed Richardson and had the authority to fire him, that chain of command placed Cox under Nixon's direct authority. When Cox defied the president, at least in Bork's view, he became insubordinate and could be fired."

During our 1997 dinner, William Ruckelshaus inscribed this June 24, 1974 photo of us, "To Jim Rogan, your youth is matched by my sideburns! You were a comer then, and now you have arrived. All the best, Bill Ruckelshaus." (Author's collection)

Ruckelshaus said that both he and Richardson had seen the showdown brewing, and they had discussed in advance how they would handle any order to fire Cox. "We both concluded that neither of us would do it if ordered. In fact, Elliot had pledged at his Senate confirmation hearing not to fire Cox unless there was significant just cause. Once the order came down, we knew after we resigned that the job would next fall to Bork, who felt Nixon did have the authority. And, of course, Bork followed through after Elliot and I resigned."

"You resigned? I always heard that Nixon fired you."

"Well," he laughed, "that is also a matter of debate." He said that after Nixon ordered Richardson to fire Cox, the attorney general went to see the president and resigned. The White House then called Ruckelshaus and gave him the order. He refused and said he would follow Richardson's example. While writing his resignation letter, the White House press office announced that the president had fired him. "The next day the White House put out a statement that I had resigned, so I guess you can claim it either way."

Ruckelshaus said he had no regrets about his refusal because he believed Cox had the power to subpoena the White House tapes. He argued that Cox's authority was to investigate Watergate wrongdoing, and if those tapes contained evidence of criminality, Cox had the legal right to seek them.

We continued our discussion until the dinner adjourned and the waiters stripped off the table linens. It took me a quarter-century to hear Bill Ruckelshaus's perspective of that October 1973 night, but it was worth the wait.

• • •

The same public sentiment that lionized Richardson, Ruckelshaus, and Cox, ginned up by a Democratic Congress and a hostile anti-Nixon mainstream media, scapegoated U.S. Solicitor General Robert Bork as the villain who fired Cox to save his job. As most press claims fashioned for emotional impact to advance a political narrative, this was and remains fake news.

After graduating from the University of Chicago Law School in 1953, Bork served stints in the United States Marine Corps during World War II and the Korean War before settling into private law practice. He joined the Yale Law School faculty and taught students such as future President and First Lady Bill and Hillary Clinton, future California Governor Jerry Brown, future U.S. Labor Secretary Robert Reich, and future Ambassador John Bolton. Bork became one of America's premiere antitrust scholars as well as an early advocate of *originalism*[6] in judicial interpretation, which found receptive listeners in later U.S. Supreme Court justices such as Antonin Scalia, Clarence Thomas, and Samuel Alito. In early 1973, Nixon tapped Bork for U.S Solicitor General, where he served until 1977. It was in this capacity, on the night of October 20, 1973, that he became acting attorney general when Richardson and Ruckelshaus vacated their positions. Believing that Nixon had the constitutional right to remove a subordinate employee, he fired Cox. Fourteen years later, while serving as a judge on the Federal Circuit Court of Appeals, President Reagan nominated Bork to a seat on the U.S. Supreme Court. The Democrat-controlled Senate turned back his nomination in a bitter and vicious confirmation hearing. Bork left the bench soon thereafter and spent the next quarter-century lecturing, teaching, and writing two best-selling books.

I never met Bork until I became a member of Congress, and that first meeting was a result of his graciousness. Dan Swanson, my boyhood friend with whom I used to cut classes to go meet famous politicians, had become an internationally recognized antitrust attorney. When Dan visited me in Washington, he asked for a favor. He wanted to meet Judge Bork, the god of antitrust law. Could I set it up?

I didn't know Bork, so I did what the brassy kid still within me might have done back in the old days. I picked up the phone and called him. He not only agreed to meet us, but he insisted on coming to my office instead of the other way around. "Congressmen are busy," he said. "I have all the time in the world."

I always respected Judge Bork for his immense legal talents.

---

6   *Originalism* asserts that judges interpret the U.S. Constitution based on the original understanding of its framers, and by the common meaning of the words and phrases in the law at the time of ratification. Bork argued that the judge who looks outside the original meaning of the Constitution "always looks inside himself and nowhere else." Dennis J. Goldford, *The American Constitution and the Debate Over Originalism* (Cambridge: Cambridge University Press, 2005), 174.

By the end of our first visit, I counted him as a friend. Despite his somewhat dour appearance, with that scraggly chin beard and unkempt hair, he proved as delightful as he was brilliant. In the years following that first meeting, I had the pleasure of sharing the stage with him at a couple of conferences and speeches, as well as enjoying an occasional private lunch. He was always available for advice or help, and I treasured the relationship. When HarperCollins published my first book in 2004, *Rough Edges: My Unlikely Road from Welfare to Washington*, Bob wrote the leading endorsement for the book's dust jacket: "Jim Rogan's story of his journey from poverty as an illegitimate son of a mother on welfare to House Manager in the Senate impeachment trial of President Clinton is at once an inspiring and rollicking good tale."

Whenever we talked, he always looked forward, not backward, and when we did speak about politics, he steered the discussion to the dangers facing America's survival as a republic. The only time I recall discussing the Saturday Night Massacre was at our first meeting. Since Dan came with me on those long-ago sojourns to meet Richardson, Ruckelshaus, and Cox, Bob was unlikely to avoid the topic when meeting two Watergate junkies.

I asked him about the common perception that he was the "bad cop" of October 20, 1973—the guy who fired Cox to ingratiate himself with Nixon to save his job. He answered without acrimony or defensiveness. "Elliot, Bill, and I had all discussed the situation both before and after Cox announced he would not comply with the president's demand to withdraw the subpoenas," he said. "It's true that the attorney general and the deputy attorney general had a different legal opinion than I on the legitimacy of Cox's course. They felt Cox was within his power to defy the president. I believed that as a subordinate employee of the president he was bound to follow the orders of his superior. He was subject to dismissal if he refused.

"Once Cox held his press conference, Elliot and Bill both told me they would refuse to fire Cox if ordered to do so by Nixon and that they would resign. As I said, I felt the president had the authority, so I told them that if the directive came to me, I would fire him and then I would resign as well. Elliot pleaded with me to reconsider resigning. He said that the Department of Justice could not afford to lose its top three officials in one fell swoop, and that my resignation would create chaos in the upper echelons of the DOJ."

He said that he based his initial resignation consideration on legal, and not moral, grounds. Because the president was empowered constitutionally to fire Cox, he felt no moral reservation about his decision. His motivation for considering resignation was personal: he did not wish to appear as a stooge doing Nixon's bidding. He reconsidered only after Richardson's and Ruckelshaus's pleas. He stayed at the helm to prevent DOJ disarray, not to preserve his job.

The long-accepted narrative of Bork's self-preservation motive in firing Cox is both untrue and unfair, and yet it continues to this day despite Richardson's testimony at Bork's 1987 Supreme Court confirmation hearing. Richardson confirmed for the senators that he and Ruckelshaus both pleaded with Bork not to resign. "We thought his leadership of the department was going to be critically important in a situation of enormous stress," he told the senators, "and we were genuinely alarmed by the possibility that if Ruckelshaus's and my resignation were followed by a chain reaction, we could end up with the chief of the messenger service as the acting attorney general."[7]

Fittingly, Judge Bob Bork's last word on this episode appeared in his memoir published posthumously. In this final work, he recalled that immediately after the Cox firing, he met with Nixon in the Oval Office. Surprisingly, Nixon had not anticipated the joint resignations of his top DOJ officials, and their actions left the president very distraught. He concluded that since Nixon hadn't planned these events—he had blundered into them—the more

---

7   *The New York Times*, September 20, 1987, https://www.nytimes.com/1987/09/20/us/ruckelshaus-supports-the-nomination-of-bork.html (accessed June 17, 2019).

appropriate description for the events of October 20, 1973 wasn't *The Saturday Night Massacre*:

It was *The Saturday Night Involuntary Manslaughter*.[8]

With Judge Robert Bork in my congressional office, 1997 (Author's collection)

• • •

Not long before Bob Bork died, I was going through some of my old political memorabilia collection when I found the index card signed for me in the 1970s by Richardson, Ruckelshaus, and Cox. Since I had not visited Washington in years, I mailed the card to Bob and asked him to complete the historic memento by autographing it. He did so and returned it with a charming handwritten note. The opening line of his final letter to me read, "These signatures bring back a few memories."

"And," he added, "some of them, believe it or not, are pleasant."

---

8   Bork, *Saving Justice*, at 84.

• • •

After losing a U.S. Senate race in 1984, Elliot Richardson returned to his law practice. In 1998, President Clinton awarded him the Presidential Medal of Freedom, the nation's highest civilian honor. He died at age 79 of a cerebral hemorrhage on New Year's Eve 1999.

In his post-Watergate years, Archibald Cox taught law, chaired the liberal advocacy group *Common Cause*, served on many bar and legal committees, and argued two more cases before the United States Supreme Court. He died at age 92 of natural causes on May 29, 2004.

William Ruckelshaus spent the decades after Watergate engaged in multiple private and public activities, including return stints in government under Presidents Reagan, Clinton, and George W. Bush. In 2015, President Obama awarded him the Presidential Medal of Freedom. He died at age 87 of natural causes on November 27, 2019.

Judge Robert Bork died at age 85 of heart disease on December 19, 2012.

Nothing ever came of the 1973 investigation of Agriculture Secretary Earl Butz. He remained in office for three more years until a series of verbal gaffes led to his resignation in October 1976. He stayed active in governmental and agricultural affairs for the next thirty-five years until his death at age 98 of natural causes on February 2, 2008.

13

Speaking of Watergate....

Besides the principal players in the Saturday Night Massacre, I met many other figures involved in the Watergate scandal, including the federal judge presiding over the trials, two of the burglars, several high-level administration officials imprisoned for their roles, and the key congressional officials investigating it. Snatches from some of those experiences follow.

• • •

"MAXIMUM JOHN"

When I was a teenager, it took me almost a year to save enough money to make my first trip to Washington, D.C. in 1975. Before leaving I wrote to certain leaders I admired (and some I didn't) and asked if I could meet them during my visit to get advice on entering the law and politics. Surprisingly, more agreed to see me during my week there than I had time to visit. One of the first to welcome me to the capital was U.S. District Court Judge John J. Sirica.

The son of an Italian immigrant barber, Sirica worked his way through law school the hard way: as a boxer and sometimes sparring partner for world heavyweight champion Jack Dempsey. He practiced law for three decades before President Eisenhower nominated him for the U.S. District Court for the District of Columbia in 1957, where he served for years in anonymity. His reputation for notoriously harsh sentences in criminal cases earned him the nickname among lawyers, "Maximum John." In 1973, after the grand jury handed down Watergate indictments, Sirica (then the senior judge) assigned those cases to himself, and he quickly became America's most famous jurist. In the case of *United States v. Nixon,* he ordered the president to comply with Special Prosecutor Archibald Cox's subpoenas for taped Oval Office conversations. Nixon appealed, but on July 24, 1974, the U.S. Supreme Court upheld Sirica's ruling. This led to the release of incriminating tapes that caused Nixon's congressional and public support to collapse, and he resigned the presidency two weeks later. That same year *Time* magazine named Sirica as their "Man of the Year" because, in the editors' opinion, he symbolized the rule of law during the lawless scandal. I visited Sirica soon after the jurors handed down their final guilty verdicts against the Watergate defendants, including Nixon's former senior aides H.R. Haldeman and John Ehrlichman, and former U.S. Attorney General John Mitchell.

On my first day in Washington, I walked from my hotel to the D.C. federal courthouse, where a security guard escorted me to Sirica's rooms. After a brief wait, the judge came off the bench. He greeted me in the reception area, and then he invited me into his private chambers. The short, stocky man with a firm handshake slipped out of his black robe, put on a sports jacket, and invited me to sit with him.

News photographs of Sirica always depicted him as stern and foreboding, and I knew of his reputation as a heavy sentencer. My expectations of him matching this persona faded quickly. He was friendly and gregarious, and he examined me at length about my first impressions of Washington. Moreover, he appeared genuinely interested in my answers. I told him that I planned to start courses at a community college the following week, and that I hoped to attend law school one day. He spent considerable time encouraging me to pursue a legal career, and then he analyzed the pros and cons of the various California law schools that he thought I should consider attending down the road. My only disappointment in meeting him came when he said that he could not discuss the Watergate cases with me. Because the appeals process had not yet run, judicial rules precluded him from talking about them. "But come back in a couple of years and we'll talk our heads off about it," he added.

For Jim Rogan, a fine young man, who I believe is destined to be a great lawyer someday. Good luck! 11/28/75
John J. Sirica

With U.S. District Court Judge John J. Sirica in his chambers, Washington, D.C., September 9, 1975 (Author's collection)

Before our meeting ended, Sirica called in a law clerk to take our picture. As we posed behind his desk, I noted a political curiosity. In his spacious chambers, this Republican-appointed judge had only one framed autographed photo on display, and it was not a memento of any GOP notable. Former Vice President Hubert Humphrey, the 1968 Democratic presidential nominee who lost the presidency to Nixon, penned a sentiment of admiration on his portrait to Sirica.

As I thanked Sirica for making the time to see me, he wished me luck in school and in my later career pursuits. Putting his hand on my shoulder, he said, "Just take it one step at a time, Jim, and you'll come out on top."

• • •

In my desire to take Sirica's advice and come out on top, I attended community college for two years, and then finished my B.A. degree at the University of California at Berkeley. When the time came to apply to law schools, I needed letters of recommendation. [Note to reader: By now, I'll bet that you know where this is going.]

I wrote to Sirica and reminded him of our meeting. I also sent him a copy of our photo together, the one on which he wrote, "To Jim Rogan, a fine young man who I believe is destined to be a great lawyer someday." Since he expressed in writing his confidence in my future legal abilities, I asked him to put his money where his mouth was and give me a recommendation letter. To my surprise, he did, and it helped.

In the fall of 1979, I began my studies at the UCLA School of Law. On my first day of classes an assistant dean pulled me aside and told me that ever since my application arrived, he wanted to know something:

"How do you know my hero, Judge Sirica?"

• • •

THE BURGLARS

On June 17, 1972, police apprehended five burglars who broke into the Democratic National Committee offices at the Watergate building. Most people who know about Watergate do not remember that the famous break-in was their *second* illegal entry into the DNC offices. The team had broken in a month earlier and planted listening devices to spy on the Democrat leadership. When the electronic bugs failed, they went in a second time on June 17 to fix the problem.

One of the burglars, James McCord, was a former CIA agent

in charge of security at Nixon's national reelection campaign committee (the "Committee to Reelect the President," or CRP). G. Gordon Liddy, a lawyer and former FBI agent who later worked in both the Nixon White House and at the CRP, oversaw the operation and monitored the burglars' progress from a nearby building. A grand jury indicted McCord and Liddy (among others), a jury convicted them for their roles in the burglary, and Judge Sirica handed down heavily disproportionate sentences on these first-time non-violent offenders: twenty-five years for McCord, and twenty years for Liddy. (By comparison, in the 1970s the average parole release for killing someone was seven years.) At these sentencings, Sirica imposed what he called "provisional sentences," meaning that he would consider a significant reduction if the defendants cooperated with prosecutors. McCord wrote a letter to Sirica and acquiesced, while the defiant Liddy remained silent. When the dust settled, Sirica reduced McCord's sentence from twenty-five years to only four months, but he refused to reduce Liddy's twenty-year term. Liddy ended up serving far longer in prison than any other Watergate defendant. After fifty-two months in a federal penitentiary, President Jimmy Carter commuted his sentence in 1977 "in the interest of equity and fairness based on a comparison of Mr. Liddy's sentence with those of all others convicted in Watergate related prosecutions."

Shortly after his release from prison, McCord published a memoir of his Watergate role.[1] Dan Swanson and I attended his book signing event at a San Francisco bookstore in 1974.

Outside stood a single protester carrying a sign depicting an unflattering Nixon caricature and captioned, "Don't Buy Books by Crooks." The message had no impact, because by the time McCord arrived there was a crowd of fifty people in line. He smiled and

---

1   James W. McCord, Jr., *A Piece of Tape: The Watergate Story—Fact and Fiction* (Washington: Washington Media Services, 1974).

nodded as he sat behind a small table stacked with copies of his book, and he stood to thank the purchasers individually. After signing each book, he slid inside its cover a subscription form for his just-inau-gurated monthly news-letter. He was friendly, but he declined to answer any Watergate questions, replying only, "It's all in the book."

When my turn came, McCord signed my book and then rose to shake hands. Dan tried to take a picture of us, but the flashbulb on my cheap plastic camera failed to fire. When Dan asked if he could replace the flashbulb and try again, McCord told him to take his time. It was no problem.

With the man who knew all about mechanical failures: James McCord and me, B. Dalton's Bookstore, San Francisco, August 30, 1974

Once Dan snapped the photo of us, I apologized for the faulty flashbulb delay. McCord winked at me. "Don't worry about it," he said. "Trust me—

"*—I know all about mechanical failures.*"

• • •

THE PLUMBER

I was a freshman congressman in 1997 when a Washington pro-ducer for a radio talk show called and invited me for an in-studio interview with the host, G. Gordon Liddy, the former head of the Nixon White House's so-called "Plumbers Unit"—a group of political operatives tasked with investigating enemies and plugging press leaks. Would I be willing to appear?

Hell, yes.

I arrived at the WJFK studio a few minutes before my segment began. While waiting in the control room I watched Liddy at the microphone excoriating liberals, squishy Republicans, and any number of my colleagues he deemed cowardly for voting for various government expansions. During a commercial break, the producer escorted me into the broadcast booth and introduced me to Liddy. He welcomed me, asked an assistant to get me coffee, and then he directed me to put on the pair of nearby headphones. The director threw him the cue and we went live on the air.

We did a couple of segments covering various current issues, none of which I remember now. When my interview ended, I took off my headphones as he broke for news and a round of commercials. While off the air he thanked me for coming, and as we said goodbye I told him, "I know that there are a lot of G-Man fans [Liddy's radio nickname], but I think these make me the original." Then I handed him two old letters that he wrote to me from his prison cell when I was a teenager in the 1970s. As he read them, his face registered shock.

"I sent these to you?"

Yes, I told him. I felt his sentence unfair and I wrote and told him so. I also offered to send him magazines or cigarettes if he needed them. Liddy had written me those two letters from prison thanking me for my kindnesses to a prisoner.

Putting down the letters, he exclaimed, "I just can't believe this," and then he asked me to put back on the headphones. He held me over for another few segments while he read the letters to his audience, and then he had me recount the circumstances of our correspondence. He seemed genuinely moved by the letters, and his gratitude overflowed.

When our interview ended finally, the show broke for a final

In-studio with the G-Man, WJFK, August 1997 (Author's collection)

commercial. He embraced me, shook my hand enthusiastically, and told me, "You always have a home at this station. I'm here for you—no matter what."

"Gordon, given the mysterious legends that surround you, I am very glad to have you for me instead of against me."

Still gripping my hand, he leaned in close and locked his dark, intense eyes on mine. "You can count on it, my friend. I'm here for you *for anything.*"

A few weeks after our interview, he sent me two signed photos taken of us. My favorite was the one on which he wrote, "When Jim Rogan speaks the G-Man listens!" I called and thanked him for his thoughtfulness. During our conversation, I got in a Watergate question that I had wanted to ask during our interview, but the opportunity never arose: with the burglary in progress, how did he learn that the jig was up?

"When McCord and the Cubans [the other four burglars] went in, I was in a nearby hotel monitoring the operation," he told me. "I stayed in communication with both the burglars inside the DNC offices and with the lookouts watching for police from across the street.

"At one point my lookout asked me if any of our Cubans were dressed like hippies. I told him no. 'Well,' he said, 'there are guys in the building dressed like hippies and they're carrying guns. They're moving upstairs to the offices.' That's when I knew that undercover police had arrived and that we had been compromised. I tried to radio the Cubans to tell them to abort the operation and get the hell out of there, but they had turned down their radios and couldn't hear my warnings. After a few tense minutes, I heard the voice of one of the Cubans over my radio. He whispered, 'They got us.'

"When Baldwin [Alfred C. Baldwin III, a lookout] radioed to me that police were converging around the building, I took as much of our electronics gear out of my command post that I could carry. The next day I went to my office at the Committee to Reelect the President and shredded everything, including a stack of consecutively serial-numbered $100 bills."

I asked how much it worried him that an accomplice might implicate him in the crime once the police arrested the burglars and foiled the operation. He replied, "Late that night, when I finally got home, my wife was in bed asleep. She awakened and asked me what kind of day I had. I told her, 'Not so good,' and that I might be going to jail." When I asked how she reacted to the stunning news, he laughed and said, "You know, I really don't remember. After I told her that, I climbed into bed, and I went right to sleep."

• • •

THE CHAIRMAN

On July 27-30, 1974, the House Judiciary Committee debated and voted to approve three articles of impeachment against President Nixon. As a teenager, I watched the live coverage as the committee chairman, Peter Rodino (D-NJ) cast the final "aye" vote on each article. Like Judge Sirica, he became one of the Watergate heroes in the eyes of the press and public.

Twenty-five years later, I served on the same committee as the mounting evidence of lawbreaking moved its members toward impeaching another president. With that possibility looming, House Speaker Newt Gingrich asked me to conduct a private analysis of previous congressional Executive Branch investigations going back to Watergate, and then recommend to him how the House should proceed in any impeachment inquiry against Bill Clinton. One of the people I placed on my interview list was the long-ago retired former chairman, Peter Rodino.

Born in 1909, the decorated World War II veteran won a congressional seat in 1948. He remained largely unknown until seniority elevated him to the Judiciary Committee chair in 1973, just as the Watergate scandal began engulfing the White House. Cast in the center of this hurricane, he earned praise for his leadership during the contentious hearings. He retired from Congress in 1989 and returned home to New Jersey. Ten years later, when I called on behalf of Speaker Gingrich and asked to meet him, the former chairman (now almost ninety) still taught at Rutgers Law School.

Of all the interviews I set up at Gingrich's request, Rodino's consent proved the most elusive. Since he didn't support any impeachment move against Clinton, he told me in advance that he had no interest in cooperating. After my continued prodding, he agreed to an interview for no more than thirty minutes. Candidly, I would have accepted any imposed limitation. Having watched the live television coverage of his Nixon hearings, it felt otherworldly to anticipate interviewing him from my position as a member of the same committee facing the same issue.

It was in May 1998 when I met Rodino in his small Rutgers faculty office. The short, elderly man with thick eyeglasses was all business as he offered a perfunctory handshake and then motioned for me to sit across the desk from him. He introduced me to his stone-face faculty colleague seated alongside him, and then explained his presence: "I asked him to join us because I want a witness to our discussion," Rodino said, and then he signaled for his colleague to turn on a small tape recorder.

Rodino ran out the clock by launching into a thirty-minute filibuster that, in essence, lectured me against any GOP move to impeach Clinton. When the thirty-minute cassette tape switched off automatically, Rodino ended his monologue as his colleague announced my time was up. Rodino stood and said goodbye.

"Mr. Chairman," I said as I rose, "I appreciate your making time to see me. I also appreciate your keeping two promises to me."

"Two promises?"

"Yes, two. You met with me today for half an hour; that was promise number one." Then I handed him a piece of paper: "Here is promise number two," I said.

When I made that first trip to Washington as a teen in 1975, Rodino was still the Judiciary Committee chairman and fresh off the Nixon hearings. He was on my list of people that I wrote and asked to meet. He replied with an apologetic letter stating that he was out of town that week, but he promised me a raincheck someday. Yet another memento from my boyhood political memorabilia collection saved the day. Rodino stood in silence reading the letter he had sent me twenty-three years earlier, and then he looked up and asked, "Was this to you?"

"Yes, sir. As I said, two promises. Thank you again, Mr. Chairman." I turned to leave.

"Hold on," he called. "Don't go. Have a seat." He kicked his faculty witness out of his office, invited the two committee staffers that accompanied me to Newark to join our discussion, and closed his office door. Three hours later, we were still talking about Watergate, presidential impeachments, and mistakes to avoid if the House moved forward.[2]

---

2   My 1998 meeting with Rodino and the specific advice he offered is set forth in my memoir of the Clinton impeachment. See James E. Rogan, *Catching Our Flag: Behind the Scenes of a Presidential Impeachment* (Washington: WND Books, 2011), 71-78.

Rodino felt skeptical about our ability to have any degree of bipartisan cooperation with the Democrat minority given the current hostile political climate and divided public opinion surrounding the Clinton scandals. Bipartisanship, he said, was the key ingredient for the country to retain confidence in the process. Any inquiry without it was doomed. He credited his success in the Nixon hearings with the minority committee Republicans cooperating with him. During Watergate, he and the ranking Republican on the committee, Ed Hutchinson, reviewed jointly the tapes of Nixon's secretly recorded Oval Office conversations. "When we listened to the first tape," he recalled, "we heard Nixon calling Jews 'kikes' and Italians 'guineas.' I told Ed Hutchinson I'd never report those remarks, and I didn't." He and Hutchinson also agreed to share the committee's subpoena power, so that no subpoena would issue without both men approving it. To the practical extent possible, he urged us to seek bipartisan support, and to approach any impeachment the way that he approached the Nixon impeachment—as a constitutional question, and not a partisan one. Otherwise, the public would believe that respect for the process took a back seat to tawdry politics.

He issued a warning in the event we followed through on impeachment: the press and the White House would conduct merciless investigations of me and of any other Republican involved in it, and they would not hesitate to smear me if I had any closet skeletons. He said the Republicans did the same to him during the Nixon impeachment, but he credited his decades in Washington with toughening his hide and not letting it get to him. "I came up the ranks alongside hardball masters like Lyndon Johnson and Bobby Kennedy," he said with a grin as he pointed with his thumb to faded signed photographs on his wall of both men. "And believe me, those were two tough sons of bitches." He added that Nixon's team also played for keeps in this realm: "I later learned that Jeb Magruder [Nixon's imprisoned former special assistant] approached a fellow convict, former New Jersey Congressman Cornelius Gallagher, while both were inmates in the federal penitentiary. Magruder allegedly promised Gallagher a presidential pardon if he would help produce dirt to 'get Rodino.'"

Rodino called it "a quirk of fate" that he hired a young lawyer for the committee, twenty-six-year-old Hillary Rodham. "She used to bring her boyfriend Bill Clinton around," he recalled, "and she once introduced him to me as a future president. They had it all planned out, even then," he said with sarcastic emphasis.

A quarter-century later, he grew emotional recalling his vote to impeach the president of the United States. "When the clerk called my name, my voice was almost inaudible. When it was over, I left the committee room, went to my private committee office, and I called my wife. I told her, 'I hope I did the right thing.' Then I sobbed like I never sobbed before."

During our lengthy discussion, he kept brushing aside my concern that he might be tiring. In fact, as it grew late, he invited us to come home with him for dinner so that we could continue the conversation. Had our leadership not needed me back in Washington for votes, I would have cleared my schedule and accepted the offer. I promised that the next time I visited New Jersey I would call him. "Okay," he admonished with a laugh, "but don't take another twenty-plus years to collect that raincheck."

Rodino's most significant advice came as we said our goodbyes. He told me that before Watergate, he had spent all his years in Washington as an unnoticed congressman voting the Party line and trying to help his district. Then, in June 1972, longtime Judiciary Committee Chairman Emanuel Celler lost his primary race in a stunning upset. That November, Democrats held the House and Nixon won reelection in a landslide. Because of seniority, Rodino took over as chairman, and soon thereafter Watergate revelations bombarded the Capitol. The senior House Democratic leadership argued against letting the biggest political story in history land in the lap of an untested chairman. "They panicked," he told me.

"Congressional party leaders pleaded with Speaker Carl Albert to yank away my committee's responsibility for Watergate and give it to a special committee or a select committee." Despite this pressure, Speaker Albert remained steadfast and kept the inquiry before the Judiciary Committee. Since any impeachment put Albert in the line of presidential succession, he did not want to make the Democratic caucus vulnerable to accusations that they changed the rules to dump a Republican president and replace him with a Democratic one.

"Once Carl Albert made that decision," he stated, "he told everyone who asked about impeachment that 'Peter's my man.' He never had any hand in selecting committee staff, he never interjected

With Chairman Peter Rodino after collecting my twenty-three-year old raincheck, Rutgers Law School, New Jersey. 1998 (Author's collection)

himself in the committee's operation, and he didn't make any statements about impeachment to reporters, and certainly not like the ones Newt Gingrich is making now. Anytime a reporter asked

Carl Albert about Nixon's impeachment, he told them, 'Go talk to Chairman Rodino.'" His voice then grew firm as he imparted this final advice: "That's why, under no condition, should Newt Gingrich be involved in any way. Tell him to get out of the picture and keep quiet about impeachment."

As an aside, the experiences and advice Rodino shared proved so helpful that Chairman Henry Hyde, along with Speaker Gingrich, adopted his recommendations in full. During the House Judiciary Committee's debate and vote on the Clinton articles of impeachment, Chairman Hyde reiterated repeatedly that our committee followed what he called "The Rodino Rules."

• • •

My opportunity to return to Newark didn't come until I accepted a speaking invitation at Rutgers in 2005. I debated calling Rodino as I had promised. After all, it had been seven years, and with him now almost ninety-six, I doubted that he would remember me. Besides, if he did remember, I expected that he'd probably be unhappy with me over my significant role in impeaching the president he didn't want impeached. However, I had made a promise. Despite my reservations, I dialed his home number.

He came on the line and, to my great relief, he remembered me instantly, and then he heaped praise for the job I did in the Clinton impeachment. He said he felt that I always conducted myself with fairness and dignity. My dual fears of calling proved baseless. When I suggested we get together for dinner during my visit, he declined with an apology, saying that he was recovering from major surgery and was unable to receive visitors anytime soon.

During the call, he prodded me at length to share with him my experiences as a Clinton impeachment trial prosecutor. Interestingly, the more we talked about politics and my time on his former committee, the more he perked up. "You know," he said, "when you get up this way maybe you could pick up dinner and bring it over. I think I could handle that much of a visit." Still later, as he grew more chipper, he started suggesting nearby Italian restaurants where we might venture. The more he talked about getting out of bed and going someplace, the more intent he appeared to do so.

The only melancholy note sounded when I asked about his recuperation. "I served in Congress for forty years," he told me with heaviness in his voice. "I chaired the House Judiciary Committee for fifteen of those years. Now I'm healing from major surgery and nobody from Washington calls to see how I am doing. In fact, the one guy who does call is a congressman with whom I never served, and he's in the wrong Party to boot. I guess this shows that no matter how big you were when you were there, when you're gone from Congress life goes on. The people there forget you quickly." With that, his voice cracked.

Trying to lighten the moment, I reminded him of my post-impeachment reelection defeat a few years earlier. "In my Democratic district," I said, "everybody was so mad when they voted me out of office that the sooner they forget me, the safer I'll be!" He chuckled politely, but the sadness remained. I took another shot at cheering him: "Mr. Chairman, you left Congress more than fifteen years ago. Yet, when the House of Representatives faced the grave duty of considering another presidential impeachment, a Republican-controlled Judiciary Committee adopted *your* precedents, because you set a standard for fairness that has long outlasted your service. In fact, Henry Hyde kept saying that we Republicans relied on 'The Rodino Rules' to ensure fair, orderly, and constitutional proceedings. That's not a bad legacy for a kid who grew up in a Jersey tenement."

His optimism returned. He looked forward to our dinner, and he assured me that he'd be well enough not only to get out of bed, but also to take me to his favorite Italian restaurant. We picked an evening in late May, and he promised to be well enough to keep the date. "You know," he told me before signing off, "I think I'll get up right now!" After we hung up, I reflected on how close I came to not calling.

To this day, I'm very glad that I did.

• • •

THE TELEVISION STARS

After winning a forty-nine-state reelection landslide, President Nixon had no time to enjoy his second term that began on January 20, 1973. Inaugurated alongside him that month was a chain of events that led to the unraveling of his presidency. Five days earlier, the four Cuban burglars arrested at the Watergate complex pleaded guilty. By month's end, a jury convicted James McCord and G. Gordon Liddy for their roles in the break-in. A week later, the U.S. Senate, by a vote of 77-0, created the Select Committee on Presidential Campaign Activities (nicknamed the Watergate Committee) to investigate the scandal. Beginning that May and lasting to year's end, the television networks covered the hearings live during the day and then rebroadcast them at night. According to the Senate's Art and History Office, this gavel-to-gavel exposure delivered the proceedings "to the living rooms of millions of American households. Only one month after the hearings began, an overwhelming majority of Americans, 97 percent, had heard of Watergate."[3]

Not only did the hearings make Watergate a household word, the coverage also had the collateral effect of turning the committee's seven members (four Democrats and three Republicans) into television stars. The biggest pop icon of the group was the chairman, Senator Sam Ervin (D-NC), whose Southern drawl, bouncing bushy eyebrows, downhome sayings, and self-minimizing "I'm just an ole' country lawyer" endeared him to the national audience.

In reality, the ole' country lawyer earned his degree from Harvard

---

3   https://www.senate.gov/artandhistory/history/common/generic/Feature_Homepage_
WatergateHearingBegins.htm (accessed June 28, 2019).

Law School. Born during the Cleveland Administration in 1896, he fought overseas in World War I, practiced law, and served later as a state legislator, judge, and a U.S. congressman. While an associate justice on his state's supreme court, the governor appointed him to fill a vacant U.S. Senate seat in 1954. As a freshman, he served on the special committee that recommended censuring their colleague, Senator Joseph R. McCarthy. Almost two decades later, when the Senate created the Watergate Committee, Ervin became chairman.

During and after these hearings, the press bathed Ervin in coverage bordering on hagiography, so much so that his name still evokes memories of a stalwart civil liberties champion. Left buried in that sentimental mist was his earlier Senate record. In the 1950s and 1960s, Ervin opposed the Supreme Court's *Brown v. Board of Education* decision that ended racial segregation in schools, and he joined the southern congressional opposition to every civil rights bill of that era. During the Nixon hearings, most Americans were unaware of this blot because the press routinely ignored it. Even when he died in 1985, the *Los Angeles Times* remembered him as a senator who "symbolized to the nation a latter-day Diogenes bent on finding the truth."[4] With such fawning coverage, it's no wonder that as the hearings progressed, "Uncle Sam" fan clubs sprouted up across America.

How successfully had the press obscured Ervin's pro-segregation, anti-civil rights record during and after Watergate? A month after he retired from the Senate in January 1975, and at the zenith of his popularity, he accepted a speaking invitation from the students at the University of San Francisco. At a leftist college campus in the country's most leftist city, the students received him as the conquering hero who helped topple the despised Nixon. His visit occasioned the only time I met him.

When the 78-year-old former senator arrived at the War Memorial Gymnasium, 3,000 students (at $2 a ticket) joined in a

---

4   *The Los Angeles Times*, April 24, 1985.

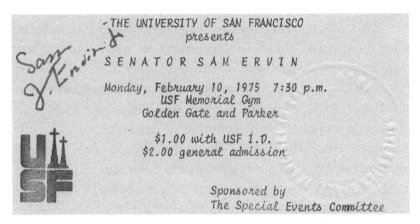

The University of San Francisco presents

Sam J. Ervin

S E N A T O R   S A M   E R V I N

Monday, February 10, 1975   7:30 p.m.
USF Memorial Gym
Golden Gate and Parker

$1.00 with USF I.D.
$2.00 general admission

Sponsored by
The Special Events Committee

My $2.00 ticket to the USF event February 10, 1975, signed for me by Sam Ervin (Author's collection)

thunderous ovation, which they repeated when he ambled to the lectern. "When I first went to the Senate," he began, "I received some very good advice from former Vice President Alben Barkley. He told me, 'Always speak extemporaneously.' However, I will depart from that practice tonight by reading from a prepared text." He then spread out his notes and delivered a dull lecture on the origins of the Bill of Rights.

After listening to his dry speech, and then comparing it to his lively Q&A with the students, I understood why Barkley gave him the advice. Once liberated from a text, the same magnetic charm that appealed to television viewers came to life.

The students wanted to discuss Watergate. When one asked if Ervin believed Nixon truly guilty, the senator thundered, "Nixon was guilty—he was guilty of assassinating the rights of the American people." He also criticized President Ford for pardoning Nixon a few months earlier, saying Ford acted prematurely and that he should have let justice take its course. "The soundest principle of government," he intoned, "is that all men stand equal before the law. It is wrong that underlings are sent to jail while the chief goes unwhipped." Then, with a grin, he added, "Mind you, I am not advocating we whip anybody in particular!" When the laughter subsided, he added, "Only Almighty God can pardon sin, but Mr. Nixon still denies he ever sinned."

Another student asked if he had read the current bestselling book about Watergate, *All the President's Men.* "That reminds me of a story I heard back home," Ervin replied. "A fellow down in a North Carolina jail went to the prison library and asked if they had *All the President's Men.* 'Not yet,' said the librarian, 'but at the rate they're coming in, we soon will!'"

A few weeks after Ervin's San Francisco speech, I wrote to him at his home in Morganton, North Carolina. I told him I attended the function, and I asked if, in the light of Watergate, he had any

My father, who was an active Practitioner at the North Carolina bar for sixty five years, gave me this sage advice when I entered his law office many years ago: "Salt down the facts; the law will keep." Inscribed August 14, 1975, for Jim Rogan, with all good wishes.
Sam J. Ervin, Jr.

"Salt down the facts; the law will keep." Senator Sam Ervin speaking at the University of San Francisco, February 10, 1975 (Photograph by the author)

advice to impart for a young man bent on law school and politics. A few weeks later, he replied, "While Watergate was a great tragedy, it eventually taught the American people that we have the wisest system of government on earth. It particularly shows the wisdom of the Founding Fathers in separating the powers of the president, the Congress, and the courts. When the president proved faithless to his constitutional obligations, the Congress and the courts remained faithful to theirs."

Along with my letter, I also sent a photograph I took of him that night and asked him to sign it for me. He returned it with this guidance for a budding lawyer penned on it: "My father, who was an active practitioner at the North Carolina bar for sixty five years, gave me this sage advice when I entered his law office many years ago: 'Salt down the facts; the law will keep.' Inscribed August 14, 1975 for Jim Rogan, with all good wishes, Sam J. Ervin, Jr."

• • •

I spent thirty years trying to ask the Watergate Committee's ranking Republican member, Senator Howard Baker, about his experiences investigating the scandal. The chance came when both of us were out of Congress. As they say, better late than never.

The son of a Tennessee congressman, Baker served in the Navy during World War II, and then he returned home to practice law. When he won a U.S. Senate seat in 1966, he became Tennessee's first Republican senator since Reconstruction. Later, as the ranking Republican on the Watergate Committee, he asked the famous open-ended question about Nixon: "What did the president know, and when did he know it?"

I first met Baker when he came to San Francisco for a speech in 1975. Although he appeared before a sold-out crowd that day, he talked about foreign policy, not Watergate. At that time, he was contemplating a 1976 presidential campaign, so he wanted to accentuate his foreign policy experience rather than harping on the scandal that devastated a presidency and crushed Republicans in the 1974 congressional midterm elections. He avoided Watergate in his speech, and when asked about it during the Q&A, he deftly deflected the inquiry into a foreign policy answer ("The Nixon years, although tragedy ridden, will be remembered favorably for detente with the Soviet Union."), and then he meandered into an analysis on the Middle East.

The only time he addressed a political question directly during this talk was when asked about his 1976 presidential ambitions now that Nixon's vice president, Gerald Ford, was in the White House. "If you are asking me if I would *like* to be president, the answer is yes. If you are asking me if I will *run* for president, the answer is I don't know. It depends on what others do. Ask me six months from now." He said he would not challenge Ford for the GOP nomination if Ford chose to run for a term in his own right. "President Ford is a good friend of many years," he noted. "There are many things he has done that I agree with. There are some things he has done that I have disagreed with."

I next met Baker when I served in Congress almost twenty-five years later. Along with Peter Rodino and others, I sought his advice for my Clinton impeachment project assigned to me by Speaker Gingrich. Although I hoped to hear him intersperse his suggestions with personal Watergate vignettes, the closest he came was in drawing vague parallels between the Nixon and Clinton impeachment proceedings. A few days later, Speaker Gingrich and Judiciary Committee Chairman Hyde joined me in a second meeting with Baker at the Capitol. He reiterated for our leadership what he told me initially: unlike Watergate, where the minority Republicans cooperated with the Democrats to flesh out the truth, the current Democrat minority opposed Clinton's impeachment bitterly. Their goal was not truth seeking, it was delay and obstruction. Thus, trying to replicate the Watergate model promised failure for any Clinton impeachment inquiry before it began.[5]

---

5   For my diary notes of my meeting with Baker, Gingrich, and Hyde, see *Catching Our Flag*, 82-83.

Because Gingrich had requested secrecy for our meeting to avoid media curiosity, when the briefing ended, Baker said he would slip out of Gingrich's office unnoticed by the press. I offered to show him through the back exits to avoid reporters. He brushed me off with a look of disdain. "Rogan," he said, "if there's one thing I learned in all my years in Congress, it's how to get out of an office without the press knowing."[6]

• • •

It took me five more years before getting the chance to talk to Baker about his Watergate experiences. When I was U.S. under secretary of Commerce, I led an American delegation to Tokyo to sign on behalf of the U.S. the Trilateral Agreement on Intellectual Property Protection with my counterparts from the European Union and Japan. On my last day in Tokyo, and along with my chief of staff Wayne Paugh, I paid a courtesy call on Baker, then the U.S. Ambassador to Japan.

Wayne and I met with Baker in his spacious embassy office. He had aged much since he and I last met before Clinton's impeachment. His hair was white, he was overweight, and his stooped body moved slowly. Before joining him for coffee, he showed us the memorabilia adorning his walls, which included photographs from his Senate days and with various presidents, along with the Presidential Medal of Freedom awarded him by Ronald Reagan.

After catching up on current politics and other news, Baker shared a few memories of Watergate and Nixon. "After the Senate selected me as the ranking member of the Watergate Committee," he recalled, "I went to visit Nixon at the White House. Back then, I thought that Watergate was nothing more than a Democrat witch-hunt against him. Besides, I liked Nixon. I was his friend. When I ran for the Senate he came to Tennessee and campaigned for me, and we always had a great working relationship.

6   *Id* at 83.

"I visited him in his office in the Old Executive Office Building. As we discussed the role of the new Senate Watergate Committee, Nixon told me not to worry about anything reaching the Oval Office. 'I have no skeletons,' he assured me. I felt relieved and confident that would be the case.

"At the time, I was also good friends with Nixon's attorney general, John Mitchell [later imprisoned for his role in the scandal]. We had once done some legal work together. John had left the Justice Department to help run Nixon's 1972 reelection campaign. Since individuals associated with Nixon's campaign committee were implicated in the burglary, as I was walking out the door, I mentioned offhandedly that I hoped Mitchell would have no Watergate problem. Nixon's casual smile disappeared, and his face became firm. He paused, looked down, and then he said, 'Well, John might have a problem.'

"I had arrived at the White House that day intending to support the president against a witch-hunt. Now, I rode back to the Capitol stunned by his answer. I decided that I'd have to follow the facts no matter where they led. I had to get to the truth."

As for his relationship with Chairman Sam Ervin, he said, "Sam and I both got along, but we were never buddy-buddy. He was very friendly, but he was also very partisan." He walked across the room, picked up a framed photograph of the committee, and then showed it to Wayne and me. "Here's a picture of all seven of us from 1973," he said as he shook his head. "Now, only three of us are still alive."

When asked what role, if any, he played in pushing Nixon to resign, he replied, "Once Nixon lost in court and surrendered the tapes of his Oval Office conversations, the so-called 'smoking gun' tape told me it was over for him. If he did not resign, he would be impeached. On August 8, 1974, the Senate Republican leader, Hugh Scott of Pennsylvania, asked me to join him, Senator Barry Goldwater, and House Republican leader John Rhodes. They planned to visit the White House and tell Nixon that he needed to resign. I turned them down. 'That's not my place,' I said. They went without me and told Nixon his congressional support had collapsed. If he did not resign, he would be impeached and removed from office. Nixon resigned the next day."

Wayne asked if he remained in contact with Nixon after his resignation. "We stayed in occasional touch," he said. "About a year after he resigned, he called and invited me to dinner at his home in New Jersey. We spent a few hours together that evening talking and reminiscing. I thought it very odd that, of all the subjects we covered, he never once raised the issue of Watergate, his possible impeachment, or his resignation. This was odd because I shared in some responsibility for him resigning. It was as if it never happened.

"Years later, near the end of the Reagan Administration and when I was Reagan's White House Chief of Staff, Reagan was preparing for a summit meeting with the Soviets. I called Nixon and asked him to come to the White House to brief Reagan before we left for the summit. Nixon balked at the request. He hated the press, and he didn't want to come to Washington and give them a chance to write about him. I persisted and he finally agreed. I brought him into the White House quietly through the Diplomatic Reception Room and up to the third floor. When Nixon and Reagan met, Nixon delivered a brilliant and lengthy briefing on the Soviet-U.S. relationship, and he suggested how Reagan should approach the negotiations. Amazingly, he did it without any notes before him.

"After the briefing, I was escorting Nixon back through the White House. We walked down the hallway where the paintings of former first ladies hung on the walls. He stopped when we reached the formal portrait of his wife Pat. He asked if he might have a moment. I stepped away and left him to his thoughts. He stood gazing at her painting for several minutes. As he turned to leave, he told me, 'You know, I've never seen her painting until now.' It was a touching moment."

The hour we spent with Baker went by quickly. After leaving the embassy, as Wayne and I walked back to our hotel, I asked if Baker appeared sorry to see us go. "You sensed it, too?" Wayne asked. "I felt the same way," adding, "Think about it. Here's a guy who was a senator for almost twenty years. He was the son of a

Listening to Watergate memories from Ambassador Howard Baker, the U.S. Embassy, Tokyo, November 7, 2003 (Author's collection)

congressman and the son-in-law of a famous senator.[7] He was Senate majority and minority leader. He ran for president himself, and he was Reagan's White House chief of staff. Now he's stuck in Tokyo surrounded by a bunch of career foreign service diplomats. How often do you think he gets a chance to talk politics out here with anyone who gets it? Hell, yes, he was sorry to see us go."

I especially liked Wayne's analysis for a personal reason. After spending decades since boyhood pestering politicians to talk to me about their careers, perhaps my historic curiosity, for once, proved more of a boost than a bother.

• • •

Of the seven original members of the 1973 Watergate Committee, only one remained in the Senate when I arrived as a freshman congressman a quarter-century later. Daniel Inouye (D-HI) was more than a senator. He was a respected war hero.

---

7   Everett Dirksen (1896-1969) represented Illinois in Congress for thirty-six years, and he was the Republican leader of the U.S. Senate from 1959 to 1969.

Born in 1924, Inouye enlisted when World War II broke out. He joined the U.S. Army's fabled 442nd Infantry, a regiment comprised mainly of Japanese Americans. By war's end, the 442nd became the most decorated unit in U.S. military history. Inouye's valor in combat contributed mightily to this legacy, and his Congressional Medal of Honor citation speaks for itself:

> While attacking a defended ridge guarding an important road junction, Second Lieutenant Inouye skillfully directed his platoon through a hail of automatic weapon and small arms fire, in a swift enveloping movement that resulted in the capture of an artillery and mortar post and brought his men to within forty yards of the hostile force. Emplaced in bunkers and rock formations, the enemy halted the advance with crossfire from three machine guns. With complete disregard for his personal safety, Second Lieutenant Inouye crawled up the treacherous slope to within five yards of the nearest machine gun and hurled two grenades, destroying the emplacement. Before the enemy could retaliate, he stood up and neutralized a second machine gun nest. Although wounded by a sniper's bullet, he continued to engage other hostile positions at close range until an exploding grenade shattered his right arm. Despite the intense pain, he refused evacuation and continued to direct his platoon until enemy resistance was broken and his men were again deployed in defensive positions. In the attack, twenty-five enemy soldiers were killed and eight others captured. By his gallant, aggressive tactics and by his indomitable leadership, Second Lieutenant Inouye enabled his platoon to advance through formidable resistance, and was instrumental in the capture of the ridge. Second Lieutenant Inouye's extraordinary heroism and devotion to duty are in keeping with the highest traditions of military service and reflect great credit on him, his unit, and the United States Army.[8]

---

8   https://history.army.mil/moh/wwII-g-l.html (accessed July 4, 2019).

Returning home from the war as an amputee, Inouye became a lawyer, and then he won election to both houses of Hawaii's territorial legislature. When Hawaii won statehood in 1959, he became its first congressman. Three years later, he moved up to the U.S. Senate, where he served for the next fifty years.

Inouye was another Watergate Committee member that I met in my teens when he came to San Francisco for a speech. The hearings, which dominated the national news for months, had recessed recently by the time he came to town in December 1973.

Once again, with my friends Dan and Roger, I waited for a politician with my tape recorder in hand. When I saw Inouye enter the San Francisco Hilton, I approached him with my right hand outstretched reflexively while introducing myself. Then I noticed his empty right coat sleeve hanging limply at his side. I had forgotten that he had lost his right arm in combat. I felt embarrassed immediately, but he reached over with his left hand and grabbed mine. He told me he was running late for a reception, but he stopped long enough to answer a couple of my Watergate questions.[9]

ROGAN: Senator Inouye, so far four senators have called for the president's resignation, including yourself.

INOUYE: Uh-huh.

---

9   When I dug out the tape of this interview, I discovered another interview I had conducted that night with a local politician attending the Inouye reception. California State Senator George Moscone had announced previously that he would seek the 1974 Democratic nomination for governor of California. Dan, Roger, and I interviewed him about his campaign. I still remember the overwhelming smell of alcohol on his breath as he talked merrily about his race and his expectation of winning. His bid for the nomination failed ultimately, but he went on to win election as San Francisco mayor in 1975. On November 27, 1978, in one of the most shocking events in the city's history, San Francisco Board of Supervisors member Dan White murdered both Moscone and fellow Supervisor Harvey Milk in their City Hall offices.

ROGAN: Do you think that if Gerald Ford is [confirmed as vice president], there will be more pressure from senators, particularly Republican senators, to oust Mr. Nixon? [10]

INOUYE: Well, I have no idea. I haven't discussed this matter with the Republican senators. It might happen. It might not.

ROGAN: With this new revelation of an [18-½ minute gap in a critical White House tape]—this obviously hurts Mr. Nixon's credibility—do you think there is anything he could do now that would let him be able to effectively govern? Is there anything he could do now to restore confidence?

INOUYE: I think it would be very helpful if the president turned over all the tapes to the court and to the Select Committee instead of hanging on to some. And further, I think it would be very helpful to the president if he presented himself either to the court or to the committee and say, "I am ready for any questions you may have."

After the brief interview, we walked with Inouye to the reception, and he made a comment to me that he repeated in his speech later that night: "When Democrats are corrupt, they look for wine, women, and song. Here, the corrupt were seeking to steal our government."

Over twenty-five years later, Inouye was still serving in the Senate when my fellow House Managers invaded that chamber for over a month to prosecute the Clinton impeachment trial. Near the end of the case, and during a recess in the proceedings, I walked

10   After Vice President Spiro Agnew resigned in October 1973, Nixon nominated longtime Michigan Congressman Gerald Ford to replace him. At the time of my Inouye interview, Ford was awaiting congressional confirmation to the post. He became vice president a week later.

over to Inouye's desk and showed him the photograph of me interviewing him decades earlier. "I can't believe it!" he exclaimed, and he insisted that I recount the details for him.

He teased me about my inheriting presidential impeachment responsibilities during my freshman term, and then he shared this story of his own introduction to Congress:

"When Hawaii became a state in 1959, I was elected as its first congressman. Since it was a special election, I arrived in Washington and joined a Congress already in session. This was only fourteen years after World War II ended, and there was still plenty of anti-Japanese bigotry around. My election made me the first American of Japanese ancestry ever to serve there, and quite a few congressmen snubbed me when I first showed up.

"The Speaker of the House back then was Sam Rayburn, a gruff, no-nonsense Texan who had served in Congress for almost fifty years. Rayburn called me forward into the well of the House

Interviewing Senator Daniel Inouye, San Francisco, December 1, 1973 (Author's collection)

and told me to raise my right hand to take the oath of office. Of course, I couldn't do that, because I had lost my right arm in combat. When I raised my left hand instead, I heard congressmen and visitors in the gallery weeping. In that moment, I think the bigotry began fading.

"Anyway, after I took the oath, I wanted to meet Rayburn, but he left the chamber after swearing me in. Over the next few weeks, I kept looking for a chance to introduce myself to him, but the opportunity never came. Then, about a month or so later, I was standing in the lobby of the Longworth Building talking to someone on the payphone. I saw Rayburn walking down the hallway alone and in my direction. Here was my chance. I got off the phone, approached him, and said, 'Mr. Speaker, I'm sorry to interrupt, but I wanted to introduce myself. I'm Dan Inouye, the new congressman from Hawaii.'

"Rayburn was a very dour-looking and serious man. He looked me in the eye and said, 'You don't need to introduce yourself to me, Dan. I know who you are.'

"You do?

"'Of course, I know you,' Rayburn said. 'How the hell many one-armed Japs do you think we have in Congress?' Then he continued on his way."

A few senators had gathered around and had joined me in listening to Inouye's story. When he reached the climax of his Rayburn yarn, everyone erupted in laughter—

—and nobody laughed harder than Dan Inouye.

• • •

There are more stories I could share of other Watergate figures I met or knew, but I don't want to wear out my welcome with the reader on this topic. I'll close this chapter with a final observation. When I began these reflections, I wrote that *Watergate* was a word so ubiquitous throughout my life that it required no explanation. Upon reflection, perhaps that is an overstatement.

Only six years after the infamous Watergate trials ended, I was in my final semester at UCLA Law School. One evening I was playing racquetball at the newly opened John Wooden Recreation Center with a beautiful young woman I was trying to woo, Jeannine Gallant. She was an undergraduate senior and a fellow UCLA Co-Op resident. When our game ended, we stepped out of our court just as the two men playing on the adjoining court did the same. I nodded a greeting to the middle-aged man, fit and tanned, accompanied by a younger man that I assumed might be his son.

As Jeannine and I walked away, I said, "Do you know who that man is? That's H.R. Haldeman."

"Who?"

"H.R. Haldeman. He was Nixon's White House chief of staff, and he went to prison for Watergate."

"He went to prison? For what?"

"For Watergate, you know, Watergate, the scandal that led to Nixon's resignation."

She thought for a moment, and then she said, "Oh, Watergate! Sure, of course—

"—We studied that in our history class."

• • •

U.S. District Court Judge John J. Sirica died of a heart attack at age 88 on August 14, 1992. My youthful reverence for him took a hit when Special Prosecutor Leon Jaworski's files, along with other records, became public many decades later. They showed that Sirica held over a dozen secret meetings with prosecutors during the Watergate trials, and that he used his rulings and sentencing discretion to facilitate the government's case against the defendants. If true, such conduct violated his ethical duty to remain impartial and to ensure that both sides received a fair trial. Author Geoff Shepard, who laid out the case against Sirica, Jaworski, and Archibald Cox for multiple due process violations, wrote, "Had any one of these incidents...come to light at the time, it would have necessitated resignations, removals, and possibly disbarments. [These facts emerging] some four decades later...completely taint the Watergate verdicts and render them indefensible as a matter of law."[11] None of this minimizes my appreciation for the kindness Sirica showed me long ago, but, sadly, it tarnishes the patina of my early admiration for him.

After serving four months in prison for his role in the Watergate burglary, James McCord owned and operated a security firm and remained out of the public eye for the rest of his life. He died at age 93 from pancreatic cancer on June 15, 2017. He lived in such anonymity that the press did not learn about his death to report it until 2019.

Aside from his two decades as a syndicated radio talk show host, G. Gordon Liddy's post-prison career included best-selling author, popular lecture circuit habitué, television and motion picture actor, and founder of a counter-surveillance firm. I appeared on his radio show a couple of times more, with the last time in 2012. During that final interview, he sounded old and tired, and his edginess was gone. He retired soon afterward.

Sadly, the dinner plan I made with Peter Rodino following his surgery was not to be. A few days after we spoke on the telephone, he died at age 95 on May 7, 2005. For the second time, he left me with a raincheck.

After leaving the Senate, Sam Ervin returned to North Carolina and wrote his memoirs, practiced law, and even made a record album sharing his down-home philosophy, reading poetry, and speaking the words to a Simon and Garfunkel song. He died at age 88 of emphysema on April 23, 1985.

Howard Baker retired as U.S. Ambassador to Japan in 2005. He returned home and practiced law, co-founded a non-profit think tank, and served on multiple boards focused on domestic and international affairs. He died at age 88 from complications after

---

11   Geoff Shepard, *The Real Watergate Scandal: Collusion, Conspiracy, and the Plot That Brought Down Nixon* (Washington: Regnery History, 2015), 63. Shepard's book contains multiple sources showing that Sirica used his courtroom as an adjunct operation of the prosecution.

suffering a stroke on June 26, 2014.

Two weeks before Daniel Inouye reached the fiftieth anniversary of his joining the U.S. Senate, he died at age 88 of respiratory complications on December 17, 2012.

H.R. Haldeman, Richard Nixon's former White House Chief of Staff, served eighteen months in federal prison for his role in Watergate. After his release, he became a successful author, real estate developer, and businessman. He died at age 67 of abdominal cancer on November 12, 1993.

14

The Big Ticket

When I served in Congress, I was antagonistic toward the United Nations. Whatever usefulness it might once have had (a hypothetical point I was not prepared to concede), I saw it as a bloated army of bureaucrats gorging from the U.S. tax trough and then using the subsidy to bash America, legitimize corrupt and murderous regimes and pave the way toward a centralized one-world socialist empire. Back in my Washington days, had I found enough like-minded allies, I would have sought to defund the United Nations, sell their East River headquarters, deport to Geneva its teeming ensemble of international leeches, and let them pursue their leftist Utopia on someone else's dime.

Given my instinctive hostility toward the world organization, it might surprise you to learn that I participated in two major milestones in United Nations history, and for all I know I might be the only person still around to have done so. No, I didn't attend its 1945 formation, which was more than a dozen years before my birth. However, I did attend both the twenty-fifth *and* fiftieth anniversary celebrations of the founding of the U.N., and, of course, I have stories to share from both events.

• • •

In June 1970, I was a twelve-year old boy fascinated by history and government who had never met any political figures. I read a story in the local newspaper announcing that international dignitaries would mark the twenty-fifth anniversary of the 1945 signing of the United Nations Charter at the site of its birth, the San Francisco War Memorial Opera House and the adjacent Veterans Building. This unique powwow, practically in my backyard, sounded irresistible to a history junkie, so I conscripted my fifth grade best friend (and fellow politics enthusiast) Jon Jacobs to join me in an adventure: attend the anniversary celebration and, maybe, meet some world leaders.

This grand scheme appeared stillborn soon after conception. I called San Francisco Mayor Joseph Alioto's office and learned that the host organization had distributed the limited number of public tickets long ago, and when they did, they went to dignitaries and not to schoolboys. Without any plan for attending the security-heavy festivities beyond youthful determination, Jon and I resolved to crash the June 26, 1970 event.

Our first hurdle involved overcoming a power higher than a Security Council veto: parental consent. Jon and I recognized that most mothers would be reluctant to deposit young boys in the middle of a felony-ridden major metropolitan city, let alone encourage their plan to commit a criminal trespass into a fortified international confab. That we hoped to execute our scheme without either an adult chaperone or admission tickets would no doubt add to maternal angst. Having synthesized the likely response to any entreaty, we bypassed Mrs. Jacobs and Mrs. Rogan and instead approached Jon's father. Mr. Jacobs enjoyed a spirit of adventure, and he proved a willing coconspirator in our plot.

On the big day, Mr. Jacobs drove us from Pacifica (the suburb in which we lived) to the Polk Street entrance of San Francisco City Hall. Jon and I had picked City Hall as our drop site only because we had no idea where the Opera House was located. We never investigated that detail during our planning, but we assumed everything would be near the city's political nerve center. That we made a lucky guess was evident when we arrived and saw scores of black stretch limousines lining every nearby street for blocks, countless world flags fluttering from poles encircling Civic Center Plaza, and mobs of people in suits walking toward City Hall.

Jon hopped out of his father's car. I followed carrying my plastic Kodak Instamatic camera, a flashbulb cube, and a pen and card in case I had the chance to score a famous autograph. Mr. Jacobs wished us luck. "You boys stay out of trouble," he yelled out the window, and then he drove off down the street. We were on our own.

"By the way," Jon asked as the family car sped away, "how are we getting home tonight?" I shrugged. In our excitement, we had also neglected to secure a ride back to Pacifica, and Mr. Jacobs, no doubt assuming we had worked out that detail, never asked us before leaving. It being too late to worry about that fact now, off we went in search of tickets.

City Hall, a French Renaissance architectural masterpiece occupying two full city blocks, captivated me as we entered. Modeled after the United States Capitol, its iron, copper, and gold leaf outer dome actually stands forty-two feet higher than its Washington counterpart. I had never seen the inside of a building as ornate or as crowded, with hundreds of well-dressed official-looking people surging through the rotunda toward the Van Ness Avenue exit. They all seemed to know where they were going, so Jon and I joined the flow. We eavesdropped on random conversations hoping to glean useful intelligence. One man mentioned to his companion that incumbent President Richard Nixon, and maybe even former President Harry Truman (who officiated at the first U.N. meeting in 1945), might make surprise visits today. We later learned the exciting rumors were false, but not before we had spent the rest of the day straining our eyeballs searching for a familiar presidential profile inside every passing limousine.

Another man in the crowd wearing cameras and press passes around his neck stood nearby. Assuming a reporter would know everything, I approached him, told him why we came, and asked for his advice. Dick Donovan of the San Francisco Chronicle obliged: "The Opera House is just behind City Hall," he said, "so you're very close to where you want to be. I don't know if you can get tickets this late, but if you boys want to get pictures or autographs, go to the Veterans Building next door to the Opera House." He said that if we waited at that entrance, we might catch a glimpse of U.N. Secretary-General U Thant when he arrived to view the original 1945 charter. "But you'd better hurry," he added, "because he should be there in a few minutes." Jon and I rushed out of City Hall, crossed Van Ness Avenue, and located the day's centers of gravity.

A small courtyard separated the Opera House and its adjacent twin structure, the Veterans Building, both of which opened in 1932. On June 25, 1945, delegates meeting in the Opera House voted unanimously to adopt the charter creating the United Nations. The next day, President Truman and other dignitaries attended the signing ceremony at Herbst Theater inside the Veterans Building. On this silver anniversary, while everyone else surged into the Opera House, Jon and I entered the Veterans Building. We positioned ourselves just inside the south door and did as Mr. Donovan suggested: we waited for U Thant.

Born in Burma in 1909, Thant worked as an educator and journalist before embarking on a diplomatic career. Rising to the rank of Burmese ambassador to the United Nations, in 1962 he became secretary-general following the death of his predecessor, Dag Hammarskjold, in an airplane crash. Thant won re-appointment to the position for a full term four years later. His tenure marked tough times, including the Cuban Missile Crisis, the war in Congo, the 1967 Arab-Israeli war, and Vietnam.

While waiting, and for the second time that day, Jon asked a problematic question: "Do you know what U Thant looks like?"

"Actually, no. Do you?"

"No. How will we recognize him?"

In our rush to see Thant, we hadn't contemplated this, and now there was no time to investigate the deficiency. The sound of distant police sirens became apparent, and with it came police and security guards from nowhere swarming toward the entrance. Moments later, they reversed direction and headed back toward us. Although I couldn't see who was inside their human shield, I knew Thant must be buried somewhere in the middle of that scrum.

It proved surprisingly easy for a short, fast-moving kid to duck and weave under the guards' legs and arms. When I popped up in their midst unexpectedly, I found myself facing a thin, elderly, bespectacled man with a dark complexion, gray hair and wearing a neatly tailored suit. Since he was the only man in the group that was not a burly white guy built like a linebacker, this had to be Thant.

Suddenly, I froze. How do I ask for an autograph in Burmese—if there is such a language? Hoping he'd understand my desire, I said nothing and shoved a card in front of him. Thant took the blank card and inspected both sides. A quizzical look crossed his face. "Oh, no!" I thought. "I forgot to hand him this!" I waved my pen in front of his face, and then I pretended to write in my palm while speaking *very* slowly, hoping that he might grasp my combination of pantomime and rudimentary English: "Auuuuu—towwww—graphhhhh, pleeeeese?"

For all I know, this illegible scrawl says, "Beat it, kid," but I accept on faith it says, "U Thant," since it's the autograph he signed for me on June 26, 1970 (Author's collection)

"Oh, I see," he replied. "You want my autograph. Very well." Thant took the pen, signed my card, and then handed both back to me.

No opportunity to thank him presented. As soon as the pen and card made the return trip to my hand, a guard grabbed me by the shoulders and heaved me outside the security wedge. Thant and his entourage disappeared inside the display room to inspect the original charter, which was preserved inside a glass case beneath a painting of the 1945 signing ceremony.

A couple of minutes later, as Thant headed back to his motorcade, I got close enough to snap a couple

U.N. Secretary-General U Thant, San Francisco, June 26, 1970
(Photograph by the author)

of pictures, but poor Jon had no luck replicating my autograph conquest. A guard held him back from approaching the secretary-general as the entourage breezed by us and exited the building.

• • •

The mild physical manhandling notwithstanding, we had scored a coup encountering the secretary-general despite his heavy security detail. Given this achievement, we hoped getting inside the U.N. session would be just as easy, but our hopes dashed after circling the Opera House perimeter. Every door was either manned or locked, and our pleas to the doorkeepers at the main entrances proved ineffective.

After casing the building again, Jon and I stood at the iron fence in front of the twin buildings' courtyard and watched for an unguarded moment to slip into a side door. Alas, even had we spotted one, the locked gate appeared impenetrable.

While we stood at the fence, growing frustrated in our ambitions, an old man staggering down the street stopped next to us. "What's going on here, boys?" he slurred. He had bloodshot eyes, and the liquor smell almost overpowered me. As I began explaining the day's significance, he turned away and stared through the gate at the slow-moving black limousine inside the courtyard that was now coming toward us.

"Well-l-l-l," he called out as the car neared us, "Hello-o-o-o-o, Ronnie!" I looked over and saw California Governor Ronald Reagan riding alone in the rear seat. As his car rounded the turn in front of us, Jon and I waved and called to him, hoping he might stop for us. Reagan saw us, smiled broadly, and returned our wave as his car went by, and then it continued circling the courtyard and exited the west gate. Reagan had just finished delivering welcoming remarks to the session, and now he headed back to the airport.

A half century later, I still remember the impression left from this first in-person sighting of the future president. On television and in photographs Reagan always looked tanned and ruggedly handsome, and that was true when I saw him in 1970. What surprised me was how heavily lined his face appeared, and how the camera never captured those deep wrinkles. This was not my observation alone. As Reagan's car drove by us, the old drunk remarked, "Je-e-e-e-sus, he looks like a r-r-r-r-inkled old p-r-r-r-rune!"

"Good old Ronnie!" our new companion belched as Reagan's car disappeared, and then he started patting his pockets. "Hey, boys," he asked us, "anyone got an extra smoke? You don't smoke? Well, okay, see you later." With that, the fellow toddled away.

Seeing Ronald Reagan in person thrilled me, and I owed it all to a passing wino.

With Reagan gone, Jon and I resumed trying to solve our Opera House entry problem. We approached the north entrance door and pleaded our case to the ticket-taking usher. He refused politely, but he gave us ceremonial programs distributed to each guest as a consolation.

With all other options now exhausted, and with the afternoon

The Honorable Joseph L. Alioto
Mayor of the City of San Francisco

and the

San Francisco Citizens' Committee
for the Twenty-fifth Anniversary of the United Nations

welcome you to the
Meeting commemorating the
signing of the United Nations Charter

Friday, the 26th day of June 1970, at 2:00 p.m.
War Memorial Opera House, San Francisco

Admit One

551

Success! My ticket to the twenty-fifth anniversary of the United Nations, June 26, 1970, later autographed by San Francisco Mayor Joseph Alioto (Author's collection)

clock ticking toward the ceremony's adjournment, we played our final ace: begging. Everyone leaving the ceremonies now encountered two zealous boys tugging at their sleeves: "Hey, lady, excuse me, if you're not coming back, may I have your ticket...? Hey, mister, are you coming back? If not...?" People ignored our entreaties, but eventually two exotic women wearing colorful flowing dresses and bindis in the middle of their foreheads took mercy. They smiled, removed tickets from their purses, and handed them to us.

We did it! Had those tickets been made of gold, I don't think we would have valued them more. Seconds later, Jon and I were inside the Opera House and walking unmolested past a phalanx of the same guards that had stymied us all day.

The ceremonial program was nearly over by the time we settled into balcony seats. Dignitaries occupying a long table on the stage included Mayor Alioto and Charles Yost, the United States' ambassador to the U.N. Alioto in person interested me far more because I saw his image plastered daily on TV and in newspapers. Two years earlier, at the 1968 Democratic National Convention, Vice President Hubert Humphrey had considered selecting Alioto as his running mate, and a run for governor in the next statewide cycle was on the mayor's to-do list. The gregarious Alioto thrived in city politics despite allegations of mafia ties leveled by *Look* magazine, a bribery indictment by a grand jury, and other baggage that never suppressed the city's overall affinity for him.

Alongside the colorful Alioto, Yost appeared milquetoast, but his was a lifetime of diplomatic gravitas. In 1945, he helped draft the original U.N. Charter, and he attended the original San Francisco organizing conference that year. At the post-World War II summit held in Potsdam between President Truman, British Prime Minister Winston Churchill, and Soviet leader Joseph Stalin, Yost served as secretary-general for the conference. During the 1940s and 1950s, as a career ambassador, he served in various world hotspots, including Czechoslovakia, Greece, Laos, France, Morocco, and Syria. In 1969, President Nixon called him out of retirement and named him to the U.N. post.

Mayor Alioto created a traffic jam while signing this program for me, June 26, 1970 (Author's collection)

Jon and I arrived in time to see Yakov Malik deliver his speech (in Russian). Unlike the dignitaries onstage who wore earphones listening to a simultaneous translation, we tried in vain to follow along with an advance copy of his remarks printed in English. Another career diplomat, Malik helped negotiate an end to the post-World War II Berlin Blockade. Serving as the Soviet Union's ambassador to the U.N. from 1948 to 1952, he returned to the position in 1968.

The event wound down soon after Jon and I secured our tickets. When we saw a group of news photographers rush from the auditorium, we followed them to where they congregated outside in the courtyard. We arrived in time to see Thant depart, and then Alioto, in separate limousines.

It had been an exciting day, but the time had come to figure out a way home to Pacifica. As we walked down the street pondering the dilemma, I saw Alioto's limousine stopped at a nearby traffic light. "Come on, Jon!" I said, and we ran over to his car and knocked on the rear window. Alioto looked up with a start, and then he rolled it down. Jon and I leaned inside his car and asked him to autograph our programs.

"Sure, boys," the genial mayor replied, and penned his name neatly on both of them.

The streetlight had changed to green before he started signing, so by the time he finished, the cars trapped behind kept honking for his driver to get moving. Unflustered, Alioto handed back the signed programs, wished us luck, and then started to roll up his window. Before it closed completely, I knocked again, and he reopened it. I leaned inside and asked a longshot, impulsive question:

"Mayor Alioto, is there any chance that you're driving to Pacifica right now?"

• • •

As I write this, the calendar has marked five decades since Jon and I had our U.N. San Francisco adventure. To this day, neither of us can recall how we ever got home that night (it wasn't in Alioto's limousine). What we do recall with great fondness is the shared memory of two boys embarking on an afternoon history spree

Commemorative postal cover issued by the United Nations on its twenty-fifth anniversary, postmarked in San Francisco, June 26, 1970 (Author's collection)

and leaving fingerprints behind on a small corner of that amazing day.

• • •

U Thant declined appointment for a third term as U.N. secretary-general and retired in 1971. He died of lung cancer at age 65 on November 25, 1974.

Charles Yost served as the United States ambassador to the United Nations from 1969 to 1971. He wrote and taught until his death from cancer at age 73 on May 21, 1981.

Yakov Malik served as the Soviet Union's ambassador to the United Nations from 1948 to 1952, and from 1968 to 1976. He died at age 73 on February 11, 1980.

Joseph Alioto served as mayor of San Francisco from 1968 to 1976. He ran for governor in 1974, but he lost in the Democratic primary to a future four-term governor, Edmund G. "Jerry" Brown, Jr. Alioto returned to his law practice and engaged in civic affairs until his death from prostate cancer at age 81 on January 29, 1998.

The day after Jon and I attended the 1970 U.N. celebration, I wrote a letter to Governor Reagan in which I recalled for him the day's events. I asked if he remembered waving to us, and I told him we had tried flagging down his car to get his autograph. Many months later, a large envelope arrived for me from his Sacramento office. Inside was a nice letter apologizing for not stopping the car, along with two signed photographs for Jon and me and a request that I deliver Jon's gift on the governor's behalf. In the interim months between my writing Reagan and his reply, my family had moved from Pacifica and I lost touch with Jon. It took some thirty years for us to reunite and renew our old friendship.

And, yes, I delivered Jon's gift belatedly—from the former president of the United States.

At the end of Jon's and my 1970 U.N. adventure, I told him I planned to attend the fiftieth anniversary in 1995. As it turned out, exactly twenty-five years later, on June 26, 1995, I was back at the San Francisco Opera House for the silver anniversary celebra-

I didn't get to shake hands with Governor Reagan at the U.N. celebration in 1970, but later that year he sent me this consolation autographed photograph (Author's collection)

tion. Of course, with me there is always a story behind such events, but to read it, you need to turn the page.

15

Repaying a Favor

The first time that I attended a quadranscentennial United Nations birthday event, I was a twelve-year old boy panhandling an admission ticket. Twenty-five years later, as an elected California legislator, I went as part of our state's official delegation. My colleagues teased me for being the only Republican in our eleven-member deputation. "I hope this means you've seen the globalist light," chided Assemblywoman Juanita McDonald (D-Los Angeles).

"Juanita, if ever I see the light, it won't be shining from a one-world beacon. Besides, I only came to take a walk down Memory Lane."

What a difference a quarter-century makes. When I arrived on that bright June 1995 morning, the scene looked just as it did in 1970. Large U.N. flags flew over the Opera House and Veterans Building, police blocked off the surrounding streets, rows of black stretch limousines lined every avenue, and hundreds of uniformed and plainclothes police posted everywhere in sight. Approaching the very door where Jon Jacobs and I had bummed admission tickets twenty-five years earlier, I couldn't suppress my smile while presenting my VIP pass. "Welcome, Assemblyman Rogan," greeted an usher. "Please follow me. You're a guest at the private breakfast preceding the conference."

After the reception, and on the way into the auditorium, I

found myself walking alongside an old pol that I recognized from my youth. Elected the year before I was born, George Christopher, to date San Francisco's last Republican mayor, served two terms (1956 to 1964). He enjoyed another historical footnote: he was the running mate of one future president, and he lost an election to another. In 1962, he ran unsuccessfully for California lieutenant governor on the GOP statewide ticket headed by former Vice President Richard Nixon. Four years later, he ran against political rookie Ronald Reagan for the Republican gubernatorial nomination.[1]

The stocky eighty-eight-year-old ex-mayor displayed a spring in his step as he returned greetings with enthusiasm and warmth to those who recognized him. This surprised me pleasantly, because my previous encounter with Christopher over twenty years earlier was less than ideal. He had been out of office for more than a decade in 1973 when I showed up unannounced at his Folsom Street office and asked his secretary if I could meet him. As a young kid interested in politics, I wanted to question him about his career and the leaders he knew, especially Nixon and Reagan. She made clear her displeasure. "He's not in," she barked, "and even if he were, you'd need an appointment. Do you have one?"

"Well, no, but I'd like one."

"Take this and call back in an hour." She scribbled her phone number on a piece of paper, handed it to me, and then she told me to leave.

When I called back as instructed, she still sounded annoyed when she put my call through to her boss. Christopher's voice

---

1   After dispatching George Christopher in the primary, Ronald Reagan went on to trounce incumbent Governor Pat Brown that November. Over lunch decades later, Brown told me that his 1966 campaign team viewed Christopher as their chief political threat, and that they thought Reagan would be a "pushover." Brown ended his point with a pensive observation. "You know," he told me as he stroked his chin, "That guy [Reagan] has made an entire career out of having us Democrats underestimate the son-of-a-bitch." James Rogan, *And Then I Met...Stories of Growing Up, Meeting Famous People, and Annoying the Hell Out of Them* (Washington: WND Books, 2014), 207-208.

boomed into my telephone earpiece, "Young man, why do you want an appointment with me?" I told him I wanted to talk about his career and get his autograph.

"Can you be here in a few minutes?"

"Sure!"

"Then come now, *so we can get this over with.*" Click.

That didn't sound too inviting.

When I returned, the secretary brought me into Christopher's small wood-paneled office. He shook hands, signed an autograph, and then he said, "Nice to meet you, well, goodbye." Now grasping mentally for some hook to get him talking about his career before he ejected me, I pointed to the bronze Nixon medal I saw on his desk as he pressed his hand into the small of my back and steered me toward the door. "Hey, that's the official 1969 inaugural medal!" I said. "I have one, too. I saved my money and ordered one from the Inaugural Committee. It's in my collection. By the way, Mr. Mayor, you know President Nixon. What can you tell me about him?"

Christopher's hand kept steering. "In 1962 I was Nixon's running mate when he ran for governor. We both lost." A final shove and the door closed behind me.

"No wonder," I grumbled.

At today's U.N. anniversary, Christopher showed none of that earlier impatience. We chatted on the way inside the auditorium. I found him charming so, for old times' sake, I asked him to sign my invitation. He pulled out his pen and wrote his name across the front, and then he handed it back. "You know," he told me, "this might have meant something to someone a long time ago, but not anymore. Those days are long gone."

"That will never be true, Mr. Mayor, to a fourth-generation San Franciscan like me. We all remember you."

"Hey, if he's gonna sign that, then let me sign it, too!" With that, the current mayor, Frank Jordan, took my invitation and penned his signature alongside Christopher's. The two men

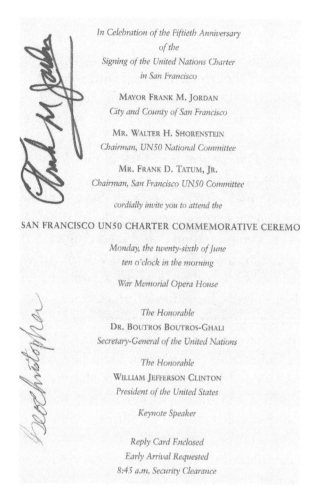

In Celebration of the Fiftieth Anniversary
of the
Signing of the United Nations Charter
in San Francisco

MAYOR FRANK M. JORDAN
City and County of San Francisco

MR. WALTER H. SHORENSTEIN
Chairman, UN50 National Committee

MR. FRANK D. TATUM, JR.
Chairman, San Francisco UN50 Committee

cordially invite you to attend the

SAN FRANCISCO UN50 CHARTER COMMEMORATIVE CEREMO

Monday, the twenty-sixth of June
ten o'clock in the morning

War Memorial Opera House

The Honorable
DR. BOUTROS BOUTROS-GHALI
Secretary-General of the United Nations

The Honorable
WILLIAM JEFFERSON CLINTON
President of the United States

Keynote Speaker

Reply Card Enclosed
Early Arrival Requested
8:45 a.m. Security Clearance

My invitation to the fiftieth anniversary celebration of the U.N., June 26, 1995, autographed by San Francisco Mayors George Christopher and Frank Jordan (Author's collection)

embraced, and then they walked down the aisle together to their seats.

As a side note, the next time I saw Frank Jordan was on the front page of the newspaper five months later, which was just a few days before the voters rejected his reelection bid. A photographer was present during Jordan's radio interview with two local "shock jock" deejays who impulsively challenged the mayor to strip and join them in the shower to sing Frank Sinatra's *My Way* as they soaped and scrubbed each other. Jordan obliged, hoping that the bathroom stunt might lighten his image with voters. The only soft side of Jordan that the photograph memorialized was his flabby white body and man-boobs on display while showering with two naked men. He went down to defeat.

Even in San Francisco, at least back in the 1990s, voters tolerated only so much.

With guests now seated and awaiting the start of the program, the audience broke into spontaneous applause. I didn't know what precipitated the demonstration until I looked upward and saw, in the balcony just overhead, President Bill Clinton arrive. His sunburned face looked beet-red against his gray-white hair. He waved, the house lights dimmed, and the formal ceremony began.

During the processional of the 155 permanent U.N. representatives, I spotted one of my heroes, President Lech Walesa of Poland, seated in the audience. As an electrician and a shipyard labor activist during the 1970s and 1980s, Walesa led the labor movement that eventually helped end the Soviet communist chokehold of his country. Along with Ronald Reagan, British Prime Minister Margaret Thatcher, and Pope John Paul II, Walesa was one of the moral titans that contributed to the toppling of that retched totalitarian empire. Awarded the Nobel Peace Prize in 1983, Walesa won election to Poland's presidency eight years later.

Another person I enjoyed seeing during the program was the emcee, newsman David Brinkley. In the 1960s, I grew up watching NBC's nightly *Huntley-Brinkley Report*. A staple of network news for over forty years, Brinkley displayed his dry wit throughout the ceremony. When he introduced U.S. Ambassador to the U.N. (and future Secretary of State) Madeleine Albright, he commented, "Madeleine Albright was a foreign policy advisor to Adlai Stevenson, Walter Mondale, Michael Dukakis and Bill Clinton." Then, with a smile and a slight bow to Clinton in the presidential box, Brinkley deadpanned, "Three losers and one winner."

Archbishop Desmond Tutu, another Nobel laureate for his work in ending South African apartheid, delivered the invocation. A variety of speakers then took their turn on stage, including U.N. Secretary-General Boutros-Boutros Ghali and poet Maya Angelou. U.S. Secretary of State Warren Christopher told the story of how, as a young Navy ensign stationed in San Francisco, he attended the original 1945 U.N. founding ceremony. "Now, fifty years later," he added, "every American president since Harry Truman has worked with the U.N. to make better the world in every way. No longer are we faced with superpower confrontations." He then introduced Clinton, noting that he was America's first president born after World War II and the founding of the U.N. "President Kennedy's proverbial torch has been passed to his generation," Christopher said.

Clinton recounted the founding of the U.N. in the midst of a world war. "Some of those founders are still with us today," he said, and then he asked the surviving delegates to the 1945 conference to stand. A handful of old men scattered throughout the audience rose to great cheers.

In his prepared remarks, Clinton both praised and chided the United Nations. When he called it at times bloated, wasteful, and often ineffective, I elbowed the guy seated next to me. "He's got that right," I said approvingly. The stranger frowned at me in silence. Oh, well, to each his own. Anyway, just as I contemplated that Clinton and I agreed about the U.N., he doused our budding accord by adding, "Turning our back on the U.N. is no solution. It would be shortsighted and self-destructive. It would strengthen the forces of global disintegration. It would threaten the security, the interests, and the values of the American people.... Today, we face no Hitlers or Stalins, but we do have common enemies—enemies who share a contempt for human life and human dignity and the rule of law."

"We sure do," I commented to the stranger still seated next to me, "and today they're all members of the U.N.'s Human Rights

Council." That comment triggered a fiercer dirty look.

When Clinton finished his speech, an announcer declared the ceremony adjourned and a technician turned up the house lights. When the room illuminated, the recipient of my running U.N. commentary bolted from his chair and hustled toward the exit before I could offer any valedictory remarks.

• • •

With the proceedings concluded, I departed the Opera House and stumbled into a déjà vu vortex. Two young boys, about the age that Jon Jacobs and I were when we planted on that very spot twenty-five years earlier, stood outside holding cameras, pens, and index cards. "Do you see any famous people?" I heard one boy ask the other. I asked what they were doing.

"We came to get autographs and pictures," one replied.

"Did you get inside the ceremony?"

"No, we couldn't get tickets."

"Follow me, boys." I told the doorkeeper that they were my guests and he let them enter. I retrieved for them a couple of leftover official programs and then pointed out for them the remaining dignitaries. "Go get your autographs, have fun, and I'll see you back here in 2020." They thanked me as they ran off to collect their mementos.

No thanks were necessary. I was just paying back the favor done for Jon Jacobs and me by two women wearing bindis a long, long time ago.

• • •

Former San Francisco Mayor George Christopher died at age 92 of natural causes on September 14, 2000.

Boutros Boutros-Ghali served as secretary-general of the U.N. from 1992 to 1996. He died at age 93 on February 16, 2016.

David Brinkley died at age 82 on June 11, 2003 of complications after suffering a fall.

Warren Christopher served as U.S. secretary of State from 1993 to 1997. He died at age 85 of cancer on March 18, 2011.

Poet Maya Angelou died at age 86 of natural causes on May 28, 2014.

Assemblywoman (later Congresswoman) Juanita McDonald, my dear friend with whom I served in both Sacramento and Washington, died of colon cancer at age 68 on April 22, 2007.

• • •

Jon Jacobs and I had planned to attend the seventy-fifth anniversary celebration in San Francisco on June 26, 2020, but a worldwide COVID pandemic caused its cancellation. Not deterred, we've already booked our hotel reservations for the city's U.N. centennial on June 26, 2040.

If you happen to be there on that day, and you encounter two wobbly old men standing outside the front door pleading for your admission ticket, be charitable.

16

El Diablo

During my freshman congressional term, I attended a memorable invitation-only luncheon in the Capitol's wood-paneled Rayburn Room. Ten or so round tables, with twelve people seated at each, dotted the intimate chamber. The guest list placed me at a small table that included the speaker of the House of Representatives, a European prime minister, two Nobel Peace Prize laureates, and the president of the United States.

One would think that any one member of this eminent group would monopolize the moment. Amazingly, none of them held our table's center of attention. They ceded the floor willingly to an elderly senator many years past his prime. Even more remarkably, he outshone the others without trying. It came naturally. Whether one loved or hated him, and millions aligned into both of those camps during his half-century of public life, Senator Edward Kennedy (D-MA) commanded the spotlight of any stage on which he stood.

Penning my memories of the last of Ambassador Joseph P. Kennedy's and Rose Fitzgerald Kennedy's nine children and the youngest brother of two assassinated political legends, President John F. Kennedy and Senator Robert F. Kennedy, leaves me conflicted. As a conservative Republican congressman, I opposed everything that he trumpeted. During his nearly five decades in the Senate, he favored statism and Washington bureaucracies over individual freedom and local control. He showed little regard for the constitutional rights of unborn children or law-abiding gun owners. His character assassination against one of America's great jurists, Robert Bork, has left a lingering stench over every subsequent U.S. Supreme Court confirmation hearing. All of these reasons are insignificant when compared to the night in 1969 when, after leaving an alcohol-fueled party with a young female campaign staffer, he drove his car off a Chappaquiddick bridge and into a deep pond. He freed himself from the wreck, and after trying unsuccessfully to locate her, he left the scene. Then, the unpardonable: he failed to summon the help that might have saved her.[1] Presuming her dead, he returned to his hotel, dried off, tried establishing a fake alibi, and telephoned political cronies to strategize damage control. He waited almost eleven hours before reporting the accident to police. A week later he pleaded guilty to leaving an accident scene and received a wrist-slapping suspended two-month jail sentence.[2]

Chappaquiddick proved the most notorious example in his lengthy string of continuing personal excesses. His drinking and womanizing fed the tabloids for years, but unlike mortal politicians, he never faced any meaningful accountability for these bohemian escapades. Unfazed Massachusetts voters returned him to the Senate repeatedly, while his detractors fumed endlessly over two apparent

---

1   Trapped inside Kennedy's car, Mary Jo Kopechne may have found an air pocket and remained alive for some time before suffocating. Some estimates claim she lived for an hour. See, e.g., The History Channel, *Ted Kennedy's Chappaquiddick Incident: What Really Happened?* September 4, 2018 (accessed September 21, 2019): "Kopechne likely did not die instantaneously, but her final moments remain a mystery. When John Farrar, a diver for the local fire department, found Kopechne's body the morning after the crash, its positioning suggested she had remained alive for an unknown period after the car went underwater. Her face was pressed into the footwell, and her hands gripped the back of the front seat, as if she had been trying to push her head into a pocket of air." Others dispute that she remained conscious for any appreciable amount of time.

2   The former prosecutor in me suspects he delayed reporting to give his blood alcohol level time to dissipate. As a former prosecutor himself, he knew that a traffic fatality caused by a drunk driving U.S. senator was political hemlock: goodbye White House; hello jail.

sets of rules: one for Kennedys, one for everyone else. Republicans despised this Lucifer of the Left who personified unrestrained government and unrestrained bad behavior.

I came to Washington as one of Speaker Newt Gingrich's conservative foot soldiers in the war against Big Government, so there was every reason for me to abhor him politically and personally. And yet—

—I liked Ted Kennedy. There. I said it.

In truth, I couldn't help it. I remained too in awe of the unimaginable sweep of history that he witnessed and represented. The combined forces of heredity and boyhood sentimentality doubtless fed my contradiction. Born into a low-income, all-Roman Catholic and part-Irish family, during the 1960s we venerated the Kennedys. On our living room wall hung two framed pictures: Pope John XXIII and John F. Kennedy, whose 1960 election broke the chain of political bigotry against Irish Catholics. He was our president and our hero.

And then, Dallas. At age six I watched on our black-and-white television a previously unimaginable display of horror and sorrow during that long November 1963 weekend. News coverage of the funeral only compounded the heartbreak: the beautiful young widow, looking both dignified and lost, holding the hands of their two infant children. The three-year old boy saluting his father's flag-draped casket as it rolled past him. The slow procession to Arlington National Cemetery. The lighting of the gravesite's eternal flame. JFK's assassination exposed me to the unrestrained tears of my longshoreman grandfather who had taught me that tears were not an emblem of manly firmness.

JFK's brother Robert, later a U.S. senator, picked up the torch. When he ran for president in 1968, hopes rose again for a restoration of what Lee Harvey Oswald had snuffed so cruelly five years earlier. Then, in another flash of gunfire, Bobby Kennedy's brief campaign ended. Another flag-draped casket. Another widow with small children. Another procession to Arlington. Those not old enough to remember it cannot comprehend living in a decade that opened in such promise and then dragged to a conclusion in repeated, raw grief.

After Bobby's murder, there stood Ted Kennedy, the last brother, the final link to the twice-shattered hopes of millions. No ordinary senator now, upon him fell the uninvited inheritance of romanticized expectations. An aura of inevitability encircled him. The White House was now *his* destiny as long as another lurking potential inevitability, the threat of which hovered over every public appearance, didn't strike first.

Even the 1969 Chappaquiddick tragedy, as bad as it was, didn't seem to preclude this expectation. He won reelection to the Senate easily in 1970, and

Elect ROGAN Delegate

1980 DEMOCRATIC NATIONAL CONVENTION PLEDGED TO SENATOR EDWARD M. KENNEDY

23d CONGRESSIONAL DISTRICT
CAUCUS MAY 4,1980 [1PM]

#100 Moore Hall
UCLA CAMPUS

When I was a UCLA Law School student, I had printed these handmade fliers promoting my candidacy to be one of Ted Kennedy's California delegates to the 1980 Democratic National Convention. Look carefully and you will see the hip beard I sported (and the cigar) back in the days when I paid my way through law school as a bartender on Hollywood's rowdy Sunset Strip (Author's collection)

national polls always showed him as the leading choice for the Democratic presidential nomination in 1968 (post-RFK assassination), 1972, 1976, and 1980. As importantly, these polls also showed that the voters forgave him for Chappaquiddick. With time salving the wound, and after saying no three times, in 1980 he said yes. To *Camelot* sentimentalists, and to a new generation of Kennedy fans, his time had arrived. Finally, America called another Kennedy.

Only America didn't call.

As it turned out, the polls *were* correct: voters did forget about Chappaquiddick, but only until his presidential candidacy gave them a reason to remember it, and then they didn't like what they recalled. Losing the Democratic nomination (along with a long-worn cloak of inevitability), he never again sought the White House. He returned to the Senate and carried the liberal standard for three more decades.

• • •

By the late 1990s, Kennedy was the Senate's third most senior member, but his presidential timber days were long gone. His black hair had turned white. The athletic physique of the 1960s had given way to a paunch draping over his belt buckle. His straining suit coat button always appeared ready to liberate itself into someone's eye. His once angular face had grown puffy, and small broken red blood

Standing under Washington's portrait, Ireland's Prime Minister Bertie Ahern toasts the United States at a St. Patrick's Day luncheon. Among those depicted at the table are President Bill Clinton and Speaker Newt Gingrich; appropriately, Ted Kennedy is at far left and I am at far right. U.S. Capitol, March 17, 1998 (Author's collection)

vessels landscaped his eyes and cheeks, which was a common trait that I noticed on heavy drinkers during my bartending years. And yet, during that Rayburn Room luncheon, none of this mattered to the president, the prime minister, the House speaker, the Nobel laureates, or to me. I saw it in their faces, and they would have seen it in mine had they bothered noticing: *I'm sitting here talking to Ted Kennedy.* His presence at our table opened the door to a time warp that we entered gladly.

Coming from my background, and then serving in Congress with an icon of my youth, the pull proved too intoxicating. I couldn't help it. I liked Ted Kennedy, and at the risk of my right-wing passport's permanent revocation, I'll confess another heretical disqualifier from my future entrance into the eternal gates of Conservative Valhalla:

He liked me.

• • •

On January 14, 1999, a couple of hours after I delivered my two-hour opening statement at the start of the Clinton impeachment trial, I appeared on CNN's *Larry King Live* talk show. King asked what I first thought after stepping to the lectern and facing both the U.S. Senate and a worldwide television audience. I replied that when I looked up from my notes to speak, what I saw made me flinch (I've never watched the video to see if my momentary distraction was apparent to the viewing audience). There sat Ted Kennedy at his desk, arms folded, studying me. It transported me back to a spring morning in 1971 when I cut classes in the eighth grade and waited outside a TV studio, along with two other classmates, to meet him when he arrived for an interview. He shook our hands, signed autographs, and then posed for a picture with us before disappearing into the building. He looked far different then: young—only thirty-eight, trim, and with slicked-down dark hair. On that morning, nobody could have convinced me otherwise: I had just met the future president of the United States. I can't remember a bigger thrill from my boyhood.[3]

During my teens, I saw Kennedy on other occasions when he came to the San Francisco Bay Area. In late 1972, I worked part-time as a stock boy at King Norman's Kingdom of Toys in Oakland's Eastmont Mall. The store's owner (and my boss), King Norman, groused like hell when mall security made him close early on the day Kennedy spoke before an indoor rally in front of the nearby J.C. Penney department store. King Norman let me off work to get a spot close to the stage where Kennedy addressed a huge crowd in support of Democratic presidential nominee George McGovern.

Two years later, Kennedy came to Contra Costa County to campaign for Democratic congressional candidates. I couldn't afford the $7.50 reception ticket, but I learned that his chartered plane would land at Buchanan Field, a small airstrip only a hundred feet from the hotel's back door. I waited behind the cyclone fence and saw Kennedy's little blue Cessna land. He waved to the small crowd standing with me, and then he went into the hotel for the reception. I tried to sneak inside unsuccessfully, so I returned to the fence and joined those waiting to glimpse his departure.

Things had changed at the landing strip during my brief absence. A few minutes before Kennedy returned to his plane, a single-engine yellow Grumman taxied and parked next to the blue Cessna. Two stunning young women wearing revealing and exotic evening gowns exited Kennedy's Cessna and boarded the Grumman. A local Party official standing next to me had helped organize the event. I pointed out to him the two women who looked, shall we say, *overdressed* for a noontime seven-buck-a-person hot dog and beer reception.

"Who are they?" I asked.

---

3   The complete story of my meeting both Ted Kennedy and the 1968 Democratic presidential nominee, former Vice President Hubert H. Humphrey, on that day in 1971 is recounted in my book, *And Then I Met...*, 7-11.

"They're for Teddy," he told me. "For later. You know."
I knew.

• • •

In 1997, shortly after my family and I arrived in Washington, we attended a summer ice cream social held for members of Congress in the courtyard of the Russell Senate Office Building. The day was muggy and hot, so ice cream proved a welcome treat for my five-year-old twin daughters, Dana and Claire. As they stood near the counter enjoying their cones, Kennedy walked up and ordered cones for himself and for a young girl in a wheelchair that he pushed into the reception. He caught sight of my daughters. "Look at these beautiful little girls!" he said, and then he introduced himself to me,

"Look at these beautiful little girls!" Ted Kennedy speaking to my twin daughters Dana and Claire (lower left corner) as I introduced them (my wife Christine retreated from the scene surreptitiously), Rayburn Senate Building courtyard, June 19, 1997 (Author's collection)

as if that were necessary. We struck up a brief conversation about adjusting to D.C.'s whirlwind lifestyle.

My wife Christine slipped away diplomatically from us before I could introduce her. She had no interest in meeting a man she had disliked for decades. When a photographer suggested taking our family's picture with Kennedy, I looked to where she had moved and pleaded with my eyes for her to return and join us. She shook her head and disappeared into the crowd.[4]

• • •

I saw him occasionally during my first term in Congress. He was always friendly, but I was mindful that I was just another in a parade of the hundreds of congressmen and senators that had come and gone during his nearly four decades on Capitol Hill. It wasn't until the Clinton impeachment trial and my prolonged stay in the Senate chamber that I came to know him. Even though he opposed impeachment vigorously, he always listened to my presentations attentively, and sometimes he walked over during breaks to slap me on the back, congratulate me, or tell me that my arguments had impressed him. I think he admired my moxie as the only House Manager from a solidly Democratic district, which made taking on Clinton a near-guaranteed death sentence for me at my next election.

On the last day of the trial, and in my closing argument, an unanticipated bond cemented between us. I told the story of how it happened in my 2011 impeachment memoir, *Catching Our Flag: Behind the Scenes of a Presidential Impeachment*:

> When I finished [drafting and polishing my closing argument], I felt satisfied that it summarized the reasons why I helped impeach Clinton and why this principle was more important than my political survival. If any historian of the future cared to know why I volunteered for this mission, I wanted this speech to be my answer from the grave.

---

4   Stick with the story—Christine will soften later.

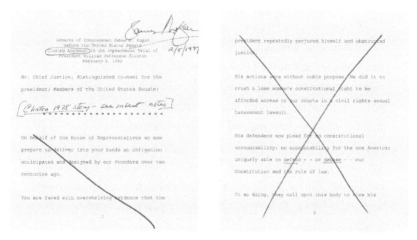

The first two reading copy pages of my intended closing argument in the Clinton impeachment trial, February 8, 1999. A television commentator's overheard claims caused me to "X" out most of my prepared speech moments before its scheduled delivery (Author's collection)

I rushed back to the Senate and arrived as Asa Hutchinson [gave his fifteen-minute closing argument]. This left little time for reflection since the schedule had me following Asa. I wandered into the Marble Room to catch my breath and steel my nerves. The voice of a commentator coming from a nearby television caught my attention: "These House Managers don't care about Bill Clinton the man," he intoned. "They don't care about what impeachment has done to him or to his wife and daughter."

"You son of a bitch," I growled at the television screen. One of our young staffers walked over and turned it off.

"That's just one guy talking," he said, trying to console me.

Maybe so, I replied, but he was saying what millions of Americans thought, and that frustrated the hell out of me. Suddenly, my "answer from the grave" speech no longer appealed to me. Within moments, I had drawn a big black "X" across every page of the first half of my prepared text.

"Congressman," a guard said, "you're up."

When Asa concluded, Chief Justice Rehnquist recognized me. Carrying my now-obliterated speech, I walked to the podium and...extemporize[ed] much of [it].... I now had a focused purpose: addressing the false but pervasive notion that none of us cared about the personal toll of impeachment:

Mr. Chief Justice, distinguished counsel for the President, Members of the Senate: For me, perhaps the most poignant part of this case came on the day former Senator Dale Bumpers addressed us in defense of President Clinton.

The thing that touched me most about his presentation was when he talked about the human element of what this impeachment proceeding has meant. It touched me because it reminded me that this appreciation for the difficulty is not limited solely to Democrats in this chamber. I am a House Manager and a Republican, but that was not always the case. I used to be a Democrat. Being a House Manager in the impeachment of President Clinton has been especially difficult for me, and I would like to tell you why.

Twenty years ago, in December 1978, I was finishing my last semester of college and I had just applied to law school. I was waiting for my application to be accepted somewhere. That month I was a delegate in Memphis to the Democratic National Midterm Convention. At that time, President Carter was halfway through his term and he was not very popular with the Party faithful. In Memphis among the delegates that year was a great deal of sentiment that a current member of this body should challenge Carter for renomination.

When I spoke those words, I looked to the rear of the chamber at Senator Edward Kennedy (D-MA), who leaned back in his chair smiling and nodding at me. He was perhaps the only person in America who knew where I was going with this story.

The delegates to that convention had an overwhelming desire to see Senator Ted Kennedy run for the presidential nomination. In retribution for his popularity, the Carter White House froze out Senator Kennedy from all the proceedings. He was not invited to address the convention and his name appeared nowhere in the program, so the delegates did something on their own. At the scheduled policy workshop on health care, the delegates invited Senator Kennedy to fly out that day and address them. He came that afternoon and left Memphis as soon as he finished speaking.

I had gone to a workshop earlier that morning where President Carter appeared personally. Only 200 or so people came to hear him. In contrast, Senator Kennedy's workshop had to move to a larger auditorium because over 2,000 people came to hear him.

Kennedy kept nodding his head and continued grinning. His smile grew when I said he outdrew President Carter's audience ten-to-one.

As I said, Senator Kennedy came, he spoke, and then he left. However, I stayed even though most people left when Senator Kennedy did. I stayed because I wanted to meet the young fellow moderating the program. He fascinated me. He was bright, articulate, and in control. He didn't look much older than I, and here he was already the attorney general of his state, and now the governor-elect.

After that workshop, I walked up to the moderator and introduced myself. He spent the next fifteen minutes encouraging me to go to law school and stay active in politics.

His name was Bill Clinton.

I never have forgotten that day twenty years ago when then-Attorney General Clinton took time for a young fellow with an interest in the law and politics. And I have never forgotten in recent years the graciousness he has shown my wife, my children, and me when we have encountered him.

This has been a very difficult proceeding for me and for my colleagues. Our presence here isn't out of personal animosity toward our president. It is because we believe that, after reviewing all the evidence, the president of the United States obstructed justice and committed perjury. He has violated his oath of office; in so doing, he sacrificed the principle that no person is above the law. Personal considerations cannot control under those circumstances.[5]

With my extemporaneous story completed, I concluded what remained of my prepared remarks. After Chief Justice Rehnquist adjourned the proceedings, Kennedy bounded down the aisle and pumped my hand with enthusiasm as he gushed about the great job I did. He put his arm around my shoulder and led me to an unoccupied corner of the chamber. "You know," he told me, "I remember that convention well, and I remember how Carter and his people treated me. Bill Clinton has told me that workshop story at least a dozen times since he became president, and he tells everyone that it was the first time he and I ever met. Whenever he tells it, I always say I remember him very well. The truth is that I remember the convention and the workshop, but I have no recollection of meeting Clinton that day when he moderated the panel. Since he has told the story with great relish so often, I don't have the heart to tell him."

"Your secret is safe with me, at least until I write my memoirs," I told him.

Kennedy laughed. "Fair enough!"

I handed him a manila envelope. "I've been carrying this into the chamber every day of the trial to show you. This is the first chance I've had. You might get a chuckle from it." Kennedy opened it and removed the eight-by-ten color photograph taken of us in 1971 when my junior high buddies and I cut classes to meet him. Kennedy's face registered surprise when he saw it.

"Are you kidding?" he asked. "This is really you? I'll be damned!

---

5   James Rogan, *Catching Our Flag*, 392-395.

"What the hell happened to you?" With my buddies (from left) Dan Swanson and Roger Mahan, Senator Ted Kennedy, and your correspondent, San Francisco, May 16, 1971 (Author's collection)

What campaign was this from?"

"No campaign. You came to town and I wanted to meet one of my political heroes. This photo has been hanging in my office for decades, and it hangs there now."

"You'd better take it down or you'll get primaried next year!"

Kennedy led me around the chamber as he showed the photo

to every remaining senator. Phil Gramm (R-TX) studied it carefully. "This is you and Rogan?" he asked in mock seriousness. "Well, Rogan hasn't changed much, but Ted, what the hell happened to you?!"

After he ran out of senators to whom he could show the photo, we sat in an alcove and continued our conversation. "I just can't believe we met way back when, and now here we are in this impeachment trial," he told me as he returned the photo. "Will you get me a copy of this? I want to show everyone on my staff." (I delivered a copy the next day.)

He questioned me about my family, where I grew up and went to school, and how I got to Congress. He appeared intrigued to learn that I was the illegitimate son of a single mother who was a convicted felon and who later raised her four children on welfare and food stamps. When I told him that my high school expelled me, I went to work in my early teens, and later I bartended my way through law school working on Hollywood's Sunset Strip, he shook his head in amazement. "I just can't comprehend how tough that must have been," he said, and then he grew pensive: "I wish my own children, nieces, and nephews could hear this story. They don't know what it's like to have to fight for things like this."

Before we parted for the evening, he insisted that I bring my wife and daughters to visit with him. "I've met your daughters, the twin girls, right? But have I ever met your wife?"

"Uh, no." I didn't tell him about her disappearing act at last year's ice cream social. I promised to bring everyone over to meet him, but as I made that pledge I contemplated silently how many glasses of wine I'd have to pour into Christine before I could coax her into meeting *El Diablo*.

• • •

Five days after the Clinton impeachment trial ended, I boarded my regular early morning direct flight from Washington to Los Angeles on American Airlines #77 out of Dulles Airport. I took my usual coach seat, opened my briefcase, and started poring through the thick stack of briefing materials that I always saved for cross-country flights. Soon after takeoff a flight attendant that I knew handed me a new boarding pass. "We have an open seat in first class, Congressman Rogan. We've just moved you there."

"Really? Are you sure?"

"I'm sure," she replied. "You have more fans on this crew than you know." She led me to an empty aisle seat in the forward cabin.

To reach my upgraded surroundings I had to step through the trash pile gathered around the feet and ankles of the man in the seat across the aisle from my new one. He held his newspaper opened and in front of his face, and he appeared oblivious to his clutter that had metastasized into the walkway.

I settled into my plush seat and didn't look up from my briefing papers for the next few hours while trying to ignore the frequent distractions of the messy guy crumpling and tossing more papers on the cabin floor. Whenever the rubbish around his feet leeched too far into the aisle, a crewmember appeared and collected the litter.

Halfway across the country, and while still absorbed in my work, a cabin attendant wheeled out the beverage cart. As she parked it next to me, I heard a slight crash. "Oh, shit!" yelled the untidy fellow.

"I'm so sorry!" exclaimed the attendant. She handed him stacks of napkins to blot the full glass of orange juice that she had just spilled on his lap. He raised his bulky frame out of the chair and hustled unhappily to the restroom while the woman in the seat next to him grabbed fistfuls of crumpled newspaper from the floor and wiped his seat. When he returned a few minutes later, his entire lap and rear pants seat bore huge wet stains. The attendant proffered more apologies as he plopped back into his chair.

I waited until he finished grumbling about the mishap to his seatmate, and then I leaned over and asked him, "So, have you seen any good impeachment trials lately?" Ted Kennedy looked back, recognized me, and then we both laughed. We had sat together for three hours, yet we were so engrossed in our respective work that we hadn't noticed each other.

He asked if I was heading home for the weekend. Yes, I told him, but without my family. This was a working weekend in my district for me. "What about you?" I asked. "Will you get any R&R in California?"

"Nah," he said, and then he rubbed his thumb and forefinger together, indicating it was a fundraising trip. "I'm gearing up again." Although he had not announced his intentions formally, he told me that he planned to run for another term next year. He expected the Republicans to field "another Mitt Romney-type against me, so I need to get my campaign bank account into shape."[6] He told me his Massachusetts Senate race would cost him up to $5 million.

"That's chickenfeed. My *House* race will cost twice that much." (It did.)

He warned me to guard against the strains of a congressional job on family life, especially with young children at home. "When I first went to the Senate, I tried to have my wife bring the kids to the Capitol most evenings for dinner. We used to have picnics or play soccer on the grass outside the Senate. I also brought the kids with me on campaign trips or to evening events so that we could spend more time together. Make sure you take time for your family, trust me on this one." He renewed his invitation to bring my family over for a visit.

Ignoring the nagging cough that plagued him, he seemed content to sit back and talk during the remainder of the flight. Of course, I had many questions for one of the most powerful men ever to serve in the Senate:

6   In his 1994 reelection race, Kennedy faced multimillionaire businessman Mitt Romney (later Massachusetts governor, presidential candidate, and U.S. senator from Utah). Although 1994 proved to be a difficult year for Democrats nationwide, and throughout most of the Kennedy-Romney campaign polls showed the race very close, by Election Day, Kennedy pulled ahead and won a comfortable 58 to 41 percent victory.

- On running for the presidency generally:

"It really is a four-year commitment. After the 1956 Democratic National Convention [when JFK made a last-minute and unsuccessful bid for the vice presidential nomination], my brother Jack ran full throttle for four years. He went everywhere and spoke to every group, large and small. He never stopped running for that four-year period, and that was before the days of dozens of presidential primaries. Back then, there were only a few primaries."

- On his first Senate race in 1962:

"I ran for Jack's old seat against the heirs of two other long-standing Massachusetts political families: Eddie McCormack and George Lodge. Jack beat George's father for the Senate in 1952, and George's great-grandfather beat my grandfather for that same Senate seat in the early 1900s. After I won the election, Eddie, George, and I became good friends, and I became especially close to Eddie. When he died last year, I was the main speaker at his funeral."

- On his previous offers of the Democratic vice presidential nomination:

I said that I recalled in 1976, as former Governor Jimmy Carter's campaign for the presidential nomination picked up steam, Party regulars pleaded with former Vice President Hubert H. Humphrey (the 1968 Democratic presidential nominee) to enter the primaries and challenge him. News reports teased that Kennedy had said privately that he would accept the second spot, but only if the Democrats nominated Humphrey. National Democrats grew ecstatic over a possible Humphrey-Kennedy combination. I asked if he would have really run with Humphrey had HHH entered and won the nomination. He shook his head. "No, I never wanted that job. I was offered it twice: Hubert offered it to me in 1968, and George McGovern offered it in 1972. I turned them both down."

"You only get bragging rights on turning down Humphrey in '68. Turning down McGovern in '72 doesn't count. He asked everyone to be his running mate."

"Okay," he conceded. "Let me rephrase. I was asked once in 1968, and I was begged once in 1972!"

• On a peculiar piece of political memorabilia in my collection: I asked about a 1958 Massachusetts campaign brochure. It touted Foster Furcolo for governor, John F. Kennedy for U.S. Senate, and John F. Kennedy for treasurer. "Did Jack run for both offices? Was the treasurer slot some sort of Party or honorary office?"

"Hell, I forgot all about that guy!" he said. "That was a different John F. Kennedy. This other guy with the same name as my brother ran for treasurer that year to capitalize on Jack's name. When the voters found out they thought it was cute, but only to a degree. They were amused when he ran for treasurer, but when he ran for lieutenant governor later it stopped being funny, so they dumped him."

"Since you're a history buff," he told me, "you need to visit my favorite room in Washington if you haven't already: the Old Caucus Room in the Russell Senate Office Building." When I told him that I had walked over to Russell one day just to look in there, he nodded. "There is so much history in that room. That's where the Senate held their Teapot Dome hearings from the Harding Administration scandals.[7] Senator Sam Ervin held

---

7   During the Harding Administration, Interior Secretary Albert Fall had approved oil leases at the Naval Oil Reserve No. 3 located in Teapot Dome, Wyoming. The leases went to friends at low rates and without competitive bidding. The Senate investigated the scandal, and Fall went to prison for accepting bribes, becoming the first cabinet member sentenced to a penitentiary. "In the days before Watergate, one historian called [Teapot Dome] 'the greatest and most sensational scandal in the history of American politics.'" Robert W. Cherny, *Graft and Oil: How Teapot Dome Became the Greatest Political Scandal of its Time.* History Now: American History Online, http://www.gilderlehrman.org/historynow/historian5.php (accessed September 29, 2019).

the Watergate hearings there in the '70s. It's also where Jack announced his presidential candidacy in 1960. So did Bobby in 1968. He announced in that same room...." His voice trailed off.

While we talked and he reminisced, the same flight attendant who spilled the orange juice earlier brought her cart down the aisle again. Unbelievably, she spilled another glass of orange juice on the man seated in front of me. "Oh, I'm so sorry," she told her latest victim as she reached for the now dwindling napkin stack. Kennedy's laughter exploded through the cabin as he pointed to me.

"Okay, Rogan, you're next!"

"Oh, no I'm not, Ted. I can guarantee it."

"What makes you so sure?"

"She's a Republican!"

"That explains it! A conspiracy! Now I know why I'm gonna smell like a goddamn orange all day."

As we began our initial descent into LAX, his aide handed him several snapshots depicting him with admirers and asked that he sign them. He lowered his tray and used it as a desk while scrawling inscriptions onto each. When he finished, he told his aide about our 1971 picture. "I wish I could show it to you," he told her. "What a great photo."

"Here you go," I said as I retrieved it from my briefcase. I had put it there earlier and had forgotten to remove it. She studied it carefully, and then she held it up to compare us then and now.

"Don't say another word!" he admonished her while laughing at his own joke.

I asked him if the autograph on my photo was genuine or whether a secretary had done the signing duty for him long ago. He scrutinized it. "It sure looks like my writing," he said. "I used to carry boxes of photos on planes and into committee meetings. I'd spend hours signing them for people. I don't like to do it anymore. I'm about six months behind on these requests. Everyone from visitors to interns wants them. It's too damned much work for me nowadays. It slows things down when I have to pose for pictures with people and then sign all of them."

"But I see you're still doing it."

"Well, people like getting them, I suppose." Ironically, at that moment two passengers from coach came forward and interrupted. "Excuse us, Senator Kennedy, but we're huge fans. When we land, may we take a picture with you? It would mean so much to us!"

"Sure. I'll wait for you at the gate."

"And ladies," I added, "after you get the picture developed, be sure to send it to him. He loves autographing them!"

When we landed, I helped him on with his too-tight coat and offered him a ride, but he had a driver waiting to take him to his hotel. As we parted outside the airport, he reminded me, "Don't forget to bring your wife and daughters for a visit. I'm looking forward to seeing them."

"I don't know if I should. They might want a signed picture, and that will set you back six months and six seconds."

• • •

Before I leave the story of my plane ride with Ted Kennedy, I must share a final vignette from the experience. During my in-flight discussion with him, the flight attendant who had upgraded me earlier to first class brought me a request: "Congressman, I hate to bother you, but our captain is a big admirer of yours. He doesn't want to disturb you, but he was wondering if he could come out and say hello."

"Of course, I'd be honored."

A few moments later, a tall, handsome man with a gleaming smile approached and shook my hand. If ever someone looked as though Central Casting had assigned him to portray a dashing pilot, it was Charles "Chic" Burlingame. After introducing himself, he told me, "I'm a huge fan of yours from impeachment. I watched as much of it as I could when it was on television. I can't tell you how proud I was of you and the other House Managers. I was graduated from the Naval Academy and I later flew fighter jets, so serving my country means an awful lot. You guys served your country." As the captain kept lavishing praise upon me, he appeared oblivious to my distinguished colleague's presence. I waited for him to take a breath so that I could introduce them, but the captain never noticed him and continued his monologue:

"It made me very proud to see you standing up for the flag that I fought to defend, *not like those cowardly bastards in the Senate.*"

My face twitched. "Oh, no," I thought, "he doesn't see who's seated across from me! I need to alert him!" I tried interrupting and signaling Ted's presence, but he persisted unabated: "Those senators disgusted me. They turned their backs on the rule of law and on the Constitution." By now, it was too late to mitigate the damage, so I let the captain finish his speech. When he concluded, I smiled and used my hand to direct his attention to my right:

"Captain Burlingame, allow me to introduce you to my colleague, Senator Edward Kennedy."

The captain looked at Kennedy, gave him a dismissive head nod, and replied, "Oh yeah, hi." He then turned back to me. "Anyway, Congressman as I was saying, you guys were the heroes...." Ted returned to his pile of work and didn't look up again until Captain Burlingame repaired to the cockpit.

• • •

After the impeachment trial ended, I never followed up on Kennedy's twice-offered invitation to bring my family for a visit. I wanted very much to go, but I didn't want to attach to his busy schedule a nuisance obligation likely made in polite haste.

Later that year, I obtained a rare 1952 Congressman John F. Kennedy for U.S. Senate campaign flyer. As much as I wanted to keep it for my political memorabilia collection, I thought Ted would appreciate it. I had it framed and delivered to his office. The next day a letter arrived thanking me for the gift, along with yet another offer to bring my family for a visit. Before I could respond, he followed up with a call and asked that we put a date on the calendar—now.

• • •

For our visit with Kennedy, we agreed to meet his aide in the Senate Reception Room. From there she would escort us to his private "hideaway office," a secluded sanctuary hidden behind unmarked and locked doors. These hideaways are the coveted havens reserved for only the most senior senators. Unlike the cramped, pantry-sized quarters available for mid-level seniority, the elders treasure these accommodations for their luxurious views and their proximity to the Senate chamber.[8]

We arrived at the Reception Room just as the Senate adjourned for the day. A number of departing senators came over to meet Christine and my daughters, including Orrin Hatch (R-UT), a friend who had embarked upon a longshot quest for the 2000 Republican presidential nomination. As we shook hands I teased, "Orrin, aren't you president yet?"

"No," he replied, "because I don't have your endorsement." I asked how the Senate's voting schedule impacted his ability to campaign nationally. He complained that the prolonged sessions kept him from visiting key states like Iowa and New Hampshire. Then he lambasted his colleague and fellow GOP contender John McCain (R-AZ) for missing important votes regularly to campaign. "What really burns me up about McCain is that he loves to run down the institution and all of us. He builds himself up at our

---

8   After Kennedy died, a scramble ensured among the Senate's higher-ups to see who would inherit his hideaway office. See, e.g., Alexander Bolton, *Hatch Wins Kennedy's Hideaway*, The Hill, June 21, 2011, https://thehill.com/homenews/senate/167481-hatch-wins-kennedys-hideaway (accessed September 26, 2019).

expense, and then he skips votes to campaign. A few of these votes have been really critical. It's not right and I think it'll come back to haunt him."[9]

Kennedy's assistant arrived and took us to the Capitol's third floor, through the Senate Press Gallery, and down a maze of hallways. As I rounded the final corner, I saw Kennedy standing in front of his hideaway waiting for us. He laughed as he shook my hand, bellowing, "I got all the way up here and realized I forgot my goddamned key!" Just as he blurted out *goddamned*, my seven-year-old twin girls rounded the corner and rushed toward us. Seeing them, he tried choking back the last portion of that sentence.

"Don't worry, senator," Christine told him. "They hear that every time someone cuts off their dad when he drives on the freeway."

When I reintroduced him to the girls, Claire's gaze, which was level with his belt, fixed on his girth. Then she looked up at him, smiled broadly, and took her finger and poked him a couple of times in the tummy. "Mister," she cackled, "you look like a big bear!" Christine gasped and I looked away in embarrassment, but Ted threw back his head and howled.

"I'll bet I do!" he said as he knelt and hugged the girls, both of whom threw their arms around the man they thereafter called "Bear."

"Adorable little girls," he said to Christine, and then the grandfather in him appeared. He took the twins by the hand. "Come on, Dana. Come on Claire. Follow me in here! I have a treat for you." He opened the door to his suite. With coved archways, an antique marble fireplace, white built-in bookcases that popped against the dark green walls and carpet, and comfortable chairs throughout, it had

---

9   Missing votes didn't haunt John McCain as Orrin Hatch predicted. Two months later, Hatch finished last among GOP contenders in the Iowa caucus and dropped out of the race. McCain won seven primaries that year, including New Hampshire, before losing the nomination to Texas Governor George W. Bush. McCain went on to win the presidential nomination in 2008, only to lose the White House to Senator Barack Obama.

a cozy, Early American charm. He led the girls to the large window that opened upon the Capitol's West Front that displayed a splendid panorama of the Washington Monument, the Lincoln Memorial, and the Reflecting Pool. "Come and look at this, girls," he said. "It's the best view in Washington." He told us that former Senator Charles 'Mac' Mathias had quartered in this office for years. "I came and visited him here once. When I saw this view, I vowed this office would be mine one day if I stuck around long enough to get seniority."

Still holding Dana and Claire by the hand, he gave us a tour of his office mementos. A wooden coffee table with a moon-shaped crescent cut out on the side fascinated Dana. She asked him if a shark had chomped down on it. No, he said, the table had been fashioned from a boat he once owned. One day, through his own negligence, he hit something that caused the propeller to blow off. It cut through the hull and left the large gouge. His children took that section of ruined hull and made a coffee table out of it for him as a reminder of his nautical close call. On the mantel and walls were displayed vintage photographs and paintings. An unfinished portrait of his elder brother Joe, killed in action during World War II, hung next to an old photograph of Ted as a little boy looking over his father's shoulder while Ambassador Kennedy read to him. Throughout the room were framed pictures of his late brothers Jack and Bobby, both in youth and adulthood, along with contemporary family photographs. A 1960 *Time* magazine cover featuring President-Elect Kennedy rested on his desk. Displayed on a nearby bookcase was the framed JFK for Senate brochure I had given him.

He led us to his fireplace and gave us a history lesson about it: "This fireplace connects two floors below to the fireplace in the office of the Senate Majority Leader. It was in that fireplace now used by Senator Trent Lott that British soldiers lit the torches that they used to burn the White House and the Capitol during the War of 1812." A natural storyteller, he enraptured my daughters with his vivid description of First Lady Dolly Madison fleeing the

White House with Gilbert Stuart's rolled-up painting of George Washington under her arm; a half hour later, the British soldiers occupied the White House and sat at her dinner table. They ate the venison and drank the wine that she had abandoned when she fled, and then they set fire to the building as they left.

He gave the girls a Coca-Cola, and then he and I examined campaign buttons. Earlier I had offered to bring over my extensive collection of Kennedy political memorabilia and told him that he could look through it and take any items that he might want for the Kennedy Library. "Oh, no," he had said, "I couldn't take any, but I would love to see them. *Please* bring them when you come."

We sat together in adjoining chairs as he reviewed each of the stacked glass-covered display cases. The first contained items from President Kennedy's 1960 race. He spent several minutes studying every item, muttering to himself: "Ah, I remember this one... Oh, my, it seems like just yesterday that I saw this. . . And look at that one...." A delegate's badge from the 1960 Democratic National Convention brought a smile, but the smile faded when he examined another case holding items issued for JFK's anticipated 1964 reelection campaign. "These were before Dallas," he whispered as if speaking to himself.

The grin returned later when he pointed to a matchbook bearing the likenesses of JFK and his running mate, Senator Lyndon B. Johnson. "Look at that, old Lyndon!" he chuckled. I asked about his relationship with LBJ. "Actually, I always got along with him," he said. "I liked Lyndon and he treated me well. He and my brother Bobby didn't like each other, so I always felt that Lyndon bent over backwards to be nice to me. I had to be careful with him because I knew he was trying to use me as a wedge between himself and Bobby.

"I remember once when he was president, he wanted a railroad bill to sail through Congress without any hearings, so he called all of us on the Labor Committee and others down to the White House. There we sat with some of the congressional titans, guys like Wayne

Morse [D-OR]. After playing it up with us, he said, 'Now fellahs, I need that railroad bill as quickly as possible. Why don't you boys just waive your hearings on the bill, get it passed, and send it to me at the White House? What about it, Wayne? Can you do that for me, Wayne?' And Wayne Morse, who was never any president's pushover, just rolled over and said, 'Well, Mr. President, I think we can do that. Don't you think so, boys?' And everyone nodded their heads in agreement. Imagine that! A president telling Congress to waive hearings and not do its job!

"Bobby leaned over and whispered to me, 'Ask for one day of hearings.' I took Bobby's cue and asked for the single day. The leadership said that was the least they could do to protect the congressional prerogative. Lyndon frowned. That one day of hearings stretched on, and the bill never did get to Lyndon's desk."

Claire took an interest in the colorful cases of red, white, and blue memorabilia, so she cozied next to Ted and looked along. She passed cases to him while he stroked her hair and pointed out to her various campaign buttons from his brother Bobby's 1968 presidential campaign. As his gaze focused on the upper row of one particular case, a blue felt pennant depicting Bobby in the lower corner caught Claire's attention. She struggled trying to sound out phonetically the large word emblazoned across it: "*Deestah—Deestah—*"

Growing frustrated, Claire asked, "Will you read me this word, Bear? It's too hard."

"Sure, sweetheart," he told her. He and I looked down to the word on the pennant where she pointed.

Claire had a cold and a runny nose that day, so when I saw drops of water start hitting the glass, I pulled out my handkerchief for her. I looked over and saw that her nose was dry as she reached up and put her arm around Ted's neck. I glanced back at him—stunned. The droplets hitting the glass had rolled down *his* cheeks. He pulled Claire closer to his side and helped her decipher the big word that precipitated the moment:

"Claire, dear," he said softly, "it says *Destined to be President.*"

"Bear, it's all right," she told him sweetly. "Don't cry. I'm here."

More than three decades after Bobby's assassination, the pain returned afresh. As Ted dried his eyes, Christine and I looked at each other and teared up watching our little girl comforting him over the sight of an old felt pennant.

His mood lightened when he examined several cases of buttons from his unsuccessful 1980 presi-

Ted Kennedy and my daughter Claire examining cases of campaign buttons from my collection. At the bottom of the photo can be seen the *Destined to Become President* pennant that he had not yet viewed. Senator Kennedy's Capitol hideaway office, November 10, 1999 (Author's collection)

dential campaign. He pointed to a large six-inch badge from that year's Democratic National Convention bearing the legend, *Kennedy in '80 For a Better Tomorrow.* "I remember these well," he said, "but *tomorrow* never quite came!" Then he tapped his finger over a badge bearing a cartoon likeness of him and President Carter and emblazoned by Carter's famous taunt, *If Kennedy Runs, I'll Whip His Ass.*

"And I remember that, too!" he laughed.[10]

"Here's one that I didn't put in the case," I told him. "I thought

---

10   When Kennedy contemplated challenging Jimmy Carter for renomination in 1980, Carter said publicly, "If Kennedy runs, I'll whip his ass." He repeated the phrase twice, and one of his staffers called reporters to encourage them to report it. The comment made headlines, but it did nothing to intimidate Kennedy from making the race.

you might like to examine it more closely." I handed him a 1903 celluloid badge with a brass rosette encircling the edge. It read *For Mayor, John F. Fitzgerald*. He studied it carefully, and then he grinned.

"You've even got Grandpa, old *Honey Fitz!*"[11] He showed us an oil painting of Honey Fitz hanging opposite his fireplace. "This has been in my family forever," he said. "He was quite a guy. I grew very close to him when I was a boy, especially since all my older siblings were away at school. He used to take me all over Boston on day trips and introduce me to his old cronies. I remember the day my Dad introduced me to Babe Ruth when I was a kid. I couldn't

Unbelievable—this Rogan family photo depicts Christine with her arm around *El Diablo*—and smiling! Senator Kennedy's Capitol hideaway office, November 10, 1999 (Author's collection)

11 John F. "Honey Fitz" Fitzgerald (1863-1950), father of Rose Fitzgerald Kennedy and grandfather to John, Robert, and Ted Kennedy. A former congressman, Honey Fitz served two terms as Boston mayor (1906-1908; 1910-1914).

wait to tell Grandpa later, because he spoke often about cheering for the Babe when he played for the Boston Red Sox."

"What was it like meeting Babe?"

"I was so tongue-tied that I didn't know what to say. I was never so overwhelmed at meeting anyone as when I was a young boy and met Babe Ruth."

"That's like an eighth-grade kid I knew who took the bus to San Francisco in 1971 and got his favorite Massachusetts senator's autograph. He was so tongue-tied at meeting him that he didn't know what to say."

"There's no comparison," he laughed. "That senator didn't smack 714 home runs!"

"No, but he played in the Big Leagues, and for a hell of a lot longer than the Babe."

• • •

The last time I saw Ted Kennedy was at George W. Bush's presidential inauguration on January 20, 2001. The Clinton regime was exiting as the GOP reclaimed the White House after an eight-year absence. The West Capitol steps filled with jubilant Republicans and glum-faced Democrats. My status as a former congressman admitted me onto the presidential platform where I waited with the assembled dignitaries for the start of the ceremony. When the senators joined us, Ted Kennedy was among them. His face looked pasty-white against his black fedora and raincoat. Later, when Bush rose to take the oath, I glanced over and noticed that Ted was not watching the investiture. His head hung low and he appeared to fight back tears. He took a deep breath, and then he looked up and watched the final moments of Bush's induction into office.

After the ceremony ended, I ran into Ted in the rotunda. He asked how my family and I were doing post-election loss. We were fine, I said, and then I grasped his arm. "When Bush raised his hand at noon," I told him, "I knew what that particular moment meant to

To Congressman Jim Rogan - thanks for showing me the wonderful collection of JFK buttons - They brought back warm memories - Best Regards E. P. Kennedy 99

With Ted Kennedy in his office, November 10, 1999 (Author's collection)

you on this anniversary. I was thinking about you and your family."

"Thanks, Jim." Placing his hand on my shoulder, he told me, "Of all the people here, you'd be the one guy who'd understood. Sometimes it seems like just yesterday, but today it seemed like an eternity ago. I guess I'm just getting too damn old."

At the time Bush took the oath that noon, it was the fortieth anniversary, to the minute, of the day a young president-elect raised his hand on the Capitol steps and then challenged his fellow Americans to ask what they could do for their country.

Before we parted, he told me that he had attended a Kennedy Library reception in Boston about a year earlier, and something happened there that made him think of me. "I was talking with a couple of young legislators about your age," he related. "They gushed with praise for my brothers and me. They told me that Jack, Bobby, and

I had motivated them to study government and to enter public life. They said that we had been their inspirations growing up, and they wanted to thank me."

"Of course," one of them told me, "we're both Republicans now!"

• • •

Edward Kennedy served in the United States Senate from 1962 until his death from brain cancer at age 77 on August 25, 2009.

I became friends with Captain Chic Burlingame, the pilot who left the cockpit to come out and praise me during my flight with Ted Kennedy. Over the next two-and-a-half years, I flew scores of times aboard AA #77 with Chic and his crew. Whenever I was aboard, he always left the controls to visit. The last time we flew together, he and I both arrived at Gate D-26 (the gate from which that flight always departed) early, so we walked over to the nearby Starbucks for coffee. We sat and reminisced about that Kennedy flight, and we laughed over Ted's red-faced reaction to Chic's uninhibited opinion of both impeachment and the Senate.

About a week later, Chic captained the same flight, American Airlines #77 leaving Dulles from Gate D-26. Soon after takeoff, terrorists stormed the cockpit and hijacked the plane. They took over the controls and crashed the jet into the Pentagon, killing all sixty-four people aboard, as well as 125 people inside the building.

The date of Chic Burlingame's last flight was September 11, 2001.

17

Hail to the Chief

When President John F. Kennedy craved a roast beef sandwich, he dispatched a White House messenger to The Monocle. Originally built as adjoining downtown Washington row houses in the 1880s, it opened as a restaurant in 1960 and became an immediate favorite of lawmakers and lobbyists because of its proximity to the Capitol.

I arrived there for lunch on a warm spring day in 1999. The maître d' with a photographic memory for congressional faces, Nick Selimos, knew my name even though we had never met. As he led me to a reserved back corner booth, I passed many tables filled with men in tailored suits and Italian shoes huddled with chairmen of powerful congressional committees, senior lawmakers, and visiting state governors. My presence drew scant attention from these clusters of power-lunch diners.

A few minutes later, another patron arrived. He resembled none of the fashionable lobbyists or blow-dried politicians saturating the dining room. The tall man wore tan corduroy pants and matching Hush Puppies (the shoes I wore in fourth grade), a red plaid zip-up jacket resembling the kind worn by hunters camouflaged in the duck blind, and a brown Gatsby-style newsboy's cap. As Nick escorted this fashion eyesore to his booth, table conversations ceased and every pair of eyes in the room tracked his destination. It wasn't his "I'm busy cleaning the garage" ensemble drawing all this high-voltage attention. The patrons knew him by sight, and in a town where people evaluate each other's influence by their restaurant companions, they wanted to see with whom he dined.

He dined with me. My lunch date was the Chief Justice of the United States.

I never met William H. Rehnquist before I came to Washington, and I only saw him from a distance on ceremonial occasions until our paths crossed during President Clinton's impeachment. Under the Constitution, the chief justice presides over a presidential impeachment trial held in the U.S. Senate, with each senator acting as a juror. Rehnquist became only the second chief justice in American history to do so, and it was out of this mutual experience that he and I met for lunch. Before I tell that story, I'll share the background leading up to it.

• • •

Born in 1924, as a young Republican lawyer Rehnquist worked at a Phoenix law firm where one of his partners, Dean Kitchell, managed Barry Goldwater's unsuccessful 1964 presidential campaign. Kitchell recruited Rehnquist's help on that race, and four years later Rehnquist signed on to Richard Nixon's presidential campaign. After Nixon's win, Rehnquist accepted a senior Justice Department position in the new administration. In 1971, Nixon nominated the forty-seven-year-old with no judicial experience to a vacancy on the United States Supreme Court. The U.S. Senate confirmed him later that year as an associate justice, and again in 1986 after President Reagan nominated him to the vacant chief justice position.

• • •

On January 14, 1999, the opening day of the Clinton impeachment trial, tension was high. Aside from the rancor and partisan division engendered by a presidential impeachment, America had not experienced one of these spectacles in over 130 years. We prosecutors felt like we were diving headfirst into a constitutional and political black hole.

House Judiciary Committee Chairman Henry Hyde told me that he wanted his prosecution team (known as the "House Managers") in the U.S. Senate chamber at 12:30 p.m. (half an hour before the impeachment trial started). He said that Chief Justice Rehnquist wanted to meet the managers at 12:45 p.m. in the President's Room, which was his temporary chambers during the trial and just off the Senate floor. When I asked Henry about the meeting's purpose, he said that the chief wanted to shake our hands and address us with words of wisdom before the trial.

"Did he say why?" I asked.

"Rehnquist wrote a book about President Andrew Johnson's 1868 impeachment, and in his research he learned that Chief Justice Salmon P. Chase did this with both the House Managers and Johnson's defense lawyers just before the start of the trial. He wants to follow the precedent. I guess he also wants to impress on all of us the gravity of this solemn constitutional process."

"Okay. I'll round up everyone."

"Listen," Henry warned, "the chief is a stickler for tradition, and he is also a stickler for promptness, so tell all the boys to be on time."

At the appointed hour, the thirteen House Managers showed up outside the President's Room as directed. Henry studied us with a quizzical expression and then he shook his head: "No, no, no! This won't do! Get in seniority order!" We looked like an unrehearsed chorus line trying to remember a complicated dance step as we figured out who needed to stand where. Finally, with Henry's sense of protocol satisfied, Senate Sergeant-at-Arms Jim Ziglar opened Rehnquist's door and announced us. We entered single file.

Until this moment, I had never been inside the President's Room, which Capitol tour brochures identify as the building's most ornate room. Living up to its reputation, it resembled a miniature Versailles Palace. The room shone in golden splendor with floor-to-ceiling mirrors, a tiled marble floor, and exquisite fresco paintings by the great Italian artist Constantino Brumidi (1805-1880), whose exquisite works grace the Capitol's rotunda and corridors. Presidents dating back to James Buchanan have used this room. Abraham Lincoln enjoyed holding court there, telling jokes and stories to senators and congressmen while he signed bills and lobbied for his legislative priorities. It was in here that Lincoln received word from General Ulysses Grant that Confederate General Robert E. Lee wished to discuss Civil War surrender terms. Lyndon Johnson signed the 1965 Voting Rights Act here, and later presidents have used it on Inauguration Day to sign their first official acts.

Entering a room vibrating with such history and beauty made the sight of the lone man standing inside it look misplaced. He wore baggy, unpressed slacks and a rumpled sport coat. Gangly and awkward in appearance, his head cocked sideways as if he suffered from a neck injury, his teeth were long and mildly tobacco-stained, but his smile was wide and friendly as he shook hands with each of us. If Chief Justice Rehnquist looked out of place in these lavish surroundings, it didn't appear to bother him.

When House Manager Chris Cannon met the chief, Chris said, "Please don't be too hard on us. We're all out of practice and have been for a long time."

Rehnquist replied with a laugh, "So am I, for almost thirty years!"

After Rehnquist shook our hands, we filed out and headed next door to the Senate's Marble Room, which was designated as the House Managers' bivouac during the impeachment trial. Henry chased us down the hallway and into there. "Come back, everyone!" he called. "The chief justice wants to *address* us! You guys left too soon!" We had forgotten that the chief wanted to impart traditional words of wisdom, so we reversed direction and headed back to his chambers. Henry stopped us again before we reached the door: "No!" he hissed. "In seniority order, and single file!" Once again, the bumbling chorus lined up before we reentered.

Rehnquist still stood in front of the desk and with the same cocked head and friendly smile. We shuffled in again and formed a semicircle around him. Henry bowed to him slightly but regally as if to signify our readiness to receive the chief's words before embarking upon this grave constitutional journey for only the second time in history. Rehnquist never stopped grinning as he made individual eye contact with each of us before he addressed the group:

"Well," he said, "have a good trial."

Silence. Fifteen seconds. Thirty seconds, maybe longer. Awkward stillness filled the room. Rehnquist remained mum (but still grinning). The managers looked at each other.

Congressman Lindsey Graham (R-SC), standing next to me, whispered, "Hey, Jim, do y'all think that all?"

"I think that's all, y'all."

Henry bowed again, and we filed out of the room.

Because I was the last man to reach the door, I found myself facing President Clinton's attorneys as they now entered to receive the chief's precedent-keeping pep talk. I held the door for them. The last one in line, Lanny Breuer, shook my hand and asked, "What did he tell you guys?"

"It's too deep to explain, Lanny. Listen carefully and soak it in. You'll remember it for the rest of your life."

• • •

Aside from the chief justice recognizing me to address the Senate each time I made a presentation, during the five-week trial (as is typical for an attorney and the judge during pending matters) I had no private contact with him during the proceeding—with this exception.

As the trial neared its conclusion, and at the end of another long session, Majority Leader Trent Lott rose to make his customary end-of-day motion to adjourn. This ritual was our nightly signal to grab our stuff, rush back to our offices, and prepare for the next day's ordeal. Once Lott began making his motion, the other managers scooped up their files and hurried from the Senate chamber. I remained behind because I was busy making notes. As I was both distracted while writing and thinking we had finished for the day, I wasn't paying attention when the White House lawyers sprang a trap. Once my team fled on Lott's cue, Clinton lawyer David Kendall sent a written motion to the desk demanding that the Senate order the managers to give the White House, by tomorrow morning, every quotation from every witness that we intended to use in our upcoming closing arguments. We had no advance notice of this motion, and Clinton's lawyers apparently timed it for when they expected our absence. It happened so fast that Kendall's brief comment to the Senate was over by the time I came out of my stupor and realized skullduggery was afoot.

Just as Kendall's sleight-of-hand drew my attention, our Judiciary Committee's chief counsel, Tom Mooney, burst through the Senate doors and threw himself into the chair next to me. "You need to get up and respond to this motion!" he barked.

"Motion? I don't even know what the hell the motion is, Tom. I just caught the last few words of it. It sounded like Kendall just asked for something crazy, like maybe copies of our closing arguments in advance. Was that it?"

Clarification was not an afforded luxury. Before Tom could answer, Chief Justice Rehnquist called upon me to offer the managers' reply. Tom grabbed my shoulders and heaved me out of the chair, pushing me toward the lectern while sputtering, "No time to explain. Besides, you're a politician. Since when do you need to know what's in a bill to make a speech about it?"

I approached the lectern hesitatingly, still unsure of what had just happened or what Kendall had just demanded. I glanced up at the robotic camera mounted above the chamber's entrance as it swung into place and pointed at me directly, which was a glum reminder that my upcoming response would be beamed to a live worldwide television audience of untold millions.

Oh, well.

"Mr. Chief Justice, distinguished counsel for the president, and members of the Senate," I began, drawing out each word slowly to buy a few extra seconds to formulate something to say. I told the Senate that Mr. Kendall's motion (whatever the hell it was) was unprecedented—unheard of in any trial except for one known instance. It happened many years earlier, when an experienced defense attorney demanded an advance copy of a rookie deputy district attorney's closing argument in a Los Angeles County criminal trial. Because she was a new lawyer, the deputy DA assumed the request was fair and so she raised no objection. The trial judge, future California Supreme Court Justice Otto Kaus, called the lawyers to the bench. Tired of watching the experienced defense attorney take repeated advantage of a greenhorn, Judge Kaus told the prosecutor, "Young lady, when opposing counsel demands to know in advance what is in your closing argument, I believe the appropriate legal response is to tell him, 'It's none of your damned business.'"

With that, and in deathly stillness, I returned to my seat.

"Can you say that on the Senate floor?" asked Tom, his forehead now beaded with perspiration.

"We're about to find out."

Apparently, the answer to Tom's question was "yes." After a heart-thumping few moments of tomblike silence, the guffaws of Senators Strom Thurmond (R-SC) and Robert Byrd (D-WV) broke the tension.

And Kendall's motion, whatever it was, failed.

• • •

Even though the senators did everything they could to scuttle the impeachment trial from under us, they announced with fanfare their magnanimity on the trial's first day: they voted to give us permission to use their "Senators Only" restroom adjacent to the chamber. The day after the Kendall motion, I took advantage of this senatorial largesse during a recess. While washing my hands at the sink, Chief Justice Rehnquist (also permitted the use of this sanctum sanctorum) sidled next to me at the adjoining basin. We greeted each other as he soaped up.

I learned at the start of this sham trial that generally accepted court rules are in flux during Senate impeachment proceedings. In essence, there are formal rules until the senators decide to break them, and then the rules vanish. Still, a sacrosanct rule in any trial is the prohibition of *ex parte* communications, meaning that the judge and a lawyer involved in the case shall have no private discussions unless all parties are present or until the case concludes. Rehnquist broke that rule with me as we washed our hands alongside each other. However, given the Senate's continued disregard of their own rules, and their fixation on rigging the trial in Clinton's favor, who was I to correct him?

"Mr. Manager Rogan," he said, "were your ears burning last night? I was talking to my dinner companions about how you handled Mr. Kendall's motion yesterday. I told my friends that you appeared to have no notice of it."

"I thought that was obvious, Mr. Chief Justice."

"And yet, without any notice, you pulled out of the hat a quotation right on point that came from an obscure judge in an obscure trial. I told my friends that it was amazing, and that you must be a walking *Bartlett's Quotations* or something. I really was quite impressed."

He was still rinsing his hands. I had already dried mine and now held open the door to leave while he finished his story. With his compliment concluded, I smiled and nodded my thanks. Stepping outside the bathroom, I replied, "Well, of course, Mr. Chief Justice, you presume that was a *real quotation.*"

As the chief justice's mouth went slack and his eyebrows arched, I let go of the door. It swung closed in front of me.

A couple of minutes later, I stood outside the Senate chamber with House Manager Asa Hutchinson (R-AR). I was reading a document inside the three-ring binder I held when Asa nudged me. "Come on Jim," he said, "there's the chief. He's ready to get started." Rehnquist was nearby putting on his robe, which was our signal to take our seats. When I saw the chief, I couldn't resist compounding the prank. I flung open the binder dramatically and pretended to practice for Asa an upcoming impeachment speech. In a stentorian voice loud enough to catch the chief's attention, I intoned with mock solemnity, "And, as Abraham Lincoln once said...." I looked over at the chief (now staring at me with a look betraying deep suspicion). I winked at him, closed the binder, and walked into the chamber.

Asa sat next to me. "What's with the Lincoln quote?" he asked.

"Nothing. I'm just driving a nice guy crazy."

• • •

On February 8, 1999, the president's lawyers and the House Managers finished their closing arguments. Both sides retired from the chamber while the senators deliberated in secret. Four days later they notified us that they had reached their verdict. We returned to the chamber for the public vote.

Minutes before this final act in the historic drama, the door to the President's Room was open. Rehnquist sat at Lincoln's desk in his shirtsleeves and with his sport coat draped over the back of his chair. He was signing various items of impeachment souvenirs for senators, House Managers, and the president's lawyers. I was the last person there, so when he finished autographing my few items of memorabilia, I told him that in a few months I intended to call him at the Court and invite him to lunch, and that I knew he would accept.

In a playful tone he asked, "Mr. Manager Rogan, you sound awfully confident. What makes you so sure that I'll accept?"

"Because, first, you're an impeachment scholar. You wrote a book on Andrew Johnson's impeachment, which means that you're dying to know what's been going on behind our closed doors. I'm the guy who can tell you, but I'll only tell you over lunch. And second, I know about your card game on Lincoln's desk. You can buy my silence by accepting my invitation."

On that last point, Jim Ziglar had told me that soon after the start of the trial, Rehnquist asked him for a deck of cards to help fight boredom while he remained stuck in the President's Room during recesses. Jim went to the Senate Gift Shop, bought a deck of cards, and gave it to the chief. A day or so later, Jim entered the President's Room and found Rehnquist and his law clerks playing poker. Cards and piles of dollar bills lay scattered across Mr. Lincoln's desk. Jim straightened up: "Mr. Chief Justice," he said, "this is the United States Capitol. As Senate Sergeant-at-Arms, I am responsible for administering the law here. Gambling is illegal in the Capitol. I'm going to leave now and return in a few minutes. When I return, well, I think you understand." When Jim reentered the room a few minutes later, the money had disappeared and the chief justice, with the expression of a little boy caught filching cookies from the jar, returned the deck.

Jim kept the confiscated pack as a unique impeachment memento.

I doubt if my "impeachment scholar" bait and my tongue-in-cheek poker blackmail made any difference to my luncheon invitation. I only know that as I turned to go, the chief called my name.

"Don't forget to call me," he said.

• • •

After the Senate acquitted Clinton, America's frumpily dressed but intellectually elegant chief justice offered his valedictory comments before adjourning the trial *sine die*:[1] "More than a month ago I came here to preside over the Senate sitting as a Court of Impeachment. I was a stranger to the great majority of you. I underwent the sort of culture shock that naturally occurs when one moves from the very structured environment of the Supreme Court to what I shall call, for want of a better phrase, the more 'free-form' environment of the Senate [Laughter] . . . . Our work as a Court of Impeachment is now done. I leave you with the hope that our several paths may cross again under happier circumstances."

Majority Leader Trent Lott presented Rehnquist with the Senate's "Golden Gavel Award," explaining that by tradition it goes to every senator logging 100 hours in the presiding officer's chair. "I'm not sure you quite reached 100 hours," Lott said in making the presentation, "but it's close enough."

Rehnquist brought down the house with his reply: "It sure seemed like it."

• • •

With this background, I return to my lunch with the chief justice.

When the man dressed more like a duck hunter than the leader of America's third branch of government arrived at my table, he treated me as an old friend. "Hi, Jim," he said as he peeled off his jacket and cap and tossed both onto the seat. He slid into the booth as Nick handed him a bottle of Miller Lite. The chief lit a cigarette, took a puff and a swig from the bottle, and then placed both down in front of him. He raised the first issue on the top of his conversation agenda:

"All right, now," he said while tapping his index finger on the

---

1   Adjourning *sine die* is the final adjournment of the legislative body without a future date to reassemble. See, e.g., https://www.senate.gov/reference/glossary_term/adjournment_sine_die.htm (accessed September 7, 2019).

table, "I want to know about that Otto Kaus quotation!"[2]

Borrowing from the classic hair coloring television ads of the 1960s, I replied, "Only my hairdresser knows for sure."[3]

He put the kibosh on my expectations of getting any behind-the-scenes tidbits from him. When I fired off my first question, he shrugged his shoulders. "I don't have any stories to share," he said. "I didn't do anything other than sit in my chair and listen during the proceedings, and then sit in my chambers during the recesses. Nobody came in and shared anything with me. My role was best described in a line from the Gilbert and Sullivan play *Iolanthe*, when the protagonist said of another character in the play that he did nothing in particular, but what he didn't do he did very well." However, he did salute the managers by saying that we did a superb job. "What impressed me greatly," he added, "was that you all did so well against highly-paid and more practiced lawyers of recent date."

"Thank you for the compliment. At least I think it's a compliment."

With that settled, Rehnquist returned to his agenda. Out came the impeachment historian in him, and for the next ninety minutes he grilled me on our strategy and tactics from both before and during the trial. The behind-the-scenes maneuvering interested him, especially the dynamics between the House Managers and 1) the Democrats who fought us in committee and on the House

---

2   People have asked me for decades whether I made up the Otto Kaus story. I have never replied beyond offering a sly smile to keep people guessing. Now, the answer. Was the quotation real? I don't know. Did I make up the story? No. When I was a young deputy district attorney in Los Angeles County in the mid-1980s, my boss Walt Lewis told me that Kaus story. I recalled it as I walked to the Senate lectern to reply to Kendall's motion. As they say, if the story isn't true, it ought to be.

3   When advertising executive Shirley Polykoff came up with the ad campaign in the mid-1950s, "Does she or doesn't she? Hair color so natural that only her hairdresser knows for sure," sales of *Miss Clairol Hair Color* shot up almost 500%. The ad proved so successful that it earned Ms. Polykoff induction into the Advertising Hall of Fame. See, e.g., https://www.nytimes.com/1998/06/08/nyregion/shirley-polykoff-90-ad-writer-whose-query-colored-a-nation.html (accessed September 5, 2019).

floor during the debate on impeachment articles; 2) the senators working in bipartisan cahoots to rig the trial outcome against us; 3) the White House defense lawyers; and 4) Clinton himself. His questions came with the rapidity of a practiced cross-examination. A sampling:

- Why did the Senate vote 100 to zero to block the House Managers from calling any live witnesses? [My answer: Cowardice. They followed the polls and wanted to make the impeachment trial go away, so they pulled out the rug from under us and prevented us from presenting our case properly.]

- Did the managers agree with this decision? [Answer: Uh, no. The GOP senators screwed us.]

- When the Senate limited the managers to only three videotaped witness depositions, why did we choose Clinton friend and confidante Vernon Jordan over Clinton's White House secretary Betty Currie (both of whom we alleged had conspired with Clinton to obstruct justice)?Did we skip her because she was a sympathetic black female? [Answer: No. We suspected Jordan might flee the country on "business" and remain absent until the trial's end, so we grabbed him while we could. We knew we could always find Currie if we needed her later.]

And so it went.

I did manage to get in a few questions of my own about his career arc. "My 1971 Supreme Court nomination surprised me," he said in response to a rare query that I snuck in. "I really didn't know President Nixon well when I came to work for him at the Department of Justice in 1969. In his 1960 campaign I booked hotel reservations for his campaign people when they blew through

Arizona, and I helped the campaign again in 1968, and then I went back to Washington after he won. Later, when we had a couple of Supreme Court vacancies, Attorney General John Mitchell and Deputy Attorney General Dick Kleindienst asked me to collect names for possible nominees. We had nightly meetings and hashed over the names that I had collected. One night they told me not to come to any more of these meetings. When I asked why, they said it was because I was now under consideration myself."

I asked about published and persistent rumors that his debilitating back problems might force his retirement. "These rumors are false," he scoffed. "Yes, I have back problems. That means my back gets sore if I sit too long. I'm not debilitated by it. When it gets sore, I stand and stretch. Everyone should stand and stretch if they sit too long. Because I do it during oral arguments, these rumors started."

With almost thirty years on the Supreme Court, I asked him if he ever considered a non-health related retirement. "I think about it. There are other things that I'd like to do and I'd rather not die in office. But I'm a Republican, so if I ever did retire, I'd want to do it with a Republican president in the White House to choose my successor."

• • •

As our lunch neared its end, I had an errand to complete on behalf of House Judiciary Committee Chairman Henry Hyde. Earlier that morning, Henry summoned me to his office. "Jim," he said earnestly, "I've heard a rumor that you're having lunch with the chief justice today. Is that true?"

Yes, I told him, we were meeting at The Monocle.

"Great! I have a favor to ask. The chief and I are *very close*. As Judiciary Committee chairman, I have oversight authority over every federal court, including the Supreme Court. I've helped him many times on judiciary issues over the years. We've also worked together on a number of panels, so I know him very well." Henry then handed me two oversized photographs taken on the last day of the Clinton impeachment trial. They depicted Rehnquist presiding over the Senate, along with the House Managers, the White House attorneys, and the senators. "Will you have the chief autograph these for me during your lunch? And be sure to tell him that they're for me, and that I'm going to frame both in places of honor, one in my district office in Illinois, and one in my chairman's office here at the Capitol."

"Sure, Henry. In fact, I have a couple of these same pictures that I wanted signed. I'll just include yours, too. I'm sure he won't mind. Do you want me to have him write anything special on yours?"

"Well, yes, ask him to sign them 'For Chairman Henry Hyde,' and have him write an appropriate inscription on them. He'll know what to write. As I said, we're old friends and I've helped him on many issues over the years."

"Consider it done."

As my lunch with Rehnquist wound down, I handed him the envelope with the photos. I told him how excited and serious Henry was about getting them back, how he wanted them inscribed, and how they were destined for places of honor. Then I hammered home the point: "Mr. Chief Justice, these are *a big deal* to Henry. He said you would know what to write on them."

Rehnquist butted out his cigarette. "Sure, no problem," he said. "Henry and I are good friends, and he's been a great friend to the Court. I'm happy to do it." He took out a pen and started writing. When he finished, I slid my two photos across the table, and he did the same for me before placing the signed photographs back in the envelope.

As we were leaving, I mentioned that the House Managers were considering a reunion dinner, and I asked if he would like to join us when we assembled for a private evening of food, drink, and war stories. He told me he would be very pleased to come, but he suggested that we invite the White House attorneys "for appearance's sake."[4]

We shook hands and said goodbye outside the restaurant. "Jim, thanks so much for lunch and for suggesting this," he told me. "I really enjoyed it."

"Mr. Chief Justice, the Monocle has a gourmet menu. You ordered a beer and a cheeseburger. You're a very cheap date, but you're welcome."

"I really did enjoy it. On the Court I get so few opportunities to talk politics with people involved in it. I wish more opportunities presented. I'd enjoy doing something like this far more often, but, well...." He didn't finish the sentence. As a former judge myself, I understood why. Judges, whether at the city or county level or on the highest court, lead reclusive professional lives. For jurists, neutrality is the coin of the realm, and no subject requires greater judicial neutrality than politics.

• • •

Henry Hyde made me promise to come directly to his office with the signed photographs, so I hurried back to the Rayburn Building. There he sat behind his large desk, an oversized Montecristo cigar protruding from his mouth. His eyes danced when I entered, and he tapped his fingertips together with the eagerness of a child anticipating a birthday gift: "Did you get it? Did you get it?"

"Did I get it? Did I *promise* that I'd get it? Then I got it! I told you I'd come through. When I make you a promise, Henry, you're in your mother's arms."

---

4   Shortly after my lunch with Chief Justice Rehnquist, I had lunch with David Kendall, one of President Clinton's lead impeachment trial attorneys. I invited him and his team to join the managers for a private reunion dinner, and I told him that Rehnquist said he would come if the White House lawyers came. Kendall received the invitation cautiously. "It sounds as if it would be a fascinating evening. I'm just not sure how President Clinton and [First Lady] Hillary [Clinton] might receive the news of a joint get-together. Let me mull this over. I'll talk to the others and get back to you." Regrettably, he didn't get back to me. We never had the joint dinner, which I still lament as a lost historic opportunity.

"Oh, that's great. Thank you, Jim. Seriously, this means so much." Reaching his hands toward me, his excitement bubbled over: "Let me see them!"

I opened the envelope and returned his photos to him. "Here you go, Mr. Chairman. Signed, sealed, and delivered."

Henry grasped the pictures gingerly, careful to handle them only by the edges. He placed them on his desk and then deposited his cigar in the nearby crystal ashtray. His smile radiated as he inspected the coveted mementos.

Then the smile faded. His visage went from joyful to quizzical as he studied the top picture. He slid it aside and examined the second. He picked up his cigar, took a puff, swiveled his big leather chair in my direction, and asked in a monotone voice, "Jim, did you read what the chief justice wrote on my photographs?"

"Well, no. He signed them for you and me, and then he put them in the envelope. I rushed over here. I never looked at them, but I told him everything that you specified about how you wanted them signed."

"Here, let me read the personal and heartfelt inscription you obtained for me." Henry again set down the cigar and picked up the photograph. He read the inscription aloud:

"To Chairman Henry Hyde, with best wishes, William H. Rehnquist."

He frowned at me. *"With best wishes!"* The words spat from his mouth. *"With best wishes.* That's what I fucking write on pictures for people I don't even fucking know!" He flung the photographs. They sailed over his desk and landed on the floor in front of the couch. His thick, Vienna sausage-sized index finger jabbed in my direction. "You failed me," he growled.

I felt disappointed that the chief didn't do a better job at composition, but I also couldn't let Henry get away with this snit. I looked at my signed photo for the first time, and then I showed it to him. "What the hell are you complaining about?" I asked. "Look at what he wrote on mine: '*To Jim, William H. Rehnquist.*' I didn't even get the '*with best wishes*' treatment. I guess that's because I'm not the chairman, and I'm obviously not the close, close friend that you are!"

The Vienna sausage now pointed to the door. "You may go," he declared in a slow, dramatic voice.

I loved Henry, but his ingratitude for something over which I had no meaningful control merited a dash of salt rubbed into the wound: "*With best wishes!* Yeah, Mr. Chairman, I can see how very close you two are. I'll bet you've really made an impact on him to get such a warm and personal inscription. Anyway, always glad to help. Call on me any time!"

"*You—may—go.*"

A few weeks later, I attended a meeting in Henry's office with several other congressmen and senior committee staff. As the meeting adjourned, I noticed one of the Rehnquist signed photos matted, framed, and centered conspicuously on the wall. I couldn't resist. "Hey, everyone, look at this great photograph taken during the Clinton impeachment, and it's inscribed by the chief justice for Chairman Hyde! Wow, Mr. Chairman, what a rarity! And look at this handwritten personal inscription, *To Chairman Henry Hyde, with best wishes.* You two must be blood brothers! He must really, really like you! That inscription says it all."

Out of respect for the memory of my beloved chairman, I decline to share his reply.

A final comment on the Henry Hyde photo fiasco. About a year later, I had lunch with Rehnquist's administrative assistant, Jim Duff. When I told Jim the story of the signed pictures, he shook his head and groaned. "You know," he said, "that's the chief. He's not a politician. He doesn't understand that congressmen and senators expect lengthy and profound inscriptions like, 'To a great statesman and defender of freedom' so they can display it on the wall and show it off. He's oblivious to that sort of thing. He thinks that if you sign a picture for a friend and you want to write something

For Jim Rogan—William H. Rehnquist. What? No *with best wishes?* What a rook! Oh,
well, here I am with Chief Justice Rehnquist in the President's Room moments before
the senators announced their verdicts in the Clinton impeachment trial (and just before
I "blackmailed" him into joining me for lunch), February 12, 1999. The chief signed this
for me during our lunch at The Monocle. (Author's collection)

nice, you write, 'with best wishes.' Do you want me to tell him? I
can get him to redo the pictures with something more akin to what
Chairman Hyde wanted."

"No way, Jim," I replied. "To be honest, I've been having too
much fun at Henry's expense over this. Let's leave things as they are."

And we did.

• • •

A year after the impeachment trial, my final 2000 reelection race was
the top-targeted campaign for defeat by the Democratic National
Committee and by President Clinton personally. Shortly before
Election Day, while I was up to my neck in political thermonuclear
war, Rehnquist called and invited me to a Supreme Court reception
honoring Chairman Hyde.

The Court's West Conference Room was jammed with dignitaries and staff. Soon after I arrived, an elderly woman approached and said that her husband wanted to meet me, but he was too infirm to walk over. Would I mind coming with her to say hello? I didn't mind at all, especially when I spotted her husband: retired U.S. Supreme Court Justice Byron White.

Born in 1917, Justice White played professional football in the NFL during the 1930s and 1940s before embarking on a legal career. Like Rehnquist, he became involved as a local lawyer in the 1960 campaign of a presidential candidate, in his case John F. Kennedy, and, like Rehnquist, he joined the new Administration in a high-level Justice Department position. In 1962, Kennedy nominated him to the Supreme Court, where he served over thirty years until his 1993 retirement.

Sitting alone on a folding chair near the door, Justice White nibbled on a dinner roll. He looked very frail, and his voice was so weak that when he spoke it was barely audible. He took my hand, shook it heartily, and then slipped his hand around mine into a 1960s-style "soul handshake." He whispered something to me, nodded and winked, and then gave me a thumbs up. I interpreted his kindness as a private signal of respect for my impeachment performance. Maybe I'm wrong, maybe not. In any event, I appreciated it.

After meeting the Whites, I encountered Rehnquist in the buffet line. He welcomed me to the reception, and then he pulled me aside. "How's your race going back home?" he asked.

"Well, it's pretty tough, Mr. Chief Justice. As you know, I'm the number-one targeted congressional incumbent, and my race has already smashed all fundraising records for a House seat. I'm fighting hard, but when you impeach Bill Clinton while representing a Los Angeles-based and heavily Democratic district with many of the Hollywood movie studios in it, you shouldn't expect congressional longevity."

"This is all unofficial, of course, but good luck in November. I'm pulling for you. When the race is over and things settle down, bring your family to my chambers for a visit and a private Court tour."

"Mr. Chief Justice, nothing would gratify me more."

I lost my reelection campaign, which was no surprise, but I still lament never taking up the chief's invitation to bring my family for a visit.

• • •

After we moved back to California in 2004, I was on a plane flight when the cabin's televised news broadcast reported that doctors had diagnosed the chief justice with anaplastic thyroid cancer. The man seated next to me said, "I'm an oncologist and a specialist in that type of cancer. That's very bad. He won't last a year."

A few months later, I attended President George W. Bush's second inaugural ceremony. There had been great speculation that the chief would be unable to administer the ceremonial oath of office because of his failing health. Yet there he stood in his black robe with its signature gold stripes on the sleeves. Although he leaned heavily on his cane and moved slowly, terminal cancer did not deter him from his duty.

• • •

Shortly before the chief became ill, I did something I had meant to do since my 1983 law school graduation but never got around to it: I applied for admission to the Bar of the United States Supreme Court. I filled out the paperwork, my sponsor signed my application form, and I wrote a check for the admission fee. Instead of mailing the completed packet, I walked it over to the Supreme Court Clerk's office to hand-deliver it.

I entered the clerk's office and stood at the counter. An officious deputy clerk approached and asked my purpose. I placed on the counter my application packet and said that I wanted to file for admission. The clerk (he wore rubber gloves—a bizarre affectation, I thought) told me that he would not touch my application or anyone else's. I would have to mail it to his office.

"You're wearing rubber gloves, so you won't need to 'touch' it. Why don't you just file it and take my check?"

"You'll have to mail it. I refuse to touch any applications."

"I would have mailed it had I known of your no-touch policy, but I'm here now and the application is complete. Besides, I'm saving you from the risk of touching filthy postal envelopes. Won't you please file it?"

"I don't touch applications. You'll have to mail it."

"My sponsor for admission is the judge who presided over my last jury trial. He's very well known. Perhaps if you looked at his signature you might change your mind."

"I don't care who is sponsoring you."

"Well, okay, but before I leave, you really need to look at my sponsor's name if for no other reason than to satisfy your curiosity." I turned over the document and pointed to the sponsor's signature. The clerk looked, blinked his eyes, and then he removed his rubber gloves and picked up my application.

"I'll file it," he said.

My sponsor was indeed the judge who presided over my last jury trial: a Court of Presidential Impeachment before the United States Senate.

My sponsor for admission was the Honorable William H. Rehnquist.

• • •

Chief Justice William H. Rehnquist served on the Supreme Court for almost thirty-four years, from 1971 until his death from cancer at age 80 on September 3, 2005.

Associate Justice Potter Stewart served on the Supreme Court from 1962 until his retirement in 1993. He died of pneumonia at age 84 on April 15, 2002, the last living justice to have served on the historic Warren Court.

House Judiciary Committee Chairman Henry Hyde served thirty-two years in Congress before retiring in 2007. President George W. Bush presented him with the Medal of Freedom later that year. He died of complications following heart surgery at age 83 on November 29, 2007.

The rubber glove-wearing deputy clerk of the United States Supreme Court who refused to touch my application died at age 56 on July 4, 2012—the first worldwide reported fatality caused by acute latex exposure.

18

One More for the Gipper

"Tell them to go out there with all they've got and win one for the Gipper."
—Ronald Reagan as George Gipp, "Knute Rockne: All American," Warner Brothers, 1940

After eight years in Washington, which included my stints in both Congress and the Bush Administration, our family began packing for our move home to California. On Saturday, June 5, 2004, as Christine and I filled boxes at our Virginia townhouse, we listened to news updates on former President Ronald Reagan's rapidly deteriorating health. Diagnosed in 1994 with Alzheimer's, as the disease progressed his wife Nancy protected both his privacy and dignity behind closed doors. Now, with the end near, reporters and camera crews assembled outside their Bel Air estate as Mrs. Reagan summoned their children to his bedside. It was nearly dinnertime when a bulletin ended the wait. At age 93, America's longest living former president died of pneumonia.[1]

Because he had stepped away from public appearances many years before his death, he had long ago faded from daily popular consciousness. Still, the finality of the news struck hard. From the first time I had encountered him in 1970 as a twelve-year old boy until my final time with him in 1996, when Alzheimer's had already robbed him significantly, his life had left an impact on me personally and professionally. I knew that his death was imminent, but when it came, it hurt like hell. In my earlier book, *And Then I Met...* I

---

1   Reagan held the record as the longest living former president briefly. The others who later surpassed him were Gerald Ford, George H.W. Bush, and Jimmy Carter.

recounted many of my meetings with Reagan over a quarter-century. In this chapter, I share my last encounter with The Gipper.

• • •

The day after he died, Reagan's office released the events schedule for his state funeral. On Monday, June 7, his casket would lie in repose at his Simi Valley presidential library for public viewing. On Wednesday, a presidential jet would transport Reagan from California to Washington, D.C. for a horse-drawn funeral procession to the Capitol. There, following a ceremony in the rotunda, he would lie in state. Friday would bring the formal funeral service at Washington National Cathedral, after which he would fly home to California for a private interment ceremony at his presidential library.

The congressional leadership invited all sitting and former members of Congress to the Capitol's rotunda for a private memorial after Reagan's casket arrived and before the doors opened to the public. Since this exclusive invitation did not include our families, and because my wife and daughters had met and loved Reagan, I eschewed my congressional prerogative. Instead, we joined the people lining Constitution Avenue to witness the procession to the Capitol.

Early Wednesday afternoon proved unseasonably hot and muggy when we arrived at our reserved viewing area in front of the White House. Thousands had already lined up to witness it. Enduring uncomplainingly both heat and a long wait, people talked, at times cried, but more often laughed while sharing favorite Reagan stories and memories.

At 6:00 p.m., a police motorcycle escort came into view, followed by a hearse and rows of limousines. The motorcade stopped when it reached 16th Street near the White House. Mrs. Reagan, holding the arm of an officer, stepped from one of the limousines and stood nearby as a military honor guard transferred her husband's casket from the hearse to a black caisson. There came an

The caisson carrying Ronald Reagan's flag-draped casket and the riderless horse bearing his backward-facing riding boots, Washington, D.C., June 9, 2004 (Photographs by the author)

unexpected smattering of cheers accompanied by people waving small flags. She smiled wanly and returned the greeting before returning to her car.

With the casket strapped to a cart, the procession started for the

Capitol. Seven horses pulled the caisson, which was flanked by representatives of each military branch. A large black stallion wearing an empty saddle followed behind. This riderless horse, in military tradition, symbolized the death of the commander. Fulfilling yet another martial tradition, Reagan's brown leather riding boots faced backward in the saddle stirrups, which represented the lost leader who never will ride again.

As the caisson carrying the flag-draped casket rolled by, silence fell over the quarter-million people lining the streets. The only audible sounds came from horses' hooves clopping against the asphalt, and the soft weeping of spectators overcome by the somber and elegant view.

· · ·

Reagan's body was originally scheduled to lie in state in the rotunda for twenty-four hours. Congress extended the time an additional twelve hours to accommodate over 100,000 people who waited in line all day and night to file past his bier. When the Capitol service ended early Friday, June 11, a hearse would transport Reagan to Washington Cathedral for the formal national funeral service. Again, my former congressman status provided me an invitation to the cathedral ceremony. I had intended to go, but those plans changed unexpectedly.

The night before the cathedral service, and while working at my downtown Washington office, I heard a news report that the Reagan family would fax only 300 invitations to family and close friends for tomorrow's private interment at the Reagan Library. Since that intimate roster excluded me, I never considered the possibility of receiving one. An hour later, my secretary handed me a one-page faxed document purporting to invite my wife and me to this very exclusive ceremony. This "confirmed invitation" looked handmade and fake, so I assumed that someone was trying to play a tasteless practical joke. I called the library and told the funeral coordinator about the "invitation" and my suspicions regarding its authenticity.

"It's no prank, Congressman Rogan," she replied. "You and Mrs. Rogan are invited by the Reagan family."

Oh, my.

I never discovered why the invitation came to me. My best guess is that Mrs. Reagan, whom I knew appreciated my work during the Clinton impeachment, added our names. The Reagan Library Foundation's former director, Mark Burson, once told me a few years earlier that Mrs. Reagan was a fan mine from impeachment and

It *still* looks phony to me: my invitation to President Ronald Reagan's interment ceremony that I received over the fax machine, Simi Valley, California, June 11, 2004 (Author's collection)

that she admired my political grit. He also told me that she grew indignant when former President Gerald Ford criticized our effort publicly and urged us to drop impeachment for a censure resolution. After Ford made this suggestion, Mark said that she never again referred to him privately as "President Ford." She called him *The Unelected One.*

For whatever reason, the invitation came. The next morning Christine and I boarded a westbound airplane for Los Angeles International Airport.

• • •

The timing was such that we could not attend both the national funeral service at the Washington Cathedral and then make it to

California in time for the private interment. Fortunately, our commercial plane came equipped with satellite capability, so during the flight we watched on television the cathedral ceremony. Once that service concluded, a motorcade transported Reagan to Andrews Air Force Base, loaded his casket onto a jet, and then it took off for the trip home.

We had a brief head start on Reagan's plane in our race to arrive at the library ahead of it and in time to attend the interment, but the horrid Los Angeles traffic almost scotched our hopes. We arrived at LAX at 1:30 p.m.; although only forty-five miles away, we sat in interminable stop-and-go traffic for a frustrating four hours. We almost didn't make it to California Lutheran University, where our invitation directed us to arrive for Secret Service screening. The words on the invitation's only bolded sentence were unambiguous: "Absolutely no late arrivals will be accommodated."

Making it there only seconds before the Secret Service sealed off the receiving area, we boarded the last private coach transporting guests to the library. As we neared our destination, I saw from my window the Air Force jet bearing Reagan's body fly low over the library before turning for nearby Point Mugu Naval Base, where an honor guard loaded the casket into a hearse bound for the library.

Our five-mile coach ride to the library provided a moving sight. Tens of thousands of people lined the route waving flags and holding aloft hand-painted signs expressing love and thanks to Reagan. Troops of Boy and Girl Scouts, kids in bathing suits, old people in wheelchairs, aged veterans in uniform, people of all races and conditions—waited under a hot sun to pay tribute when the hearse drove by.

Arriving at the library's staging area, I soaked in the surrounding pastures and red mountains, now cast in a golden hue from the sun setting over the distant Pacific Ocean. The natural beauty added to the scene's serenity and majesty. An escort led us to our seats near the gravesite, where we joined other mourners, including Reagan's three successors as California governor: George Deukmejian, Pete Wilson, and current Governor Arnold Schwarzenegger; actors Mickey Rooney, Tom Selleck, and Bo Derek; and singers Johnny Mathis and Wayne Newton.

• • •

In the six days since Reagan's death, each event of his state funeral ran on time. Now, as the service fell an hour behind schedule, a whispered rumor circulated that Mrs. Reagan, overcome by grief and exhaustion, had faltered and placed the procession on hold until she revived. We later learned this was untrue. The actual delay occurred because the crowds lining the streets along the twenty-eight-mile route from Point Mugu to the library had grown so immense that the motorcade slowed to allow everyone a better view.

It was after 7:00 p.m. when the U.S. Air Force Band began playing an instrumental prelude. The president's casket was wheeled into the garden, followed by the Reagan family and former British Prime Minister Margaret Thatcher, who looked pale and unsteady after suffering a recent stroke. Despite her condition and her doctors' objections, Lady Thatcher insisted on making the grueling flight from England to California to attend the burial of her longtime friend and ally.

The casket rested on a bier between the American and presidential flags as former U.S. Senator John Danforth (a Presbyterian minister) offered a prayer. The U.S. Army Golden Chorus sang *Amazing Grace, Battle Hymn of the Republic, My Country 'Tis of Thee,* and *America the Beautiful.* Representatives of the various military branches fired a twenty-one-gun salute, along with three volleys of musketry, before Reagan's three surviving children eulogized him.

It was his youngest child, Ronald Prescott Reagan, who concluded the tributes with comic relief: "Dad was a famously optimistic man, and at a certain point in his presidency he decided to revive the *thumbs-up* gesture. He went all over the country giving

Christine and I pay our final respects before Ronald Reagan's casket at his graveside interment ceremony, Reagan Presidential Library, Simi Valley, California, June 11, 2004 (Reagan Library video capture)

everybody a thumbs-up. One day I rode in the presidential limousine with him, and along the way he was thumbs-upping the crowd. I saw from the side window a snarling man giving Dad an entirely different hand gesture with a raised digit pointed at him. Dad saw this, and then he turned to me and said, 'You see? I think the thing is catching on!'"

At the end of these remembrances, military jets performed a flyover, with the lead jet breaking away in the traditional "missing man" formation. The Army bugler sounded *Taps,* and then the honor guard escorted the casket to the nearby tomb as Mrs. Reagan and her children followed.

The family assembled behind a partition separating the seating area from the tomb, which gave the family some privacy during the presentation of the casket flag and their last goodbyes. After the family departed, Lady Thatcher walked slowly to the casket, leaning heavily on the arm of her escort as she paid her final respects. The remaining guests then lined up behind her.

Night had fallen and most of the guests had already departed by the time Christine and I approached the gravesite. Reagan's large mahogany casket rested atop a small stand in front of the horseshoe-shaped tomb, with a lone sentry standing guard near a posted presidential flag.

We lingered briefly while offering a silent prayer of thanks for Ronald Reagan's vision and leadership. As I took her hand and led her away, I said goodbye to a man who had done so much for America—

—And who had done so much for me.

• • •

Nancy Reagan outlived her husband by almost twelve years. She died on March 6, 2016 at age 94 of congestive heart failure.

The year after Reagan's funeral, doctors diagnosed former British Prime Minister Margaret Thatcher with dementia. She died on April 8, 2013 at age 87 from complications following another stroke.

George Deukmejian served two terms as California governor (1983-1991). He died on May 8, 2018 at age 89 of natural causes.

Mickey Rooney, one of Hollywood's top box office attractions in the late 1930s and early 1940s, enjoyed a career in entertainment that spanned almost nine decades. He died on April 6, 2014 at age 93 of natural causes.

AFTERWORD

After completing eighteen chapters for this book, I showed the draft to my literary agent, Sealy Yates, and I asked him to review it and see whether it merited publication. He called a week later and told me that he liked the book but he had a question: how long did I plan to make it? With my previous book clocking in at a whopping 413,438 words (a necessity, given that it was a comprehensive historical novel on the entire 1968 presidential election), I told him that I thought I'd keep this one to a modest limit, say, oh, 135,000 words.

"No," Sealy replied emphatically. "Publishers today want manuscripts that are no more than 75,000 words. By the way, as of now, how many words is this one?"

"I refuse to answer on the grounds that it might incriminate me."

"How many?"

"Over 80,000, but I have lots more stories!"

At Sealy's ~~insistence~~ suggestion, I decided to wrap up this book and save additional stories for another sequel. So, for now, the curtain descends. Unlike the great Jimmy Durante, I don't have a million of 'em, but I do have more stories. If you enjoyed this book, then please tell your friends and family to buy a copy or two—and don't loan your copy to cheapskate acquaintances. Tell them to go buy their own.

• • •

No author's book is complete until he memorializes his gratitude for those whose support and friendship contributed to the endeavor. Thanks and appreciation to old friends Mark Karis of Karisworks LLP, who designed the book cover and interior, and Geoff Stone of ClearWords Group, who shepherded the production; my literary agent Sealy Yates; editor par excellence (and my fifth grade classmate) Jon Jacobs; Julie Heath, Vice President, Warner Brothers Clip and Still Licensing; and Scott Olsen, King Features Syndicate.

Special thanks and hugs to my family for their patience and encouragement: my wife, Christine, and my daughters Dana and Claire. Your love means everything to me.

• • •

I am always delighted to hear from readers. My website, www.jamesrogan.org, contains information on all of my books. If you wish, you can email me directly from the "Contact" tab. I read them all (unless they're unduly obnoxious) and I do my best to reply personally.

In my next book, I'll tell more stories about life in Congress and meeting the greats, including how I pranked Pope John Paul II during my private audience with him. Admit it: you're already intrigued.

Until next time, thank you for reading my book.